THE BEST OF
SPIRITDAILY
D0068320

THE BEST OF SPIRITDAILY

MICHAEL & LISA BROWN

PUBLISHING COMPANY
P.O. Box 220 • Goleta, CA 93116
(800) 647-9882 • (805) 692-0043 • Fax: (805) 967-5133

Library of Congress Number # 2002091116

Published by:
Queenship Publishing
P.O. Box 220
Goleta, CA 93116
(800) 647-9882 • (805) 692-0043 • Fax: (805) 967-5133
http://www.queenship.org

Printed in the United States of America

ISBN: 1-57918-195-3

Welcome to SPIRITDAILY

Welcome to "The Best of *SPIRITDAILY*," a compilation of some of the more interesting stories we've carried in our first year and a half of existence (May 13, 2000, to the winter of 2002). As many of you know, Spirit Daily is a daily internet news site geared toward spiritual news, and this book was conceived because of the many requests we have had from readers for back articles.

The articles are placed in no particular sequence, and without regard to dates. This book is the type that can be picked up and read at leisure and random—or in one fell swoop. Keep in mind, with the way the items are written, that they are appearing on a particular day with certain events in the world swirling around them. There are articles about self-help, personal spiritual development, the charisms, prophecy, deliverance, Vatican news, and much about the Virgin—from Fatima to Medjugorje!

Indeed, our very first day of existence was May 13—anniversary of the first Fatima apparition—and our first headline on our first full day was about initial release of the famous third secret! A month later, when the entire text of the secret was finally revealed, we were graced with having been among the first to present it to the public, and the following September 29, we dedicated the website to the Archangel Michael.

There have been so many thousands of letters. There have been so many calls. There have been so many miracles. We only hope that there are articles here you find both fascinating and enlightening, and that in some way they help on the journey to Jesus.

Michael and Lisa Brown
www.spiritdaily.com
Latham, N.Y.

Angels Over America

Do nations have angels? Is a country guided in the same way that we all have guardian angels? The answer is yes. We know this from both Scripture and private revelations. In the Book of Daniel it describes how good and evil angels battle over kingdoms, and we see similar imagery in the Book of Revelation. During the apparitions in 1917 at Fatima, Portugal, the children described an encounter with the Angel of Portugal. It is said that Michael is the guardian of Israel.

And now in a revelation from the U.S. we hear of angels over America.

According to a saintly nun from Fostoria, Ohio, named Mildred Mary Neuzil, there are at least two major angelic protectors of the United States, and she saw them in vision with great glory. One held a gigantic sword tipped with a "searing" flame. That was in his right hand. "In his left hand were held bolts of lightning that pierced all the environs of the universe," said Sister Mildred. "On the right shoulder of this extraordinary being perched a pure, white dove. From the right shoulder down to the waist towards the left side was a sort of medium wide band on which was printed, *'Power of God.'* At first the letters revealed themselves in black. Then when I recognized what the letters were they changed to such a color of gold light I could barely make them out."

He had come, the angel told her—addressing her as "sister"—"to help the people of God in their hour of need."

And so it was that America—this good nation, this nation founded on God, on liberty, on justice, this nation with the Lord in its very pledge—had become the focus of evil, said Sister Neuzil, had become the focus of attack by the enemy because it had the greatest capacity to lead mankind to God. It had fallen into sin. It had darkened. We don't have to expound all the problems here (they are all around us).

But America is good and still has a chance and angels are on the scene and over us.

They have come with great might. They are empowered when we pray. They brighten when we are good. Sister Mildred saw this during a lifetime of apparitions, and while the later ones of angels were not included, earlier apparitions of the Virgin and St. Joseph were granted an imprimatur by her spiritual director, Archbishop Paul F. Leibold of Cincinnati, who struck a medal dedicated to her apparitions, which allegedly occurred from 1938 until her death in 2000. "Follow me, people of God, brothers and sisters, as our Queen paves the way and the peace of the Lord will reign once more upon earth," said the angel—while Sister Neuzil also saw a second one that looked very much like the first and also called itself "guardian and protector of America" but around its head had what looked like bright globes of light and in his left hand chains of enormous size and weight. In his right hand were what seemed like shafts of light. He also addressed her as "sister" and said, "With these shafts of light God seeks out and binds with eternal chains the evil powers and those who have sold themselves to these enemies of God and His people. They who are chained to habits of sin through weakness but have hearts filled with guilt and repentance will have their chains broken so that they will be free once more to love and serve the Maker."

Sister Mildred said these blessed spirits seemed to be composed of light. "I could barely see any form. Their garments were of dazzling whiteness, their voices were not like any other ever heard, not audible except to the inner hearing which is indescribable. I was further informed that these two mighty Spirits would fight together side by side aided by an army of their companion Spirits."

Said the second angel: "Listen to the words and warnings of the Queen of Heaven and you will experience my protection and I will fight in your defense that with the people of all nations you can at last come to the peace of the Kingdom which is within you." On his waistband were the words, "STRENGTH OF GOD."

The third part of the secret revealed at the Cova da Iria-Fatima, to Lucia dos Santos on 13 July 1917

"I write in obedience to you, my God, who command me to do so through his Excellency the Bishop of Leiria and through your Most Holy Mother and mine.

"After the two parts which I have already explained, at the left of Our Lady and a little above, we saw an Angel with a flaming sword in his left hand; flashing, it gave out flames that looked as though they would set the world on fire; but they died out in contact with the splendor that Our Lady radiated towards him from her right hand: pointing to the earth with his right hand, the Angel cried out in a loud voice: 'Penance, Penance, Penance!' And we saw in an immense light that is God: 'something similar to how people appear in a mirror when they pass in front of it' a Bishop dressed in White 'we had the impression that it was the Holy Father.' Other Bishops, Priests, men and women Religious going up a steep mountain, at the top of which there was a big Cross of rough-hewn trunks as of a cork-tree with the bark; before reaching there the Holy Father passed through a big city half in ruins and half trembling with halting step, afflicted with pain and sorrow, he prayed for the souls of the corpses he met on his way; having reached the top of the mountain, on his knees at the foot of the big Cross he was killed by a group of soldiers who fired bullets and arrows at him, and in the same way there died one after another the other Bishops, Priests, men and women Religious, and various lay people of different ranks and positions. Beneath the two arms of the Cross there were two Angels each with a crystal aspersorium in his hand, in which they gathered up the blood of the Martyrs and with it sprinkled the souls that were making their way to God."

The incredible story of Maria Esperanza

by Michael H. Brown

She is widely regarded as the greatest living mystic. The miracles that surround her are vast — among the best documented in Church history. Not since Padre Pio, the famous Italian priest now set for canonization, has there been a thaumaturge, a "wonder-worker," of her scale. She's a seer. She's a healer. She's a stigmatist. She often exudes an inexplicably beautiful fragrance. Some even claim to have seen her in levitation.

I speak here of Maria Esperanza from Venezuela. We have had a number of stories about her, but never her background. It is a life that many predict will lead to her canonization. Rarely has a single personage embodied so many mystical gifts, and rarely has a personage stood as a beacon of hope and love (the very name "Esperanza" means hope) to people of all denominations.

She is not only a mystic with whom the world needs to acquaint itself—and will find it fascinating to *become* acquainted with — but also one whose apparition site, known as Betania, which means "Bethany," has rare Church recognition.

Thousands flock to conferences or churches where she appears (I was with her at the University of Arizona before a standing-room-only crowd of 4,000); she has been filmed by the likes of ABC and NBC; and she has been featured by major television outlets in South America. When a religious cruise recently asked her to greet it at a port in Venezuela, 16,000 accompanied her to meet the ship.

Her story?

Maria Esperanza was born on November 22, 1928. Her mother had desperately wanted a daughter (she already had three boys) and asked the Blessed Virgin Mary to grant her a girl. True to the prophecy of a local woman, who in an omen foresaw the birth of an extraordinary child, Maria was born in Barrancas on the feast day of Saint Cecilia, who is associated with music. The birth occurred while Maria's mother was taking a trip by boat and in fact arriving at a port in search of better medical facilities. It was a very painful delivery, and during her pregnancy Maria's mother had often prayed before a picture of the Blessed Mother—offering her child to Mary and promising to name the child Maria (Spanish for Mary) and Esperanza if it was a girl.

So came into the world "Mary Hope," destined to shine like a star, destined to be an instrument of heaven. She was a sick, suffering youngster who often recovered from disorders in momentous ways. Prodigious too was her yen for the spiritual. As a child she often played with dolls dressed as priests or nuns and at the age of five (while bidding her mother, who was taking a trip, farewell at the port of Bolivar City), the girl saw a smiling woman rise from the Orinoco River with a rose in her hand.

It was an apparition of St. Therese of Lisieux, the "Little Flower," and henceforth roses or their fragrance would hover about Maria. The rose St. Therese held was extraordinarily beautiful, a brilliant red flower that was "thrown" to young Maria. Her mother immediately proclaimed the rose a sign from God.

Such claimed phenomena—and soon much more—are difficult for even the seasoned believer to comprehend. They invoke legitimate use of words like "incredible." In later years many around Esperanza were to witness other phenomena related to roses, including the inexplicable falling of rose petals.

Such occurrences are regular happenings around Maria. So are "coincidences." Feast days of the saints, especially those commemorating Mary, figure prominently into her diary. Esperanza received first Communion on July 16, 1937, the feast of Our Lady of Carmel, and soon after the young Maria encountered tremendous physiological tribulation. By the age of 12 she had developed such an acute case of pneumonia that her doctor didn't think she would live more than three days, but after prayer she opened her eyes and saw the Blessed Virgin. It was not a vision; it was a corporeal apparition. According to Maria the Virgin appeared as Our Lady of the Valley of Margarita (an apparition site off the coast of Venezuela) and told the girl what medication to take. During an especially severe illness in 1947 Maria was paralyzed for several months but miraculously healed upon a vision of the Lord. "At that moment something happened, which I know for the world is impossible to believe," comments Maria—who recalls that the instantaneous healing was accompanied by a startling tremor that shook the hospital.

There were other trials in Maria's sickly early years, and during another episode Christ manifested to her and again she was healed.

The Virgin Mary told her that she had a mission to "help me to save this lost world," and so began Maria's journey. So began her life of mysticism. Her marriage was typically providential. At first she'd wanted to become a nun and entered a convent in 1954. That same year, on October 3, at the end of a Mass, she had another implausible experience. Once again, Saint Therese the Little Flower appeared and once more a rose was "thrown" to her. But this time when Maria went to catch it—as she had done as a girl of five—it wasn't a rose that landed in her hand. Instead there was blood.

It was the onset of Maria's stigmata.

"Work out your salvation as a wife and mother," the Little Flower instructed Maria, who indeed sensed that her vocation would be that of a family woman but went to Rome to live at the Ravasco Institute, which was operated by the Daughters of the Hearts of Jesus and Mary at the Vatican.

On August 22, 1954, on a visit to Caracas, Maria had a dream about a place where miracles would take place and where there would be an unusual blue butterfly. In 1956 she returned to Rome where she met her future husband, Geo Bianchini Gianni, as had also been foretold to her. The following October 13—anniversary of the "great miracle" of Fatima—the Blessed Mother told Maria she would be married on December 8, 1956—yet another feast day, this time the feast of the Immaculate Conception (and Geo's birthday). They were married that day in the choir chapel of the Immaculate Conception at St. Peter's Basilica.

No one had ever been married there during the holy season of Advent, and it was only after a cleric, Monsignor Julio Rossi, parish priest at St. Peter's, noticed the incredible aura around Maria, as well as the scent of roses. That caused him to go to Pope Pius XII, who knew of Maria and secured final approval for a ceremony in the historical chapel.

Their first child, a daughter, was named Mary Immaculada.

During these younger years Esperanza made the acquaintance of Padre Pio, the most famous mystic since Francis of Assisi, who had told people he expected to be visited by an extraordinary woman. "There is a young woman who is going to come from South America," Pio said. "When I leave, she will be your consolation." When finally they met, Maria would hear his "call" even though she was far away near Rome and she would head for his monastery at San Giovanni Rotundo on the barren east side of Italy, where despite throngs waiting to see him the aged priest called out, "Esperanza!"

On September 23, 1968, Maria had a vision of Padre Pio. "Esperanza," he said in the vision, "I have come to say good-bye. My time has come. It is your turn." As this was happening Geo watched with amazement as his wife's face transfigured into that of the Italian priest. The next day they saw in the newspaper that Pio (whose funeral would be attended by more than a million) had died.

One thing she had discussed with Pio when he was alive was her vision of a special plot of land where the Virgin Mary would appear. In the vision Maria had seen an old house, a waterfall, and a grotto.

"From 1957 until 1974, we searched for this land in all of Venezuela," says Geo, who had oil concerns and a construction business in Caracas.

Then came a visit from a friend who came to ask for help during a drought. The cattle on his land were stricken with hunger and Maria told Geo they should go see it. When they did, in March of 1974, they immediately fell in love with the picturesque hillside about an hour and a half from Caracas.

"It corresponded exactly with the vision my wife had been given," says Geo of the land known as Betania.

There was an old sugar mill on the land, and although it wasn't apparent at first, a stream and waterfall were also located on the property. Geo and his partners purchased the land and cleared the hillside. They saw it as a place for all faiths—not just Catholics. And Betania quickly became a sanctuary.

In February of 1976, while Maria was in Italy tending to Geo's ailing mother, the Virgin told Esperanza to head back for Venezuela and prepare herself for something that was to happen at Betania. Maria did as she was told and at this spot on a hillside encountered an apparition of the Virgin, who called herself "Reconciler of Peoples and Nations.

It was the onset of apparitions and miracles—in many cases extraordinary, well-witnessed manifestations—that continue to this day. The sun pulsed here as at Fatima, there were strange white forms, there was a blue butterfly that seemed to flit out from the grotto at the moment Maria went into apparition. The most momentous occurrence came on March 25, 1984, when seven successive apparitions were witnessed *not only by Maria but a total of 108 people.* In the days and months that followed, hundreds and then thousands saw manifestations at Betania or around Maria. It was this series of events that started a formal inquiry by Bishop Pio Bello Ricardo of Los Teques. Trained as a psychologist and with a tendency toward skepticism, Bishop Ricardo personally interviewed several hundred eyewitnesses, including an army general, a lawyer, an atheist, and a doctor who all claimed to have experienced the supernatural. In all the bishop took 550 formal written statements and concluded that extraordinary paranormal events were indeed taking place around Maria.

That wasn't all. The bishop himself had witnessed phenomena. He had miraculously recovered from an illness after a visit from Esperanza, and had smelled the rose fragrance.

"I have also been able to see the transfiguration which happens to her when some gold spray seems to cover her hands and face and her body," says Pio Bello. "It is a little film of gold spray. Also the phenomenon of levitation has been taking place. I have testimony from many people about the transfiguration which takes place in her, the phenomenon of stigmata which takes place on Good Friday."

After an extensive evaluation the bishop flew to Rome and confided the happenings to Cardinal Joseph Ratzinger, prefect of the Sacred Congregation for the Doctrine of the Faith, and to the Pope himself.

Heeding protocol, the bishop discerned the matter for three

years and then issued an extraordinary pastoral letter that declared Betania "sacred ground" and stated that the incidents "are authentic, they are supernatural, and they are of a divine source." It was the strongest such ruling since Fatima. Thirty-five of Venezuela's 37 bishops and auxiliary bishops supported him.

By 1993, Dr. Vinicio Paz, a local specialist, was estimating that there were 1,000 physical healings at Betania and that at least 10,000 had witnessed phenomena around Maria. One cure occurred to a doctor himself.

This was the incredible case of Dr. Vinicio Arrieta, a Harvard-educated physician who was healed of cancer and whom we have written of previously.

Others have been cured of paralysis, liver disorders, and leukemia. According to biologist Samir Gebran, a doctor of immunology and Maria's son-in-law, strange relics are found around Maria. In one case she felt compelled to go to a creek, pulled a rock from the ground, and on it was a white image of the Virgin. Another time, upon her first visit to Massachusetts—where she had mystically advised a Boston-area nun on where to build a retreat center — Maria once more felt compelled to head into a forest and told those with her to dig up a rock. When they did, they encountered an image that bore similarities to the face of Jesus.

There is no living mystic who has been affirmed by such competent witnesses. Are there detractors? Yes, as there are always detractors. But the litany, especially from those who have lived with her, seems endless. I have spoken to another son-in-law who described how he would pad downstairs in the middle of the night when he and his wife were staying with Maria and see Esperanza deep in prayer and surrounded by a large halo. Still others have encountered unearthly luminous fogs or during Mass have seen her feet rise several inches. On December 8, 1991, a Host used at Betania began to bleed as the priest held it, and in another Church-authorized miracle it has been exhibited in a special reliquary in Los Teques—where those who visit have seen images form in it and have even videotaped it turning into what looks like flames. "I had a scientific investigation conducted, and this was done by a laboratory that is totally trustworthy," says the bishop. "They proved definitively that the substance that leaked from the Host was human blood."

Most incredible are claims, again made by competent observers—doctors, a TV journalist—*that on 15 occasions a stemmed rose has pushed out from the skin near Maria's bosom.* The rose witnessed was an actual flower, red and touched with dew.

This, of course, is impossible to believe. But many are those who claim to have seen it—first a dot of red, then the bud, which unfolds as the stem with thorns breaks through the skin and causes Maria an agony they have compared to a woman giving birth. Carolina Fuenmayor, a journalist from Venevision, the major station in Caracas, has filmed it but at Maria's request will not release it until after Maria's death.

What are we to make of such accounts? Is Maria indeed a modern, female version of Padre Pio? Or is it all too much to believe?

I can only say that aside from the tremendous array of phenomena (I am only here scratching the surface), there is the fruit of love. Those around Maria—her husband, her seven children, her in-laws—are filled with joy and zeal I have never seen before. They don't want to be away from Maria and often the entire family —up to sixty—have traveled with her to the U. S. "I have seen how petals of roses appear, how there is a materialization of roses, and one smells the roses in the environment," says Dr. Gebran. "I have seen how the Eucharist materializes on her lips. I cannot give any explanation, because in her many supernatural phenomena take place. This is outside of science."

As for the stigmata, Maria's doctor, Alfonso Gutierrez Burgos, has no doubt about it. He was an eyewitness. "When I observed the stigmata, the army general was there and other people as well, so I am sure that these things are happening to her and are of a supernatural character," says Dr. Burgos. "As a doctor I examined her hands and I tried to see what kind of a wound it was. They were very fine wounds in her hands and they were swollen in the middle. They separated her skin and they hurt her very much. That was accompanied by a loss of blood, a tremendous loss of blood."

"Maria Esperanza is a very, very special person," adds Carolina Fuenmayor, the TV reporter who has witnessed both the stigmata and the rose. "She's not from this place. She's like in-between [earth and heaven]."

Only the most powerful of historic mystics have had events like Maria's, and few are those whose phenomena have been verified while they are still alive. Such claimed phenomena indeed are hard for even the faithful to accept. It is only after reading the full details or spending time with Esperanza and at Betania that one begins to integrate the realism of her experiences. Everyone who has spent time around Esperanza is as amazed at the love and unity in her family as the phenomena. Most impressive is the feeling of unconditional love and joy that pours from her. There is a remarkable cognizance—as well as an unforgettable twinkle— in her scrutinizing brown eyes. But she also carries a message of warning. The moment has arrived in which mankind must awaken, says Esperanza, in which it must awaken to the love of God. In the coming years a new light from heaven will illuminate hearts, she says, but before it does there will be hardship. She foresaw AIDS and now sees other problems, including another disease and a foreign threat to the U.S. (by two nations, one large, one smaller, who will conspire to provoke America). A "very serious moment" will arrive but humankind will survive and will be better for it and will live in the truth of God. She claims that this is *"the hour of decision for humanity."* She sees war, societal problems, and natural disasters. But she also sees a cleansing that will restore humankind. *"A great moment is approaching,"* said Esperanza. *"A great day of light!"*

Nothing is more potent against evil than pleading the Blood of Christ

By Michael H. Brown

Many are those who come to us at this time with problems that involve evil. I'm speaking about both generic evil and also problems caused by actual evil spirits. It is a time, in the words of the Virgin of Medjugorje, when the devil is "unchained," and he has caused problems for all of us. He causes divisions in our families, jealousies, anger, problems at work, anxiety, depression, and especially confusion. This is his special hallmark, confusion, and right now we see a cloud of perplexity and confusion over the U. S.

In some cases his presence is clearly discernible, while at other times he comes with great stealth. Without our knowing that it's him, he causes the anxiety, division, and argumentation. He darkens us. He does so to entire societies. He tempts us to sin. On September 11 there was not just a physical darkness from the smoke at the World Trade Center but also a shroud of perplexity and confusion that descended. And it has affected most people. More than anything we are under spiritual attack, and we need to break it. We need to dispel the darkness. We need *clarity*.

There are many ways this is done, but most powerful is through the Blood of Christ.

By meditating on Christ's Blood, by pleading it, by washing ourselves in it, we banish evil. The devil cannot take this. It's what defeated him—drop by drop—at Calvary. It's what flowed into every part of the Savior's body, and what was shed for the salvation of the whole world. It is the holiness of the soil of Israel!

And the most powerful way that we can invoke that precious Blood is during Mass. Bring your problems to church. Bring your fears. Bring the afflictions the devil causes and *break* them during Consecration. When the priest raises that chalice, or when you drink from the cup, *there* is your opportunity to banish evil. There is your chance to dispel problems or habits or attacks that haunt you. There is your chance to get in all your needs. Adore the Blood and invoke it and cover yourselves in the power that breaks all bonds and dispels all confusion. Every drop is more potent than all the evil demons can conjure. They can do *nothing* in the face of it.

Plead it all day. Plead it at the first sign of evil. If you have evil in your lives—if you're hurt, or confused, or perplexed, or frightened, or sick, or fatigued—take these matters to the Eucharist and dispel them. Plead that the Blood of Christ washes all evil from you and you'll find that bondages are broken and light shines and a curtain of darkness and spiritual blindness is lifted. This is why blood is seen in Eucharistic miracles. It is to remind us of what's behind the Eucharist; it's to assure us; it's to let us glimpse a power that transcends the entire universe.

Ask for bigger blessings

How do we make miracles happen? With belief. Trust. That's how we get answers to prayers. We need to open up. The sky is the limit. God hears us—and responds when it's in His will.

It's up to us to better appreciate how much God wants to help us and even bless us specially. Too often, we limit ourselves. Too often, we pray as if we're confined in a closet. While that's a good place to go for privacy, we're not supposed to confine ourselves spiritually, and most often we do. We set limits. We believe only to a point. We restrain the blessings God may have in store for us!

This is the message of a remarkable new book called *The Prayer of Jabez* and while we don't know what the final verdict will be on this book, and while we caution that it shouldn't be used for self-centeredness or materialism, it's seems a tremendous inspiration to better faith and more direct communication (in the name of Jesus) with God. We need to open up. We need to think big. There's no time to limit what we need to do for God, and that's the message of this book: that when we're working for Jesus, when we're seeking to do His will, He will bless us specially, He'll help us accomplish the impossible, He'll expand our territory—often in a way that's miraculous.

So too is this true in our daily struggles. There is no use allowing yourself to be oppressed by daily life. There is the need to rise above it. When we have problems, when we feel down, we need to pray as if we *know* we will be heard and we *know* that if it's right for us (if it's correct in the larger picture only the Lord can see), God will grant it.

Don't be afraid (*John* 16:24) to ask. Ask beyond what you normally expect. God loves our requests. It honors Him. He loves to bless. But we have to ask and all of us should do that every day: ask for better and bigger blessings and better and bigger ways of serving and living His glory here on earth and then forever!

Pope's exorcisms and dramatic remarks set standard

On Sunday, Pope John Paul II said the devil is most dangerous when least perceived. "Every man, in addition to his own concupiscence and the evil example of others, is also tempted by the devil, especially when least aware of it," the Holy Father said from the window of his study before praying the midday Angelus. At the same time came word that the Pope recently performed another exorcism.

To those who have argued for so long now, especially since Vatican II, that it's best not to mention the devil, and for theologians who have tended to discount the evil one (replacing him with psychology), this had to be a shocker. In one fell swoop, the Pope was indicating that we are only safe when we know where Satan is, and that we have let the devil work in the dark. Indeed, "intellectualism" has all but allowed Satan to roam the world unfettered. What was once known as demonism is now called names like "multiple personality," psychosis, and schizophrenia. While we have to be careful not to mistake legitimate mental illness for diabolical activity (there are legitimate biochemical imbalances), our society has gone to the opposite extreme and as a result has left itself wide open to assault.

At the same time, the Church, bowing to that same intellectualism (which replaced mystical theology in the seminaries), has all but neutralized ancient prayers found effective against evil. At least that's the claim of Father Gabriele Amorth, the official exorcist of Rome and one who was present at two of the Pope's exorcisms. Last June, in a startling interview with an Italian publication called *30 Giorni*, Father Amorth complained that bishops do not have experience in dealing with evil and have left the Church without proper safeguards, especially in the way of a new Ritual for Exorcists. In fact Father Amorth has called the New Ritual, which he says leaves out prayers that were used for 12 centuries, "an incredible obstacle that is likely to prevent us from acting against the demon." Among other things, Father Amorth said he was asking "that the prayers might be amended so that invocations to the Virgin, which were completely absent, might be incorporated, and that the number of prayers specifically relating to exorcism might be augmented."

"During these last ten years, two commissions worked on the Ritual," Amorth charged. "One was made up of cardinals and was responsible for the *Praenotanda*, the initial provisions, and the other was responsible for the prayers. I can affirm with certainty that none of the members of these commissions had ever performed an exorcism."

Father Amorth charged that exorcists are "very badly treated" and that on one recent occasion when 150 of them had gathered, they were kept away from an audience with the Pope. Moreover, he claims "there is not a single exorcist" in countries such as Germany, Switzerland, Spain, and Portugal—"a terrifying deficiency." "Out of a hundred French exorcists," he said, "there are only five who believe in the devil and carry out exorcisms. The rest send anyone who gets in touch with them to a psychiatrist." As a result, he claimed, many suffer the rest of their lives in torment. He said the German episcopate sent a letter to Rome declaring that there wasn't even a need for the New Ritual because exorcisms should no longer be performed. He likewise points out that the baptism of children has been watered down with its exorcism "virtually eliminated."

These are strong words. They come from someone frustrated. We can't vouch for every perspective. But we can say that the Church has stripped itself bare when it comes to exorcism—even allowing psychologists, who in large part don't believe in the devil, to determine who should be exorcised! In the new benedictionary, Amorth says references to the Lord protecting us from evil and prayers to bless schools and homes have been suppressed. "Everything should be blessed and protected, but today there is no longer any protection against the demon."

"I will tell you a story," said Father Amorth. "When I met Don Pellegrino Ernetti for the first time, a celebrated exorcist who practiced in Venice for forty years, I said to him, 'If I could speak to the Pope, I would tell him that I meet too many bishops who do not believe in the devil.' The following afternoon, Father Ernetti came back to see me and to tell me that he had been received by John Paul II that same morning. 'Holiness,' he had said to him, 'there is an exorcist here in Rome, Father Amorth, who, if he met you, would tell you that he knows too many bishops who do not believe in the devil.' The Pope answered him briefly: 'He who does not believe in the devil does not believe in the Gospel.'"

Nun and Pilgrims Saw the Virgin Mary During Jubilee Mass in Medjugorje

"I am with you," said the Virgin Mary to Medjugorje visionary Marija Pavlovi-Lunetti as part of her message from June 25th. Half an hour later she proved it by appearing in the church to a nun and to pilgrims from Bosnia and Switzerland.

By Jakob Marschner in Bosnia-Hercegovina

MEDJUGORJE, July 5th—A remarkable story which has been talked about for days has had its credibility considerably strengthened with the Franciscan nun Sister Marina Ivankovi confirming that she saw the Virgin Mary during Medjugorje's evening Mass on June 25th, the twentieth anniversary of the Virgin's Medjugorje apparitions.

Sister Marina, originally from Medjugorje but now assigned to the Croatian parish of St. Cyril and St. Methodius in New York City, tells the French nun Sister Emmanuel Maillard, based in Medjugorje, that she truly got the special treat of seeing the center of events on that grace-filled June 25th. Sister Emmanuel tells the story as part of her latest report from Medjugorje, available on www.childrenofmedjugorje.com.

"If I am told that it is not true, I know for myself that it is true and I am ready to go on the Cross for it! Our Lady has given me a very special gift and I keep telling myself with wonder: She is alive! She is alive!" Sister Marina says in the report.

The Mass had just begun when Sister Marina, standing in the doorway between St. James Church's sacristy and choir, heard a very loud cheering coming from people in the the church. She noticed Father Branko Rado trying to calm down a group of people who seemed to see something by the statue of the Virgin Mary situated to the right in the church. The pilgrims were stretching out their hands towards the statue, and out of curiosity Sister Marina went down to see what was happening.

Standing in front of the statue she saw a kind of whiteness

behind it. The light was sparkling and pulsating, and Sister Marina was overwhelmed with amazement, she says. Once again the pilgrims cried out and pointed to the same spot before them. Sister Marina says that it amazed her to see how everyone reacted at the very same instant.

Then a silhouette appeared in three dimensions. It was right behind the statue and wearing a blue-white veil, bordered by a distinct gold band covering the upper forehead as well, and so it was obvious to Sister Marina that this was the Blessed Virgin Mary herself. By this time the Gospel was being read in many languages, and the Franciscan nun bears witness that the Virgin was silently standing in an attitude of prayer with her eyes looking down, listening very attentively.

Apparently this had happened four or five times, and Sister Marina had witnessed only the last time. The day after visionary Ivan Dragievi said to Sister Marina that a pilgrim from Slavonski Brod in central Bosnia had also seen the Virgin at the same time and place. A group of pilgrims from Switzerland said they also saw her.

"I am really very happy and I feel a great need to pray. The name of Mary has become dearer to me, and I pronounce it with intense joy. Before, of course I used to pray to Our Lady, but now prayer to her has become dearer to me and more beautiful. I pray to her with more reverence now," Sister Marina says in Sister Emmanuel's report.

In this immediate way the Virgin Mary confirmed her brand-new monthly message which had been given to visionary Marija Pavlovi-Lunetti just half an hour before she appeared in the church. *"I am with you,"* said the Virgin in her message of June 25th, a message which says in its entirety:

"Dear children! I am with you and I bless you all with my motherly blessing. Especially today when God gives you abundant graces, pray and seek God through me. God gives you great graces, that is why, little children make good use of this time of grace and come closer to my heart so that I can lead you to my Son Jesus. Thank you for having responded to my call."

An experience with the Archangel Michael

By Michael H. Brown

It was the autumn of 1983. The best I can remember, it was September. I don't know the precise date. It would be neat if it had been this date, the 29th. I didn't keep a diary. But I didn't need one to recall the details.

At the time, I was living the "fast track," the high life, of New York. Although born in Niagara Falls, I had gone to Fordham, a Jesuit university in The Bronx, and had moved to Manhattan's Upper East Side after a brief stint as a newspaper reporter, during which I had been involved in the discovery of a famous toxic waste dump named Love Canal.

This had propelled my career as a writer, and at the time I was working on a book about the Mafia. I wrote about an experience from this the other day (see "A spiritual brush with a mob hitman"). It was one of many such experiences, some of which I will be sharing in days ahead. As I said, it was the fast track, and in addition to my research on organized crime, I had also written books on toxic-waste scandals, and (stupidly enough) on psychic phenomena and haunted houses. In fact I had just "investigated" a supposedly "haunted" house (in reality it was demon-infested) in the Chelsea section of Manhattan.

Anyway, I was a 31-year-old writer doing what he had always aspired to doing: writing, appearing on national TV, lecturing at colleges for excessive fees, making enough money to live in a luxury high rise and eat in the ritzy cafes every night of the week. I was what you might call a "swinging bachelor." I admired people like Hugh Hefner. I'm not proud of it. I wasn't an evil person, but I certainly wasn't good, and one Friday night that September after coming home earlier than usual I feel asleep and awoke because of an amazing dream.

In the dream I was on a bed that was like a hospital gurney, and it was in my foyer facing the door of my 12th-floor apartment.

Around me were three or four spirits with their hands over me, two on each side, as if they were praying. I wasn't allowed to look straight at them, but I had the impression they were thin pencil-like figures of light who could appear in any form they wanted. They were uttering what seemed like an ancient language. "Who are you?" I asked the one on my left, who seemed to be in charge.

"My name is Michael," said this entity (for lack of a better term). *"Now look!"* He indicated toward the door, and on that door I saw the most frightening thing of my life: the face of the devil or at least a major demon, etched and yet alive, living, sneering, full of a hatred I had never before seen and could not hope to adequately describe.

I woke up in a sweat. I paced a while, probably had a cigarette back then. Looked out the window. Below, the last of the stragglers were leaving the cafes along Third Avenue. It was probably between three and four a.m.

Finally I got back to sleep, but immediately lapsed into the same dream. It didn't seem like a dream, but more a vision. It continued where it had left off. *"I told you, look,"* said the one who had called himself Michael. *"Now say, 'Vanish!'"*

I could never imitate the power behind those words. Instantly his words had made that awful evil face on the door, the hollowed cheeks, the pointy goatee, disappear.

I didn't have the courage or faith to do what he said. Instead I woke up and this time was the most terrified of my life. It was far scarier than anything the Mafia or haunted houses could dish up. I was probably up close to an hour, smoking, wanting to call someone, pacing. But who was I to call? At the time my two best friends were reporters for *The New York Times*, which for all practical purposes meant they were atheists.

Finally I forced myself back to sleep and the dream again continued where it had left off. The one who said he was Michael told me again to say, *"Vanish!"* Somehow, I came up with the faith. I came up with the courage! When the awful face materialized, I raised my right hand and shouted "VANISH!"

Suddenly and to my amazement the face disappeared and so did the angels and I got up from the "gurney" and walked to the door. As I did I could see that where the face had been was now a set of keys. When I took them and looked at them a tag indicated the address of that haunted house in Chelsea.

I had been brushing up against evil in many ways, and now the devil was at my door.

It was part of my coming back to Christ. I hadn't been to church regularly since junior high school, but now went back. Did I! Around this time I became a daily communicant. It was almost instant. There were other experiences. I came back through both Catholicism (a church on 90th Street called Our Lady of Good Counsel), and also through a non-denominational group of pentecostals, evangelicals, and charismatics on the Lower East Side. And I came back in a big way. Although I know there are those who would question the entire experience, there was a reality to it and it wasn't evil. I believe they were angels—because right after that I learned that my mother had been invoking Michael and had bought me a statue of him (which to this day is next to the bed).

As I said, this helped lead me back to Christ, and to a journey away from secular journalism and to writing spiritual books. Eventually, it also lead to this website, *Spirit Daily*. We have been up and running since May 13, and in that time it has been amazing. We have had many thousands of "hits." We saw a peak on June 26 when by God's grace we were allowed to get a jump on releasing the third secret of Fatima (there is still a bit of newsman in me).

Today, the feast of the Archangel Michael, we are beginning official operation, and dedicating the site to the greatest of all angels, the one who saved me as he had also helped Daniel (*Daniel* 10:13), the one for whom I had been named, the one who battles Lucifer tirelessly, the one who will cast him down forever in the end (*Revelation* 12:7)—the one who has no fear as we too must have no fear at a time when we must confront the face of the devil and make him vanish from our culture with the same question, the same insistence, that Michael once spoke, with the same courage and strength as when, casting out Satan, who pretended to the Throne, the angel shouted with a voice I think I also heard, with a voice of overwhelming power, with one that should now—must now—resonate around the world: *"Who is like unto God?"*

One of the most astonishing cures reported at site declared "sacred ground" in Venezuela

One of the best documented and most astonishing medical miracles in recent times happened to a doctor himself. The doctor, Vinicio Arrieta, a Harvard-educated man who was director of the School of Medicine at the University of Zulia, experienced his phenomenon at a site in Venezuela that stands as one of the few officially approved by the Church since Fatima.

The place was Betania—which means "Bethany"—and it had been declared "sacred ground" by Bishop Pio Bello Ricardo in 1987 after consultation with the Vatican. By that year there were at least 500 to 1,000 people who'd received medically significant cures at Betania, according to medical authorities—none more dramatic than what happened to Dr. Arrieta.

In the next couple of weeks we'll be looking at a number of miraculous cures. We haven't kept up with him in recent years but the last time he gave his testimony it was best expressed in his own words. At the time he was suffering from cancer of the prostate that had spread to the lumbar column of his spine. His antigen level had been 100 where the normal value is 0 to 10. He had received two treatments of chemotherapy. "There is no possibility of a misdiagnosis," he had said. "They had given me two years to live."

But heaven—and the Blessed Mother—had other plans. Dr. Arrieta had spent all night praying with his wife and a crowd of about 5,000 on the anniversary of Fatima. At five he awoke and begged God to let him live for his two children. He announced that he was casting off his pride and pretentiousness.

"We got up at six in the morning and we broke our fast, and we sang a little song to the Virgin," said Dr. Arrieta. "At eight in the morning the solar phenomena began in which the sun lost its light—it was illuminated but it lost its light. The center part became green. It began to spin on the inside like there was a circle on the inside and then it began to come nearer to us. I began to feel an infusion, a heat within my body. I grabbed my wife and I began to scream. They thought I went crazy. I began to scream, 'I'm being cured! I'm being cured! I'm being cured!' I felt that this infusion arrived at my spinal column and to my prostate. I wasn't even looking at the clock but after this the Virgin appeared above the trees and toward the heavens as a real human being. That is to say that she had hair which was moved by the breeze. She had a face, an extremely beautiful face, a beauty that can not be described!

"The only thing that can be said is that it is like the expression of love, of the glory of God. Her eyes were blue. Her nose was very sculpted. And in her face was a candor, a love, a kindness. And in her right arm she had the Child Jesus, as if to hand Him over.

"In the other arm a rosary hung down to her knees. The rosary was completely illuminated. Five hundred other people were seeing the Virgin at that moment. I thought that I was cured. Five days later, the prostatic specific antigen was not detectable."

One of the specialists, Dr. Vinicio Paz, who made the original diagnosis, said there was "no scientific explanation" for what occurred. They did a biopsy which was also now negative. The cancer had simply vanished.

Records from old Irish observatory may offer clues on strange weather

Records at an ancient observatory in Armagh, Ireland, indicate that a strong shift in climate has occurred since the mid-1800s but may be from natural causes—and may relate to a message given around that time at an obscure site of apparition.

The logs, among the world's oldest and kept as a daily meteorological diary at Armagh since the earliest days of the thermometer, show a shift in climate during the past 150 years that included a temperature spike in the 1840s and since that time a strong upward track that many believe is responsible for a global increase in violent weather.

The observatory is in the town where Saint Patrick once preached. It's a spooky place. Astronomers who work there speak of strange noises and the limestone, decked in ivy, dates back to the 1700s.

There in a basement archive are the logs—many of which were written on parchment—and what they reveal is telling. Recording daily temperatures for more than two centuries, the diaries show that a major shift in weather began from 1840 to 1860, surged in the mid-1900s, and has been skyrocketing since the 1980s.

Scientists compare the situation with a similar swerve in climate that occurred during the Roman Empire and then during the Middle Ages.

While astronomers who have analyzed the records say that pollution may have contributed to the rise in temperatures, they believe the most likely cause is the sun and its cloud-affecting magnetic fields.

"We conclude that, possibly excluding the most recent decades, much of the warming of the past century can be quantitatively accounted for by the direct and indirect effects of solar activity," write E. Palle Bago and C. John Butler, two astronomers at Armagh, in a series of papers they sent to *Spirit Daily*.

Records show that there has been a great increase in clouds—heralding storminess—and they warn that the current trend could suddenly reverse into a cold spell as happened around 1300, before onset of bubonic plague.

The most pronounced early temperature spike occurred in 1846—the same year, as we have previously noted, that the Virgin Mary appeared in the French hamlet of LaSalette to two shepherd children. There she allegedly warned that seasons would be *"altered"* and that famine would come—which occurred soon after as the change in weather helped spawn fungus that caused the great Irish potato famine.

While temperatures leveled or dipped a bit after that, by the 1880s they were surging again and since then, except for brief respites, have heralded numerous changes in weather, including an increase in atmospheric moisture that has led to more severe blizzards, rainstorms, and flooding, along with drenching hurricanes.

According to the scientists, the increase has been more than a degree centigrade and has been accompanied by an intensification in cloud patterns. "The total cloud cover over the oceans has increased during the past century," state Dr. Butler and Bago in the papers, which include analyses not just of the old records but also tree-ring, oceanic, and satellite data. "Temperatures rose quite steeply in the period 1900 to 1940, then leveled off and indeed fell for a decade or two after which the warming has resumed till the present day," say the scientists, concluding that "this variability has, in the past, come about through natural causes not related to the activities of mankind."

It thus appears that at least to some extent forces far out of mankind's reach are causing the current gyration, which has seen hurricanes devastate Central America, typhoons last for record times in the Pacific, floods overrun parts of China, tornadoes rip through expanding parts of America, and winter storms dump record amounts of snow.

The scientists conclude that the main cause is natural because the shift occurred before large quantities of carbon pollutants were emitted by industry.

Whereas half of the temperature rise occurred from 1900 to 1940, only 20 percent of the carbon dioxide rise occurred at that time. In addition, temperatures leveled off and slightly fell for a while in the 1960s and 1970s when levels of carbon dioxide—the pollutant thought to be behind much of global warming—was quickly rising.

"That fact alone," say the scientists, "is strong evidence that some other mechanism is involved."

The "mechanism" is nature, which is controlled by God—Who through the Virgin allegedly warned in 1846 that the sins of humankind would lead to disturbances in nature. The word "allegedly" is used because it was part of the message that wasn't approved by the official Church.

But in many ways the message has been startlingly accurate. *"The seasons will be altered, the earth will produce nothing but bad fruit, the stars will lose their regular motion, the moon will only reflect a faint reddish glow,"* it said. *"There will be thunderstorms which shake cities. Nature is asking for vengeance because of man, and she trembles with dread at what must happen to the earth stained with crime."*

Grace comes in a hurry when we stop complaining

Want to surprise yourself with happiness? Want to feel a sudden infusion of grace? There's one way to do that, and it's simple: stop complaining. You'll be astonished at how much closer God is when you're grateful than when you're in a state of dissatisfaction.

To complain means to grumble, to be annoyed, to express resentment. It's one thing to speak out when there are injustices or to report a serious situation. It's another to complain.

When we complain—when we act like our lot in life is never good enough, when we are always declaring ourselves mistreated—we only give energy to whatever it is that is irritating us. Check this out. Next time someone bothers or even insults you, suffer silence. Don't mention it. Zip it. Offer the silence up. You'll be amazed: though it may cause a niggling aggravation for a short period of time, the "sting" will leave much sooner than if you complain about it!

Jesus never complained on the way to the Cross nor during the Crucifixion and His reward was Resurrection. His reward was rising to the right Hand of the Father. So it is with us. The Lord told us to take up our crosses each day and often this cross is when something irritates us and we're tempted to voice anger.

While our psychologists tell us we need to "vent" our emotions (and while there are times we *do* need to express certain problems), for the most part "venting" makes a problem worse. It makes an insult last that much longer. It fans the flames.

Worst of all is when we complain about something we have prayed for! Think about *that*. We pray for a job—and then when we get it, we're full of complaints about it! We pray to get married and then complain about our husbands and wives! We pray for kids—and then complain when we have to get up in the middle of the night!

This is ingratitude, and it's the opposite of thankfulness. It's a manifestation of pride. When we're resentful we believe we deserve better (indeed, that we *deserve* heaven on earth), and are indignant of anything less.

That's a good way of falling out of God's favor. It never works. It compounds a bad situation. It's counterproductive in the extreme. Did Mary complain in the manger? Did she complain about how little she was given? Did she complain that here she was having a Child in the most inconvenient of circumstances?

Instead of complaining we should be thanking God—and praising Him in all circumstances. Easier said than done? Yes. Much. We're all in this struggle called life. It's one big test! There are constant aggravations. But when we pass the little quizzes along the way—when we make it over one of the countless obstacles, and when we offer up our silence—there is often an outpouring of grace. This is especially true when we are silent in the face of unfairness.

When we can do that—when we can shake off even something unfair—then grace is not only powerful and not only long-lasting but often arrives in an instant.

Bishop in Argentina declares approval of dramatic messages at San Nicolas

In a rare pronouncement the bishop of San Nicolas de los Arroyos in Argentina has reiterated that dramatic prophecies and messages claimed to be from the Virgin Mary and warning the world is in "great danger" have been officially accepted by the Church. The messages, which came through a woman named named Gladys Herminia Quiroga from 1983 to 1990, warn of chastisements and say that mankind is in "very dramatic moments." But they offer the hope that what looks like a triumph of evil will soon be reversed.

"From the church point of view the messages are approved and they are finished," states Bishop Mario Luis Bautista Maulion. "The effects continue, although there is nothing official about new messages. We presume there are not more messages. If there were it would be up to the church to discern them and publish any new messages after February 1990." He adds: "The content of these messages is very spiritual. They call for conversion, prayer, and hope in a hopeless world. The consecration to Our Lady takes us to a very holy life which is the goal of baptism. It is a response to the secularism and materialism of our times."

While aspects of the apparition have met with previous positive comments from bishops, the latest statement appears to be the strongest endorsement of the prophecy itself, with use of the term "approval" taking it beyond an "imprimatur" (which is simply an acknowledgement that nothing in a message contradicts Church doctrine).

We'll have more on the content of the messages in coming days. The important point for now is the Church's stand. The reiteration is of a determination by the previous bishop, Domingo Castagna. Although the apparitions themselves have never been formally approved, Castagna announced construction of a church to serve the faithful who flocked to the apparition during his tenure and records show that along with an archbishop, Jorge Lopez of Rosario, made public statements that left little doubt that both prelates firmly believed that events were manifesting "by God through the Blessed Virgin." There have been at least ninety visits to the sanctuary by cardinals, bishops, or auxiliary bishops, according to a website devoted to San Nicolas.

The declaration of Bishop Maulion, made in response to questions formally posed by *Spirit Daily*, says the actual apparitions have not been formally approved and will not be—a curious decision in that the messages themselves have in effect been declared as supernatural missives from Mary. "What is important is the ecclesiastic discernment and the pastoral directions which are approved and are what give authority to the Church," states Maulion according to a preliminary translation. "The most important aspect of the apparitions is the spiritual fruit. They produce prayer, conversion, and other supernatural manifestations given to Our Lady in favor of her children who come to look for her and they receive a lot of graces. I believe since the beginning these apparitions have been producing a lot of spiritual fruits, which increase the faith of the people and which the Church can use to direct the pastoral life of the believers. These manifestations are like a tree that produces good fruit. If the fruit is good the tree is good. Our Lady is manifesting a lot of graces through these apparitions to a lot of people."

Some of Maulion's responses are in reply to a question about his personal beliefs. The bishop says there have been apparitions reported at San Nicolas since 1990 but that his office had not yet discerned them. Asked if there were similar seers elsewhere in Argentina, Maulion says, "There are some reported and some reports of supernatural events but the Church has not confirmed any of them."

In response to a query about sun phenomena or other miracles at San Nicolas (about 145 miles north of Buenos Aires), the bishop says "there are a lot of healing, conversions, and miraculous cures but there are so many that they have not been investigated. The testimonies of the faithful and pilgrims are very large and are attributed to the graces received from Our Lady."

When asked what he thought about prophecies concerning sin and coming chastisements, Maulion says, "All sin requires conversion and purification. It is appropriate in these times when the values are changed by the world, so it is a consequence that requires conversion and suffering at the local, personal, and national levels. Chastisements and sufferings bring us to conversion. It is through Divine intervention that Our Lady fulfills the request of Our Lord at the foot of the Cross from Jesus: 'Here is your son.' She united with her Son and, obedient to Him, brings her children to Him. Filled with maternal love, her actions are the hope for those who ask for her intercession as Mother and Queen of Perpetual Help."

According to the previous bishop as well as the rector of the sanctuary the Pope has discussed the issue and has been both very interested and "totally positive."

Approval of the San Nicolas messages joins with two other apparitions in Latin American that have been accepted in the past several decades: Betania in Venezuela and Cuapa in Nicaragua, where both the messages and apparitions themselves met formal Church approval. There are other apparition sites in South America that have been approved through the centuries but none in the U.S.

Messages claim that the majority of mankind is "contaminated" and a "warning" covers the earth

The majority of mankind has allowed itself to become contaminated and as a result the world is under a "warning," according to prophecies reaffirmed this month by a bishop in Argentina.

The messages, allegedly granted by the Virgin Mary to a woman named Gladys Herminia Quiroga de Motta 145 miles northwest of Buenos Aires at San Nicolas, are among the strongest ever approved by the official Church and exhort the faithful to spread word of judgment. "It is your duty to teach the Almighty's justice, and blessed is he who learns it," say the messages, which we present here as composites. "You must be warned, children, the plague is big. At these moments all humanity is hanging by a thread. My children, the senseless person is dead, even if alive, because he does not fear the justice of God, nor fears not fulfilling of His commandments. He wants to ignore the fact that the Lord's day and His judgment will arrive. Blessed are those who fear God's judgment."

These are the hours, say the messages, when prayer and visits to the Blessed Sacrament must be especially "fervent." Humanity is living, say the messages, in "very dramatic moments." Gladys says she was shown a vision of the world in two parts, with one of the parts representing those whose souls are being "destroyed," especially through an obsession with wealth. "A great part of the world is very far from God," the Virgin told Gladys in more than 1,900 messages. "They go ahead in everything that is materialism, and they do not advance in what is most important, in the knowledge of the Word of God. Daughter, the earth is inhabited, but it seems uninhabited. A very great darkness is over it. God's warning is over the world. Those who stay in the Lord have nothing to fear, but those who deny what comes from him do. Two-thirds of the world is lost and the other part must pray and make reparation for the Lord to take pity. My dear daughter, there is darkness and loss everywhere! My children, in the large cities of the world, atheism and total indifference toward God are to be seen. The devil wants to have full domination over the earth. He wants to destroy. The earth is in great danger."

In what can only be termed stark warnings, the Virgin emphasized materialism and pride in all its manifestations. "My children, impose nothing on your lives!" say the messages, granted between 1983 and 1990. "Do not be too ambitious, because to want much can make you forget that the only and real ambition you should have is to be able to enter God's Kingdom. Try to remember this always, as it is the only thing that matters to the Lord. Not everything is corrupt in the world, but a great part is. This great part is what must be fully and completely renewed, since they despise God. They are God's enemies. They are being used by the devil craftily and very coldly. Break the bonds to the materialistic world you live in, and join the Lord."

Reaffirming messages from other places, the Virgin told Gladys in 1988 that "the weapon that has the greatest influence on evil is to say the Rosary" and emphasized that for those who pray it is not a time for anguish but of "hope," "peace," and "fortitude." "The coming of the Lord is imminent," says a 1988 message, "and as the Scripture says, no one knows the day or the hour, but it will be, and certainly for that hour the soul of Christians should be prepared. These are hours in which your prayer must be fervent. Do you not know that prayer is a shield against evil? It is not mankind who is abandoned by God, but God Who is abandoned by mankind!"

While the alleged apparitions at San Nicolas themselves have not been formally accepted by the Church, a sanctuary at the place of revelation has been built and Bishop Mario Luis Bautista Maulion has notified *Spirit Daily* in a formal letter that "from the church point of view the messages are approved and they are finished" as of February 1990—although there may be messages since that have not yet been ecclesiastically discerned. "The content of these messages is very spiritual," noted the bishop in reiterating the approval of his predecessor, Bishop Domingo Castagna. "They call for conversion, prayer, and hope in a hopeless world. The consecration to Our Lady takes us to a very holy life which is the goal of baptism.

It is a response to the secularism and materialism of our times."

The message warning that the world was in "great danger" came in 1985—the year Fatima seer Lucia dos Santos claims the world narrowly averted nuclear war—and was followed by prophecies that continued into 1990 with equally forceful language.

Never before has a message so directly admonished followers to preach God's justice.

While there are no further details on what was meant by a "big plague," the hints of purification are followed throughout the messages by the encouragement of the Blessed Mother. "I say this for all my children: God does not want you to humble yourselves before the enemy, nor does He want you to be destroyed by him, but for you to face up to him. Fear nothing, because the Lord goes in front to each battle. May your will not shrink; be strong because you have the Presence of the Almighty. Daughter, the prince of evil pours out his venom today with all his might, because he sees that his worry reign is ending; his end is near; little is left to him. My daughter, the evil one is triumphant now, it is true, but it is a victory that will last briefly. Hurry because time is running out."

Urgent surgery canceled after executive returns from Medjugorje

When Arthur Boyle, president of Cargo Worldwide in Boston, was told there were three nodules in his lung, it came with a sense of doom. Boyle, 46 and the father of 13 children, already had undergone major surgery for cancer of the kidney.

That was in December of 1999. The nodules were found in his right lung about eight months later. With kidney cancer, that's often where it spreads, along with the brain. And all the danger signals were there: Boyle was weak, was losing his memory, and his skin felt like it was afire. Surgery was set for last September 14. A tremendous sense of doom set on the normally upbeat, athletic businessman.

Then his brother-in-law, Kevin Gill, was playing golf when a mutual friend asked how Boyle was doing and suggested a trip to Medjugorje, the village in Bosnia-Hercegovina where the Virgin Mary has been appearing since June 24, 1981 and where many healings have been reported. Within a week the three men were on the way to the remote village.

It was just ten days before the scheduled surgery. "While we were over there all kinds of things happened," Boyle told *Spirit Daily*. "Our guide, Zeljka, was supposed to set us up with Vicka [Ivankovic, one of the six seers], but she said, well, I have some bad news for you. Vicka's gone. She went to Rome to visit a sick nun."

It was bad news because the seer is known to have a gift of healing. The men went to Mass the next morning, came out of church, and went to buy some religious articles for their families. "We stopped at a jewelry store and we were shopping in there for at least 45 minutes," says Boyle, who knew that as unusual. "Guys like us go in, buy something, and leave, so something was keeping us there. I was staring down at these crosses. I had just bought all my daughters, five of them, these rosary-bead bracelets and I have eight boys and I was going to buy them all gold crosses and chains and I'm saying, 'Man, this is going to cost me a fortune.' So I'm looking at it and I say, "You know, if I can waste the money I spend on sports, hockey sticks, equipment, I can spend it on Jesus.'

"The minute I said that there was this commotion to my left and standing right to my left was Vicka. Zeljka got excited and explained to Vicka what my situation was and she prayed over me right then and there. Apparently her plane was cancelled the night before and she was stopping at this particular jewelry store to buy a rosary ring for this sick nun and she was on her way to the airport."

Afterward the men did what most pilgrims there do: visited the hill of the first apparitions, climbed a mountain that has a cross at the top, and took pictures. Photographs afterwards showed symbols and inexplicable forms of the Blessed Mother and we'll be trying to bring those to you shortly. "We had Rosary beads turn to gold, we saw the sun spinning," says Boyle, referring to the common phenomenon there of sun miracles.

After attending confession there, the depression—the gloom—left and Boyle began receiving his healing (a healing that may actually have originated months before when he was prayed over by a Massachusetts priest named Ed McDonough, who, as it happens, was also visiting Medjugorje).

Boyle knew something was going on because of a strange sensation, a pain, in his lung. "I called up my wife—I had a satellite phone—and I said, 'Get on the phone with the oncologist and arrange for another C-T scan, because something's going on. I don't know if it's worse or better or what. But before I go in for surgery, we have to have another scan.'

"She called up the oncologist and the oncologist's secretary called back and said, 'We know you want the doctor to give you a C-T scan, but listen, you have cancer, it's not like it's just going to disappear or anything, and we're going to go right ahead and have the surgery done. We're not going to give you another C-T scan.'"

At that point Boyle changed oncologists, was given another C-T scan on September 12—two days after returning from Medjugorje—and the scan showed that the large nodule they were most concerned with had "completely disappeared." Meanwhile the other two were very small and insignificant and all they would have to do was watch them. "I went to meet the oncologist," says

Are seers right when they foresee the Anti-Christ?

by Michael H. Brown

The news this New Year's was sobering: as mankind entered a new century—and more crucially, a new millennium—terrorists set off a bomb that killed many in the Philippines; churches were bombed in Yemen and Tajikistan; and Israel was rocked by explosions. In the U.S. a disturbed man tried to handcuff the Archbishop of New York and in the Caribbean a nun was killed by terrorists who entered a church during Communion.

These were not idle acts. They were orchestrated by evil. As we begin the third millennium since the birth of Jesus, His adversary is increasingly—nearly hysterically—active. His time running short, the devil is in the mood for a decisive confrontation.

Does that mean that the Anti-Christ—the "mystery of iniquity"—is also well-nigh?

That's what we have been hearing from hundreds of alleged seers. As in the Middles Ages—when Europe was about to be devastated by bubonic fever—prophets have risen on all sides proclaiming apocalyptic events.

Such prophecies have not come from places like Fatima or Medjugorje (which have stayed away from anything quite so dramatic), and here at *Spirit Daily* we have been especially wary of anything attached to the year 2000. It's the devil who seeks to confuse with expectations that are premature.

But there were strong warnings of the Anti-Christ from an alleged secret in 1846 at LaSalette, France (which maintained that the "King of kings of darkness" would rise after a series of huge natural disasters), and I have heard lesser-known seers proclaim something similar. In Ireland a seer named Christina says she saw an image of the Anti-Christ as a man 45 to 50 years old, with very piercing eyes and darker skin, perhaps Arabic. "There are many anti-christs and through them an army will unite and resurrect a leader," claimed the alleged Irish seer.

The evil, said Christina, was "multiplying." Satan was taking advantage of his "last chance," and the last chance, she said, was going to be an "awful battle." A similarly dark-complected man (with gold vestments and a short black beard) was envisioned by a second Irish seer named Beulah Lynch.

There are many others, and we must be careful to discern; events are unfolding powerfully but in a more gradual manner than many expected. Prophecies of the Anti-Christ are typical of every century. Even saints have been wrong. Saint Norbert thought the Anti-Christ would come during the 1100s and a famous monk from Fiore believed the Anti-Christ would arrive in the year 1260.

Hundreds of others have rung false alarms since.

Yet we must remain vigilant. The man of perdition will probably come sometime during the new millennium. It is the third millennium since Christ, and "three" is a significant number. If indeed Gallagher is correct, we still have not seen the huge natural disasters that precede the Anti-Christ, but there are signs that over the next several years and certainly the next couple decades such events will build.

If nothing else we're told this has been a period of special evil, and the recent persecutions—the direct attack on Christians, the way evil is coming into the open—indicates at least the spirit of Anti-Christ.

One of the most dramatic recent predictions of Anti-Christ has come from Pachi Talbott Borrero of Cuencha, Ecuador, whose alleged apparitions of the Virgin Mary gained attention during the late 1980s and early 1990s (including a personal visit from the president of Franciscan University) and who believes the Anti-Christ has actually taken on human form. She described him as a man who will work through science, is "very, very intelligent," and will at first seem both attractive and humble. In the 1990s she claimed he was still "very young." He would get people, she said, "through television and all the ways of the world. But especially to youth in music and drugs." He would bring people to egoism—an epidemic of pride, Pachi said—and mirroring what Gallagher saw, the Ecuadoran seer claimed he would "act directly in a terrible way after the punishment."

"All that I tell you is in Sacred Scripture," Pachi quoted Mary as saying. "A false prophet exists who will entangle [my little souls] saying he is God, but he is from the blood of the demon. He will betray the Father. And the one who has the heart and wisdom will realize that he carries the number of the beast, 666, on his right hand. Satan is set loose to touch my little ones, but I am that woman whom the Father announced, who will crush the head of the serpent who is Satan."

Pachi said this revelation was accented on March 4, 1990, a day after her last apparition, when, receiving visitors at her mother's home, a "nun" who appeared short, plump, and barefoot, dressed in white with a mole on her cheek, came to the door insisting on a private meeting with the young seer.

"I felt uneasy about this but she was a religious woman and I said okay," Pachi once said. "We went to my mother's room and the nun slammed the door. She said, 'Look at my feet. Look at my hands.' Her eyes were tremendously bad. Again she said, 'Look at my hands, look at my feet.' Again I saw nothing. I started to pray to St. Michael and the nun stopped talking and her eyes squinted. Her voice changed to a deep voice, and again she said, 'Look at my hands.' On her hands and feet were the stigmata. I was very scared. And in her right hand, which I thought was stigmata, appeared the number of the beast in blood—666. At that moment she tried to jump on me and she put her thumbs in my eyes."

Was that an omen—a demon in the flesh—or simply a crazed woman?

Time will tell. Whether the more apocalyptic prophecies will pan out—whether the personage of Anti-Christ is ready to appear—know this: the spirit of Anti-Christ has been in the world for more than a century and when such a spirit is present there is the chance it will precipitate. It is a time of exceptional evil and we have seen clear manifestations of the kind of persecution initiated by the spirit of Anti-Christ with demonic attacks specifically on Christians and during Mass itself at the very onset of this uncertain millennium.

Prayer brings faith and joy – even in times of chastisement

Can we still laugh? Can we still have joy?

Yes, of course we can. In fact, faith brings us to just such joy no matter what happens around us. It is a lack of faith—which comes from a lack of prayer—that leads to fear.

If you're afraid, step up your prayer life. Pray from the heart. And pray a lot longer. It's then that the Spirit comes, and how can anything be scary when we have the Holy Spirit?

Don't get us wrong: what happened—the tragedy of last week—must be mourned. It must be recognized as evil. It must also be seen as a dire warning. We never shy from reporting the serious and even evil side of this journey called life. The present hour is the most sobering since World War II and in our belief it's bound to get much more serious. Those who deny this—who don't think God chastises—must not believe in the Bible. (See *Matthew* 24. See *Luke* 21. See the accounts of Noah or Sodom or Jonah.)

But we know God is there, that after this life—no matter *what* might happen on earth—there is eternity. Life never ends; the most horrible tragedy, the most spectacular death, is but a transition. And so merciful is God that we're told by those who have experienced clinical death that the Lord often takes a soul before the actual instant of impact. Death is often more frightening for those *watching* than those who are actually going through it. There is the presence of saints. There are deceased loved ones. There are angels. It's when we're not prepared that we fear. And the best preparation is to grow in faith, love, and humility. Seek God. Forget worldliness. "If you are humble," said Mother Teresa, "nothing will touch you." If we are spiritually prepared, there is nothing to fear and there is the realization that some day in some way we all die and go on to a reality so exciting and vast it will take eternity to investigate it!

"God has created us to love and to be loved, and this is the beginning of prayer—to know that He loves me, to know that I have been created for greater things," added Mother Teresa.

Those greater things are forever and they cannot be terrorized or killed.

When we think of life in those terms it casts out fear and leads us to repentance. It's those short on faith who fall into a spiral of negative emotions. If you find yourself doing that, grab yourself by the bootstraps. Pull yourself up. Cast that fearfulness away in the name of Jesus! It works: when we cast away fear it must leave—making room for the bliss of thoughts eternal.

Can evil spirits manifest in animals?

Last August the story jumped from the pages of *The Los Angeles Times*. "Tokyo's Feathered Terrorists," said the headline over a story that described how huge crows, some measuring two feet, were haunting the world's largest city, attacking and even stalking people (waiting for them to come out of a building) like something out of a Hitchcock movie.

They swarmed on kids. They hung out near graves. Before an attack, they seemed to have summoned each other. In one case they were suspected of starting a major fire—a blaze sparked "when the birds picked up incense from a graveyard and dropped it on a nearby forest."

It was eerie stuff, and it brings forth a question: can animals be possessed? Can spirits inhabit them? Can this too be a "sign of the times"?

The answer is yes. First off, the Bible tells us of the time Jesus cast demons into a herd of swine, who then threw themselves into the sea (*Matthew* 8:32). If spirits can affect humans, why not animals? We note that in the early days of Christianity, a pope exorcised the vicinity of Nero's tomb when there were rumors of spirits plaguing the area and apparitions in the neighboring district were said to take the form of crows.

I don't think anyone needs to be reminded of the significance of animals—crows and black cats—in witchcraft.

We note what also seems like an explosion of crows in parts of the U.S. (where, as in Japan, materialism, occultism, and atheism have grown rampant).

We have seen cases where crows seem to hang around at peculiar times and seem to caw in aggravation.

We have seen times when they have fled in the face of prayer. That may sound ridiculous, but not to those acquainted with Christianity's mystical literature. In the *Life of St. Hilarion* it's stated that the saint often dealt with furious animals possessed by demons. "One day there was brought to him an enormous camel which had killed several persons," noted a famous demonologist named Father Delaporte in a classical work called *The Devil*. "It was dragged along by more than thirty men, with great ropes; its eyes were bloodshot, its mouth frothing, its tongue swollen and constantly moving; its frightful roaring filled the air with a strange and dismal sound."

Hilarion addressed the spirit with derision: "Whether thou art in a fox or a camel, thou art always the same," he said. "Thou dost not frighten me."

With that animal tried to charge him but suddenly fell to the ground.

[Let's also remember that a crow can be good—witness the one that hung out with Elijah—and that when we are thinking of spirits and birds our thoughts should fly with the doves.]

Are bishops against the supernatural?

It's like clockwork. In some part of the nation there will be a report of a weeping icon or an apparition or some other miracle and the local bishop will either ignore the situation, express immediate skepticism, or even condemn it. In many cases the hierarchy is tougher on mystical phenomena—phenomena that in some cases are at the very foundation of Christianity—than the secular media.

The instances are legion. Last fall, when a statue of St. Philomena exuded tears in Michigan, authorities rushed to indicate that they would have nothing to do with it, while in Arizona a bishop stopped a priest who wanted to exhibit a host on which an image of the Virgin Mary miraculously appeared. In New York State a priest hid a Communion host that had materialized on the hands of a woman in a chapel for fear that crowds would descend. And back in Michigan another bishop forced a priest to destroy a host that exuded blood and then turned into what looked like an actual flesh-and-blood heart.

In recent years apparitions have been rejected in at least half a dozen states and any number of other nations.

What goes on here? Why is the Church so skittish? Is there *anything* it will accept?

The faithful can't be blamed for asking such questions, and much of it is rooted in Medjugorje. There, despite overwhelming evidence (literally millions of extraordinary testimonies), a local bishop tried to condemn the apparitions and was stopped only when the Vatican intervened to save the situation. Since that time, apparition after apparition has fallen to the wayside due to negative rulings by the local bishop, and because of what happened at Medjugorje, many of the faithful assume that such bishops are similarly in error.

But are they? Do the local hierarchies have it wrong? Or do they know something we don't?

Much of the problem is in training. Many of today's priests have no background in how to approach the supernatural. The study of mystical theology has been stripped from the seminaries and replaced by the cold spiritless practices of psychology—which tends to treat claims of the supernatural as an illusion. Our priests have been raised on mechanistic philosophy. Some tell us they received no more than an hour of formal instruction on phenomena like demonic possession during their entire time at the seminary!

At seminary and then in the "logical," scientific world, they're immersed in an intellectuality that stifles the spirit.

No doubt about that. But does that mean bishops are always wrong? Hardly. In fact, often the issue goes deeper, and we have seen cases where the bishop was right despite widespread popular perception. While in the wake of what happened at Medjugorje it's easy to assume that every bishop who rejects an apparition is incorrect, that's not usually the case in situations where bishops actually set down formal rulings. Indeed, bishops have a special anointing *despite* the scientism that has been heaped on them, and this anointing often allows them to spot higher forms of deception. They are also privy to "inside" information or advised by priests who have listened to alleged seers in Confession (although this is not to say that the seal of Confession is broken).

The bottom line is that bishops must be obeyed and are often more correct than we know but at the same time may need to catch up on mystical theology. The root of Christianity is in the supernatural nature of Christ, Who most powerfully showed Himself precisely through the supernormal: healings, exorcisms, transfiguration, miracles, supernormal knowledge, and in the end apparitions. That tells us something. It tells us that we're the mystical body of Christ—not the intellectual one.

How Bernadette of Lourdes defeated Satan at her deathbed

It was 143 years ago Sunday that a 14-year-old girl named Bernadette Soubirous from the poor hamlet of Lourdes in the far southern end of France had her famous experience. It happened as she and some friends were trying to cross the River Gave near a small grotto or indentation in the rock.

"I had just begun to take off my first stocking when suddenly I heard a great noise like the sound of a storm," Bernadette was later to recount. "I looked to the right, to the left, under the trees of the river, but nothing moved; I thought I was mistaken. I went on taking off my shoes and stockings; then I heard a fresh noise like the first. I was frightened and stood straight up. I lost all power of speech and thought when, turning my head toward the *grotto,* I saw at one of the openings of the rock a rosebush, one only, moving as if it were very windy. Almost at the same time there came out of the interior of the grotto a golden-colored cloud, and soon after a Lady, young and beautiful, exceedingly beautiful, the like of whom I had never seen, came and placed herself at the entrance of the opening above the rosebush. She looked at me immediately, smiled at me and signed to me to advance, as if she had been my mother."

The devil tried to disrupt it. It has been reported that during the vision a disturbance arose behind Bernadette at the river. There were many sounds that seemed to echo and reply to each other. They were questioning, shouting, contradicting, like the voices of a crowd in tumult, as one reporter wrote. Amid the confusion one more distinct than the rest, more demanding, more menacing, cried in a furious way, "Flee! Flee!" to the Virgin, but the Virgin had only to turn her eyes towards the point of commotion for a moment and there was immediate silence.

There was also a struggle years later when Bernadette, who became a nun, was about to die.

"We should not forget," writes Leon Cristiani, "that Bernadette, of simple peasant stock like the Cure d'Ars, ended her days in the convent of Nevers, and that in her last hours she had to struggle against the devil as the Cure d'Ars had had to do throughout his life.

"As she lay dying, in fact, she displayed for a moment a great fear, and one of the nuns who was tending her heard her say very clearly: 'Leave me, satan!' But soon afterwards the little saint recovered her tranquility, and died in an atmosphere of victorious peace."

(To the grave with Bernadette went three secrets the Virgin had granted, secrets that she never revealed and that she said were not even meant to be known by the Pope.)

Boy sees the Virgin during apparition at Medjugorje as Mary said to field pilgrims' questions

Fifteen pilgrims were given a special grace during the Virgin Mary's apparition to Medjugorje visionary Marija Pavlovi-Lunetti on Tuesday: The Virgin answered whatever question they had—and told a young man that he would soon be in Heaven.

By Jakob Marschner in Bosnia-Hercegovina

MEDJUGORJE – Much to the surprise of everyone present The Virgin Mary grabbed deeply in her bag of special graces during Tuesday's apparition to Medjugorje visionary Marija Pavlovi-Lunetti. While already feeling privileged to attend the apparition in the chapel of Saint Joseph's retreat house 15 pilgrims were called forward and told that they could ask the Queen of Heaven any question they had on their mind.

"We were sitting way down in the back of the aisle when Marija pointed us out at the end of her talk before the apparition. She told us to come up in front, to kneel down and pray deeply. Then the Blessed Virgin would allow us to ask her whatever we liked," says Jack Gutierrez of Santa Barbara, California.

"I asked her if she would hold my hand and teach me how to pray with the heart. And then I heard her answer—in my heart: 'I will,' she just said," says Gutierrez who describes the clear voice in his heart as very much feminine as well as American.

"I did not sense that myself, but I was told that tears were flowing down my cheeks. And I had so much energy when I left from there," says Jack Gutierrez whose 5-year-old old son Michael Jacob was at least as privileged: He relates that he saw the Virgin Mary during the entire apparition.

"She was dressed in white and blue, and several times she smiled at me," he says.

For several weeks Michael Jacob Gutierrez has charmed his way into the hearts of quite a number of English speaking pilgrims. He prays with great devotion and he hears the Mass with an attention and interest that has impressed many pilgrims in the village. Michael is calm and down-to-earth and has a love for Christ and His Mother that makes it very much unlikely that he would ever tell a lie about the Virgin. Also it has happened before that children of Medjugorje pilgrims have got the grace of seeing Virgin Mary.

The behavior and testimony of the 5-year-old likewise serves to clarify that no child is too young for Medjugorje. In the course of his very young life Michael has been to the village five times, he clearly understands what goes on, and displays a lovely childish saintliness that speaks volumes of how much he has profited. He also confirms the importance of teaching children to pray and taking them to Mass from early on in their lives, a topic raised by visionaries Jakovolo and Ivanka Elez and covered earlier this month by *Spirit Daily*.

Also during the question session on Tuesday a European pilgrim was given guidance on her prayer life, a Mexican woman asked nothing but burst in tears from sensing the Virgin Mary's unusual closeness—and a young man from America was told that he would soon be in Heaven. His name is withheld since his family does not know of this yet, but the young man seems unaffected and nothing but happy with the news.

Among the English speaking pilgrims much discussion, meditation and attention is these days being given to the Virgin Mary's latest monthly message from March 25th. To many it has served as a wake-up call—and also as a chance to consider how time is being spent, and which priorities are at the forefront in life. It is generally agreed that the ambitious message speaks volumes of a world which is losing itself in useless materialism, but also many pilgrims have been encouraged to make still better use of the current time of grace: "Dear children, also today I call you to open yourselves to prayer. Little children, you live in a time in which God gives great graces but you do not know how to make good use of them. You are concerned about everything else, but the least about the soul and spiritual life. Awaken from the tired sleep of your soul and say yes to God with all your strength. Decide for conversion and holiness. I am with you, little children, and I call you to perfection of your soul and of everything you do. Thank you for having responded to my call," the Virgin Mary said in her last message.

Disease has risen as the scourge of our time but can be handled by prayer

Do you know somebody who is seriously ill? Or do you yourself suffer a condition that's incurable?

Odds are you do, but the point we'd like to make today is that there is no such thing as "incurable." Believe it or not, there's not a single form of cancer—even the seemingly surefire fatal ones like brain or pancreatic or lung cancer—that has not been the subject of miraculous healing. No matter what the doctor has told you and no matter how sick you or someone you know may be, there can be a healing if you pray enough, if there is enough faith, if you discipline your lives, and if it's God's will.

Although no one likes to mention it, part of the scourge of our time—part of the tribulation—is disease, and when we think of disease, nothing concerns us more than cancer. If we count skin cancer, somewhere between one of every four and one of every three Americans will suffer it, according to government statistics. In many parts of the world, the figures are similar. Although there was a leveling off and slight decrease of the death rate in the 1990s, its skyrocketing prevalence has brought us to the point where rare is the family that has not been touched by it. When we look around, especially in the way of breast or prostate disease, it seems like nearly everyone has it. What were once rare forms, like brain cancer, are now prevalent. Breast cancer is the most common form of cancer in women in the United States. In 2001, 192,000 new cases of female invasive breast cancer were expected to be diagnosed, causing fatalities in more than 40,000.

That's the bad news. The good news is that there is building evidence this disease can be defeated with a combination of good medical care, vitamins, a change in diet—and prayer. In fact, there are now some incontrovertible and tremendous cases of miraculous cures. Last year we carried a story on the case of a well-respected doctor (chief of a hospital in Caracas) who himself had very serious cancer of the prostate that had spread to his spine—often a death sentence. But he was cured in an instant after visiting the Church-sanctioned apparition site of Betania.

It was an impressive case because it was so dramatic, life-saving, and well-documented, but there are hundreds—thousands—of others. There is now no doubt that cancer and other serious diseases can be defeated. It takes faith. It takes prayer. But if it is the will of God, prayer will have an effect that is *remarkable*. Even scientific studies are showing this. A recent survey of cardiac patients conducted at St. Luke's Hospital in Kansas City, Missouri, concluded that intercessory prayer makes a scientifically noticeable difference (*see the October 25, 1999 issue of the Archives of Internal Medicine*)—and when something can show up in statistics, you know it's a powerful effect that goes beyond the numbers.

If someone prays for them, patients admitted to the hospital with heart problems suffer fewer complications, according to scientists. A study carried out at Duke University Medical Center in North Carolina found that patients who received alternative therapy following angioplasty were 25% to 30% less likely to suffer complications. And those who received "intercessory prayer" had the greatest success rate. We have friends who have seen serious breast cancer vanish, or who have fought back from other disabilities. We have seen people pop up from wheelchairs, and just recently we had the account of *a woman who had been paralyzed for 22 years* before a fantastic healing with the intercession of two Fatima seers! Many are those who feel the healing power of Christ with Confession and the Eucharist. These are *potent i*nstruments of healing. There is nothing that God will not and has not cured. There is *no such thing* as an incurable disease.

Do such things always happen? No. Often, suffering is part of God's salvation plan. Often, our time has come. But more often prayer causes *remarkable* effects. And the more we pray, the more powerful those prayers—and our faith—become. At this time when there is such a scourge, we need to pray for prevention of disease; we need to ask the Holy Spirit what food our bodies need; and we need to pray for the best route of healing if disease or other problems do strike. When the studies on prayer mention "alternative healing," they are referring to changes in diet that greatly reduce salt, fat, and dairy products, replacing them with fruit, vegetables, and vitamins. We have become so concerned with this aspect and

Vicar says Medjugorje will not be judged until long after apparitions

The Vicar General of Sarajevo in Bosnia-Hercegovina says there will be no official determination on the famous apparitions at Medjugorje until long after they have ended. In a recent interview with *Spirit Daily*, the vicar, Father Mato Zovkic, said there are no current plans to reopen an investigation into the apparitions that stalled when a previous investigative body halted due to the Bosnian conflicts in the 1990s. He said it could take "10 or 15 years" after the conclusion of apparitions for the Church to reach a final determination on authenticity.

"There is no need for a new commission as long as the seers claim Our Lady continues coming to them," said Father Zovkic. "Nothing new is happening [since the previous investigation]. The usual procedure in Catholic history in past similar cases was when the experience is stopped, after ten or 15 years, a new commission is nominated and they research what the seers say then about the experience."

That may mean such action, if it ever arrives, will come after the unfolding of "secrets" the seers say they have been given by the Virgin Mary. At least one of the visionaries has said that the Virgin will continue to appear up to and even during the onset of such events. Each has been or will be given ten secrets. Although it is commonly said that apparitions are never judged until completion, such has not always been the case, especially in recent times, when mystical claims associated with approved apparitions have continued after ecclesiastic rulings at places like Betania in Venezuela.

We called the Sarajevo diocese last month after a report came from CW News in Rome that Cardinal Vinko Puljic—president of the Bosnia-Hercegovina bishops conference, which has jurisdiction over Medjugorje—was negative toward the apparitions. CW News claimed that Cardinal Puljic had publicly complained at the Synod of Bishops that Medjugorje had created division between the secular diocese and Franciscans (due to a controversy back in the 1980s with two Franciscans) and referred to "pseudo-charisms."

This raised alarm because Cardinal Puljic has the potential for an important say in the authenticity of the apparitions—if the jurisdiction remains with Bosnian bishops. There are only four members of the conference: Cardinal Puljic; his auxiliary bishop; the Bishop of Banja-Luka; and Bishop Ratko Peric of Mostar—who oversees the actual diocese to which Medjugorje belongs and who has been strongly opposed to Medjugorje.

Usually a determination on authenticity is in the hands of that local bishop but in this case the authority of the local bishop was removed by the Vatican and given over to a national commission after the previous bishop attempted to rule negatively on the apparitions. The Vatican—which could also take the matter out of the hands of the Bosnian bishops conference—is itself monitoring Medjugorje and sent observers there last June.

Perplexing is the fact that in the official text of Cardinal Puljic's synod remarks is no mention of Medjugorje. That has raised questions of whether they were inaccurately reported or the Cardinal—who Father Zovkic said is indeed negative toward Medjugorje at the present time—made the remarks as a departure from his prepared text. If and when an investigation is reopened, said Father Zovkic, it will focus on the lives of the seers and what they have to say years after the experiences end. He said the Cardinal expects "saintliness" and would use the seers in the Sacred Heart and Miraculous Medal revelations, Saint Margaret Mary Alacoque and Saint Catherine Laboure, as points of comparison.

"The lives of the seers are very important—how do they behave later on, what do they say about their experiences, and then a final conclusion can be made," said the vicar general. "As far as I know the Cardinal did pay a private visit once or twice since he was nominated bishop, but never did he conduct an official ceremony in Medjugorje, because according to ecclesiastical rules, the local bishop should give previous permission. So the Cardinal does not go before he is asked."

Father Zovkic added that if the Cardinal referred to trouble with Franciscans in the region, he was not referring to the present pastor or priests at Saint James Parish at Medjugorje, where there have been diligent efforts to reconcile with the Mostar Bishop.

Father Zovkic noted that the local Franciscans welcomed the Mostar Bishop for Confirmation rites last spring and have allowed the diocese to review financial records indicating how money collected from pilgrims has been spent.

"Century of evil" about to close

Is it true that we have been through a special period given to the devil to test man? Was the twentieth century designed as Satan's century? And is this era of special evil about to end?

We know that every century has its evil. There is always a certain degree of darkness. There was the Roman Empire. There was Genghis Khan. But many argue that none was more evil than the twentieth century—from Hitler to abortion—and it's about to end: the last year of the century was not 1999 but is the current year of 2000.

Few believe that we can reduce prophecy to exact years—God doesn't rule by our calendar—but in general the century that is about to end was indeed a great battle. Its very onset was preceded by the rise precisely in 1900 of an occultist named Aleister Crowley—whose own mother called him "The Beast" and who was part of esoteric organizations that sought to replace Christ with a "new age."

"Thine hour is come," Crowley once railed at Christ during a satanic ceremony. "As I blot thee out from this earth, so surely shall the eclipse pass. . . Give thou place to me, O Jesus," said this deranged satanist from England. "Thine aeon is pass; the Age of Horus is arisen by the Magick of the Master."

We can laugh at such pagan egoism but what's not laughable is the cursed period that followed. When we count the number of Christians who were killed for their faith during the twentieth century (under Lenin, Mao, and Stalin), it tallies to *more than the combined total of all preceding 19 centuries.*

As for war: more than forty million died during World War Two alone—and that's not counting the horrors in the Soviet Union.

There was persecution. There were other wars. There was an explosion of worldliness. Electricity, chemicals, movies, television, automobiles, and medicines made man believe he could create utopia on earth and no longer needed God. Churches emptied, morality plummeted, and by the 1960s drugs, raucous music, and fornication—sex before marriage—became the norm. There were "gay rights." There was radical feminism. The first "church of Satan" rose in California in 1966 (check out that date!) and there was even a famous song called "Sympathy for the Devil."

It had all been predicted. A seer at LaSalette in France had warned that Lucifer, together with a large number of demons, would be "unloosed from hell," while according to legend Pope Leo XIII envisioned a century during which Satan would be granted enhanced power.

At Fatima Sister Lucia dos Santos, the sole surviving visionary from the famous apparitions, described the era as a "decisive battle," and at Medjugorje an official letter in 1983 from the parish to the Vatican reporting on the apparitions quoted Mary as saying that *"Satan exists. One day he appeared before the throne of God and asked permission to submit the Church to a period of trial. God gave him permission to try the Church for one century. This century is under the power of the devil."*

There has been controversy over that statement and once more let me emphasize: we can't hold God to precise dates. The year 2000 is a human term. The Virgin was speaking in a general manner, and this was confirmed when a priest interviewed one of the Medjugorje seers, Mirjana Dragicevic Soldo. "You said the twentieth century has been given over to the devil?" she was asked.

"Yes."

"You mean the century until the year 2000, or generally speaking?" asked Father Tomislav Vlasic.

"Generally, part of which is in the twentieth century, until the first secret is unfolded," explained Mirjana. "The devil will rule till then."

She used the word "generally." It was not an exactly dated message. It doesn't mean that Satan's power will suddenly stop January 1 at the stroke of midnight. But there's no question that evil has reached what must be close to a crescendo and that by God's grace the new century will see a purification unfold.

Many souls said to be released on Christmas from torment of purgatory

Aside from gift-giving and spending time with family and remembering the birth of Jesus, Christmas should be a day to pray for the deceased. It's on Christmas—according to two highly reliable revelations—that most souls are released into heaven and thus are in need of final prayers.

One revelation was in 1879 to a holy nun in a French convent. Identified as Sister M. de L.C., she received revelations from a deceased nun who authorities identified only as Sister O—and who at the time was herself suffering the torments of purgatory. The revelation was granted an imprimatur from the Cardinal of Baltimore, Maryland, and was approved by noted theologians such as Canon Dubosq, *promotor fidei* of Saint Therese the Little Flower. The transcripts of what she said may be the most valuable we've seen on purgatory.

"On All Souls' Day many souls leave the place of expiation and go to heaven," said the deceased nun. "Also, by a special grace of God on that day *only*, all the suffering souls, without exception, have a share in the public prayers of the Church, even those who are in the great Purgatory. Still the relief of each soul is in proportion to its merits. Some receive more, some less, but all feel the benefit of this extraordinary grace. Many of the suffering souls receive this one help only in all the long years they pass here and this by the justice of God. It is not, however, on All Souls' Day that the most go to Heaven. It is on Christmas night."

This message was confirmed in dramatic style more than a hundred years later—in 1983—when a seer at Medjugorje reported nearly the same message, and with virtually no chance of having been privy to the obscure French revelation (which had not been published). Said the Virgin at Medjugorje on January 10 of that year: *"In Purgatory there are different levels. The lowest is close to Hell and the highest gradually draws near to Heaven. It is not on All Souls' Day, but at Christmas, that the greatest number of souls leave Purgatory."*

At Medjugorje it has been said that the Virgin appears in great golden splendor on special days like Christmas, and the French nun likewise said Our Blessed Mother goes to Purgatory on her great feast days. She takes souls that are ready—and all they may need is one final Mass, or even a final prayer. Those on the "threshold" can gain Heaven that day with our help, while those in deeper parts of Purgatory will be relieved of suffering.

"There are many souls in Purgatory," said the Blessed Mother at Medjugorje. *"There are also persons who have been consecrated to God—some priests, some religious. Pray for their intentions, at least the Lord's Prayer, the Hail Mary, and the Glory Be seven times each, and the Creed. I recommend it to you. There are a large number of souls who have been in Purgatory for a long time because no one prays for them."*

This puts an entirely new perspective on Christmas. It's a time of great joy not only on earth but in the eternal and a day that our own joy must be joined with concern for those who have gone before us—who may be "graduating" that day.

Pray for them. Pray for everyone you have ever known who is deceased. Pray for every purgatorial soul on Christmas. If they don't need the prayers, the Lord can designate them to souls who do. And one day—perhaps on Christmas night—they'll be there to help you.

[Sister O's revelations are in a booklet called "An Unpublished Manuscript on Purgatory," provided by Fatima House.]

Churches fill and people pray as events tied to purification intensify

by Michael H. Brown

The concern was palpable. As we finally boarded a flight home Saturday ticket agents searched even the bags we had checked in and once airborne there was an uneasiness every time the pilot came on and the intercom crackled.

Returning home after being stranded for four days in Salt Lake City, there was the feeling that the nation had received a preview of chastisement. This is not the main event; this is an intensification. In any period of warning events come one after another, and that's what we see now: natural events interspersed with high-point crises like the attack in New York. How we spiritually respond will determine what we face next.

Let's face it: we were a great moral nation. We can be a great nation again. We're based on the trust of God. It's right there in our pledge and our anthem. We have a flag in our yard. God bless this great nation!

But please Lord wake it up. Let it face the facts. Let it note that millions saw demonic images in the very smoke and fire from the Trade Center—as if God was purging evil. It was right there in today's (September 16) Mass reading: "Then the LORD said to Moses, 'Go down, because your people, whom you brought up out of Egypt, have become corrupt. They have been quick to turn away from what I commanded them and have made themselves an idol cast in the shape of a calf. They have bowed down to it and sacrificed to it and have said, 'These are your gods, O Israel, who brought you up out of Egypt.' 'I have seen these people,' the LORD said to Moses, 'and they are a stiff-necked people. Now leave me alone so that my anger may burn against them and that I may destroy them. Then I will make you into a great nation.'"

Anyone who thinks it was a coincidence that Americans had to endure the spectacle of its financial center crumbling before its eyes must believe that everything is just coincidence.

It isn't. These are signs—not yet *the* sign, not yet *the* chastisements, but the largest precursor to date. While disasters like the Galveston flood of 1900 took more lives and while other nations have seen calamities much greater even during the last several years (20,000 may have died during mudslides in 1999 in Venezuela), the flagrancy and televised nature of the destruction on September 11 was the most startling event for the world since the assassination of JFK and came with a series of events that clearly showed it as part of a build-up.

Events are quickening and we have to realize that our nation can swiftly be incapacitated, that its seemingly advanced infrastructure can be brought to its knees overnight. It took the destruction of just two buildings to ground every plane in this great, 3,000-mile-wide nation. I saw first-hand what will happen if there is a failure in our infrastructure. I was in *Salt Lake City speaking of the dangers of chastisement* and the following morning as I waited for a ride to the airport it happened: on live TV the second plane struck the south tower. I hurried to the airport, where I learned that another plane hit the Pentagon. I was flying United Airlines and two of their planes had been hijacked. As a man announced that all flights were grounded—"locked down"—the TV near the gate was clicked off and emergency security measures were taken. The hands of a clerk trembled as I tried to get a later flight but was totally, startlingly unable.

The airports were closed, you couldn't get anyone on the phone, flight after flight was cancelled. Your only chance of talking to an actual person was to awaken in the middle of the night and hang on the line; there was no room on the trains; no good prospects of a bus; no car rentals. People were even buying used cars or renting U-Hauls in an effort to get home—that's how desperate, how helpless, how alien it all was.

On Thursday I got news that one of my closest friends, Daniel Smith of Northport, New York, an old and dear college buddy, was missing in the World Trade Center rubble.

Frustration had turned to a wrenching sadness. For the first time in a long while, I found myself weeping, unable to stop. We prayed for him. We prayed for all the dead—many of whom are victim-souls (it rains on the good and bad alike). Frustration, fear, sadness. It's not like God sends Osama bin Laden. It's a case of our pushing away the Lord's protective shield. That exposes us to evil. And it will get worse. It will get worse *unless* America learns the most profound lesson in all of this. It's not just about terrorists. It's not just about rooting them out. It's about returning to the *moral* greatness of America (forget money!). There are hopeful signs. People are praying. They are filling churches. Some are looking inward. Even the most stiff-necked have been made to take notice. Since the horrific terrorist attacks on New York and Washington, "we have noted that many more people are coming to churches," says Father Carlos Mullins, a priest at St. Philip Neri Parish in the Bronx. In a telephone call, the Argentine priest told *ZENIT News:* "We have four daily Masses in our parish; I noted, in those which I celebrated, that the church was full. In these hours, all are taking recourse to prayer as the ultimate thing that remains: to pray for those who died and for their relatives."

This is good. Pray that it continues. For God will bless America —but first it has to realize what's going on and return to His embrace.

Climate change indicates purification

By Michael H. Brown

It's now clear: Since the middle part of the 19th century, our planet has warmed substantially and the result will be more whipsawing weather, heavy winter precipitation, and "storms of the century." It's not clear if the warming will continue or reverse, but there's little doubt that it will change. The issue is now being debated among the world's largest nations, who are worried—some urgently—about the meteorological swerve.

In my book I argue that these harbingers herald a general purification. The argument is not so much whether the climate is changing, but whether it's caused by pollution or natural forces.

I'm not sure which is the case but I believe it also has to do with supernatural forces. Through history, whenever chastisements of society are about to begin, there is a change in climate.

During Egyptian times and in the latter Bronze Age it was a cooling, while during the last major chastisement—the bubonic plague in the Middle Ages—it was global warming almost identical to what we now see, followed by a downward gyration in temperatures.

Such changes are accompanied by severe weather and we are seeing it already.

Look around: storms in England, floods in Asia, hurricanes in North Carolina. A year ago phenomenal rains killed at least 20,000 in Venezuela.

Every week, it seems, brings some part of the world its "storm of the century."

Right now Sweden is experiencing its worst floods in 100 years.

No part of the world has been immune—fires out west while there are floods in the east and in India and the Pacific and Asia: strong ocean surges.

It's how God works. It's the way He always has. Throughout the entire Bible we see instances where He has used the weather to nudge mankind back to obedience and so now we see flux in climate accompanied by unusual events, whether political, military, or meteorological.

Oven-like temperatures in Israel. Drought in Egypt. When evil builds, God allows events that break the evil down.

As prophesied as long ago as LaSalette, the Catholic site where the Virgin Mary gave secrets in 1846, our seasons are altering. While scientists and politicians can debate the cause of the upward temperature trend (whether it's natural or from pollution), the trend itself is clear. Since the mid-part of the 19th century, temperatures over land have increased by 1.8 degrees.

That's a startling flux in a field where changes are measures in the thousandths.

And the result has already been wild weather. When there's more heat there's more moisture, and when there's more moisture, there's more precipitation. There is more rising air and violent wind. In Texas tornadoes have sucked the lungs out of cattle and hailstones have crashed through windows.

According to scientists I interviewed, there has already been an eight-to-ten percent increase in rainfall and half of the increase is occurring in the most intense events.

Translation: severe storms are becoming that much more severe.

Monsoons will have more rain, hurricanes will be larger, and while winters will be warmer, blizzards will have more snow. We have already seen this in Buffalo.

There will be floods and what Our Lady of LaSalette called "convulsions of water."

The 1990s saw record weather and the new century is continuing the trend with a vengeance. There were a phenomenal 65 tropical storms in the Atlantic between 1995 and 1999 and during that last year five category-four hurricanes formed for the first time as global surface temperatures hovered around 62 degrees and reports of large hailstorms tripled.

In 1999, Oklahoma saw the strongest winds ever recorded in a tornado as the number of twisters skyrocketed from 800 a year in the 1980s to more than 1,200 some years in the 1990s.

Two years ago so much rain was dumped during a hurricane in Central America that fifty years worth of infrastructure was destroyed, rivers rerouted, and corpses floated from one country to another.

The same happened in the past. During the Middle Ages temperatures increased so much that grapes were grown in England and agriculture sprung up on Iceland, along with major European floods that alternated with disease and famine.

It was a time—like our own—of increased solar activity. Small fluxes on the sun can cause changes in radiation with major effects not only on temperature but on the way clouds in the upper atmosphere are formed.

Is this why the sun is seen to spin and change color at prophetic sites like Fatima, Betania, and Medjugorje?

It was the very year of LaSalette that old parchment records show a tremendous temperature spike in Ireland.

It hasn't stopped. In fact the 1990s saw seven of the warmest years on record.

In Dallas there was a stretch of more than a month where temperatures hit 100 every single day, while in the North they're spotting southern birds like the pelican. In what climatologists said was a 1,000-year event, the thermometer stayed above 80 degrees Fahrenheit for 12 consecutive nights in Tampa during 1998, and Arctic ice has shrunken by 14 percent.

Global surface temperature is now hovering around 62, there is now a third of a degree rise in temperature every decade, and scientists fear it could rise up to another two to seven degrees by the end of this century—which would be more than we have seen in 120,000 years, if not longer.

God designed it so that our greatest joy is closeness to Him

God designed the world so that our greatest joy is closeness to Him. No matter what you seek in life, no matter how much money you have, no matter your luxury, you'll never get greater pleasure than simply lifting your heart to Him.

Think about that: the basic act of worship is the source of highest gladness. And it's free! When we seek God—when we love Him, when we *adore* Him—He draws us above all physical circumstances.

No matter what you may be going through (pain, depression, worries), if you praise God He will bring you to joy.

That's because praise brings us close to Him, and there is no joy like the joy of knowing the Lord. He sends graces that can completely defy our circumstances. He brings joy where, by the standards of the world, there should be depression. There are those in poverty. There are those who are lonely. There are those with cancer. In God they find happiness.

The opposite is true of those who ignore God and thus set themselves at a distance. Take a look around and you'll see many of the rich with grim looks. No matter what they accomplish on earth, if they don't have a closeness to God, they never find true gladness. Meanwhile those who love the Lord have the glow of well-being.

To draw close we must love Him and seek to do His will, to be what he planned for us to be. We must seek Him in everything. Then comes a joy that's indescribable. You can buy a yacht or a Mercedes—you can marry well, you can be the most powerful person on earth—but if you don't have God you have not experienced true happiness. You have missed out on that transcendental elation—that ineffable joy that put a smile on the faces of so many saints who to the world seemed poverty-stricken. Remember that smile on the face of Mother Teresa!

When we pray, we draw close to God, and He grants us feelings that can not be attained elsewhere. God is joy and when you draw nearer to Him you draw nearer to joy. It's that simple. There's nothing you can do that will bring as much happiness. And closeness comes through praise. Adore God through the day. Do it from the heart. Love Him. Praise Him over and over—ten times, a hundred times. *Praise You Jesus, praise You Christ.*

That's what will bring you joy because the Lord is joy personified.

Hidden connections: the mystical side of Christopher Columbus

by Michael H. Brown

As the secular press tries to slander him as cruel to the Indians or to take away his credit, the truth is that Christopher Columbus was not only the true discoverer of America, but also a deeply devout Christian with mystical connections.

Indeed, few know that Columbus prayed at a shrine in Spain called Guadalupe before setting off on his great journey. This was a spot where an ancient image of the Virgin had been hidden in the first centuries after the death of Christ and where she later appeared to a herdsman, telling him in 1326 to have the bishop dig up the image and build a chapel. It is believed that Columbus took a replica of the image with him on his first trip across the Atlantic, and when he arrived in the New World he named an island after Guadalupe (it is now spelled "Guadeloupe"), and soon after, the Virgin appeared to an Aztec Indian near Mexico City at a spot that was also named Guadalupe!

The devotion of Columbus was tangible. He named his ship after Christ's mother (the *Santa Maria)* and every night he and his crew sang the *Hail Mary*. According to his diary, Columbus, looking for the correct course, was guided at one critical point by a "marvelous branch of fire" that fell from the sky.

That was on September 15, 1492. Once across the Atlantic, this faithful son named the first island he came to "San Salvador" for the Savior and the second "Santa Maria de la Concepcion" for Mary, in addition to Guadeloupe and another island, Montserrat, named for another ancient apparition site near Barcelona.

Upon landfall Columbus and his men prayed the *Salve Regina*.

Thus, the first Christian prayer recited in the New World was an entreaty calling Mary the great advocate and Mother of God.

While in an attempt to take away his credit many point out the Vikings arrived in North America long before Columbus and that he was brutal with the Indians, the fact is that the Vikings never established their discovery (for all practical purposes, they simply skirted the northern regions and then left), and it was the *Indians* who were brutal. The first Caribbean natives Columbus encountered were cannibals!

Thus, despite the yearning for secular scholars to erase the mystical foundation of America, its very discovery was rooted in Christianity. Other explorers were equally devout. The Mississippi was originally called the "River of the Immaculate Conception" and the Chesapeake the "Bay of Saint Mary." Quebec was known as the "Village of Mary," and Lake George was originally called the "Lake of the Blessed Sacrament." Indians reported apparitions of the Virgin from South America to Montana, and New York State was consecrated to her before it was even known as New York.

The comet next time

by Michael H. Brown

"The asteroid that hits earth may be in there," said Dr. Paul Chodas.

We were standing in a small cramped room at NASA's Jet Propulsion Laboratory in Pasadena. I was there to find out about the comet threat. He was pointing to several small box-like racks—a shockingly makeshift compilation of radar images that could one day be the center of urgent international attention. With us was Dr. Eleanor Helin, the astronomer who heroically began some of the first official searches.

I was concerned because there had been recent "near-misses" with comets or asteroids that no one knew were coming. In 1989 an asteroid had missed earth by six hours. There had also been close buzzes in 1992, 1993, and 1994. In 1994 there was also the Shoemaker-Levy comet that hit Jupiter in 21 fragments (the most spectacular on July 16, feast day of the Virgin of Carmel, which is how Mary appeared during the last apparition at Fatima). And three years after *that* the Hale-Bopp comet hung in the sky for all to see.

That one was 30 to 40 miles wide, according to Chodas—plenty big enough to destroy life on earth. And what bothered me was that it was discovered by *amateur* astronomers just 40 months before its closest pass.

Scientists have no idea when the next such comet will show up. There are two major comet belts, and one alone is suspected of containing more than 200 *million* comets. That's the current guess. Many are "long-term" comets that are more dangerous than asteroids (space rocks that don't glow) because they're winging in from a longer distance. That's saying a lot when you consider that asteroids often move at eight times the speed of a bullet! Long-term comets make their orbits over such a long period that they're not in the history books and could surprise us by coming from a blindspot behind the sun.

Is this in any prophecies? Will there one day be at least a regional event? Does it relate to what *Revelation* 8:8 said about "something like a huge mountain all in flames" that one day would be "cast into the ocean"?

According to astronomers it wouldn't take much of a rock to disrupt our planet. They say anything half-a-mile wide or larger would kick up enough dust to shut down global agriculture.

Even in the middle of the ocean, such an object would cause a wave that would be 35 feet when it reached the coasts, and one that was several times larger would cause a crater at the bottom of the ocean and send waves all the way to the Appalachian foothills.

Yet as Dr. Helin and others pointed out, very little of the sky is monitored. She told me she was convinced earth had been hit more frequently in the past than we know, and that astronomers should study folklore as well as the Bible for such evidence.

Some believe objects struck in the times of the ancient Egyptians, causing swerves in climate around 2500 B.C. and 1000 B.C., then again around 550 A.D.—at the end of the Roman Empire. There are accounts from New Zealand of ancient fireballs and more recent encounters in South America. In 1178 a monk named Gervase of Canterbury watched an object strike the moon on the Sunday before the feast of John the Baptist. The Middle Ages, at the time of bubonic plague, was also a time of comets.

"For a long time we pooh-poohed and discouraged this sort of speculation because we would have just a little bit of information here and there, just a trace, and we would push it off the table," Dr. Helin told me. "But the more I see, the more I think there's an awful lot out there that we've ignored for an awful long time."

The long-term comets, says Helin, are the "stealth bombers in the solar system, the ones that give no warning, that are just there in your face." She said there have been times when she thought something would hit. "You put down the phone and say, 'what do I do now?" she remarked of several unpublicized asteroid scares.

Scientists believe that there are bands of debris that periodically bombard earth. They're at the very root of the word "disaster," which means "evil star" (etymologically, dis-evil and aster-star). And space is filled with them. At one stage last year new asteroids were being discovered at a rate of 24 a month! By the end of the 1990s NASA had logged 1,076 near-earth objects that are either earth-crossers or come close to intersecting our orbit—of which 405 were a kilometer or larger.

Even if we knew something was going to hit, I was told by Dr. Brian Marsden of Harvard, it would take us 15 to 20 years to devise a way of destroying it.

Some say we're centuries away from having to worry about that, while others warn that a cycle of strikes will result by 2300 from what's called the Taurid belt. And still others—a small group of scientists known in government circles as "the X-files Committee"—warn that the earth is already overdue for a rendezvous large enough to extinguish ten percent of the population.

Such an asteroid strikes earth every 100,000 years, they argue, and by their measure it has been that long or longer since the last.

The odds are always great that we won't see that but it points up the need to pray. It's God Who has kept millions of pieces of space junk away from us. We have no idea what's really out there. As one of the foremost experts, Clark R. Chapman, said, a mountain-sized space rock big enough to dramatically alter global climate "could hit tomorrow and we wouldn't even know it was coming." Meanwhile David Morrison, head of NASA's asteroid program, adds that if something comes, the most likely warning time "would be zero."

"These long-period comets are always being found," Dr. Helin told me. "Just thank God they haven't come that close."

Vatican scouts confirmed to have visited

A well-placed source in Bosnia-Hercegovina has told *Spirit Daily* that during last month's anniversary of the Virgin's first apparitions, the famous site of Medjugorje was visited by five officials sent from the Vatican. The mission was to evaluate the current situation, and according to this source the group included a cardinal.

Others have set the number of visitors at three or "several." And while there is no indication whatsoever at this point that the Vatican is ready to move on official approval of Medjugorje, it raises the question of whether John Paul II is pushing for protection of certain major apparitions sites before the end of his pontificate. Two weeks ago the Church approved apparitions reported to have begun at Kibeho, Africa, the same year as the onset of Medjugorje.

The latest visit was by members of the Congregation for Divine Worship and Discipline of the Sacraments. According to our chief source, a glitch occurred when the Vatican officials were asked to leave a house in which they were staying at Medjugorje when the owners accused them of being "spies." Fortunately, another home quickly took in the officials—one of whom indicated that he was favorably disposed toward the apparitions and that a formal investigation may be reactivated. However, a second source with contacts in Rome indicated that the visit cannot be construed as an opening or reopening of an official investigation and "is just the latest in a continuing series of confidential visits by personnel from various dicasteries within the Church that are charged with investigating claims of supernatural occurences."

We will report any official statement. Right now we can only consider the matter an intriguing development.

The history of Church investigations is a checkered one. In 1986 then-Bishop Pavao Zanic of Mostar, who had jurisdiction over Medjugorje, issued a negative report on the apparitions. That had come during tensions with Franciscans, who run the Medjugorje parish and with whom the diocese was quibbling over control of certain parishes in Hercegovina. Although initially favorable to the apparitions, animosity with the Franciscans heightened and Bishop Zanic soon declared negatively on the apparitions. While the local bishop usually has almost total say over an apparition, the Vatican rejected Zanic's negative conclusion and took away his authority on the matter, handing it to a national conference of bishops which issued a statement on April 10, 1991, saying that the inquiry was continuing and that as yet there was no proof of supernaturality. This inquiry was then interrupted, however, by a civil war.

By 1995 40,000 priests had visited Medjugorje, along with hundreds of bishops and cardinals. At one point last week, there were 150 priests concelebrating evening Mass, including a Caribbean bishop.

The tension between the secular diocese and the Franciscans continues. During our recent pilgrimage we were told that 14 Franciscan in the region had been dismissed by Bishop Ratko Peric, the new prelate who had been an assistant to Bishop Zanic and is equally at odds with Franciscans. In recent months he has sought to argue his case against Medjugorje at the Vatican. At the same time, the new Franciscan pastor of St. James parish has sought reconciliation with the bishop, who showed cordiality while conducting a recent confirmation Mass at Medjugorje.

Consecration said to have prevented nuclear war

There were two huge developments during the last week for those who followed Fatima. That's the site where Mary appeared to three shepherd children in 1917, of course, and the major drama was an announcement from the Vatican that the lone surviving seer, Lucia dos Santos, who is in her nineties and still cloistered in a convent at Coimbra, has verified that the third secret was revealed in full and that a major request at Fatima—that Russia be consecrated to her Immaculate Heart—was successfully completed on March 25, 1984, by Pope John Paul II.

Little known is the fact that Sister Lucia has also indicated the 1984 consecration prevented a nuclear war that otherwise would have occurred in 1985. She told this to Cardinal Ricardo Vidal of the Philippines upon his visit with her in 1993—and indeed 1985 was a time of severe Cold War tensions. The third secret, we must remember, showed an angel about to torch the earth.

We have reported this previously but it is crucial to mention now that the world has concerns about another nuclear event—whether a terrorist smuggling one into the U.S. or an exchange initiated from nations like India, Pakistan, Korea, or Iraq.

Something is in the wind, and we are called—especially at a powerful time like Christmas—to pray about it.

Last year the Pope entrusted the world again to the Virgin and in retrospect we now see how crucial it was for a year of such turmoil. Who knows what would have happened if he had *not* done that—and who knows how many events have been prevented since September 11 by your prayers. It is for good reason that the Pope has called for fasting—which can prevent war and suspend natural laws.

The other major development was word that Russian President Vladimir Putin is allegedly "a true Christian..." We don't know what to make of it as yet but it is claimed he goes to confession at an Orthodox church and receives Communion. At Fatima the Virgin had said that if Russia was consecrated it would be converted.

Is this true conversion?

While there are those who might argue that the Orthodox Church, though Christian, does not constitute "conversion" (since it is still separate from Rome, which gives us pause), it is a long way from the atheism that has dominated that nation for nearly a century, and new polls show church attendance gaining in Russia as it declines in the West. Russia still has a *long* way to go, but it was said at Fatima that the consecration would stop it from spreading its errors around the world.

To a significant extent, that has happened; the spread of atheism, at least from Russia, has greatly slowed; but what of the prophecy of a "period of peace"? In 1917 the Virgin had predicted that "in the end, my Immaculate Heart will triumph. The Holy Father will consecrate Russia to me, and she will be converted, and a *period of peace* will be granted to the world."

Sister Lucia indicated that those words pertained to the end of East European Communism. But it is just a "period," which by definition is a limited time, and while the 1990s indeed saw a period of unprecedented peace (at least in the global military sense, and certainly in the context of the Cold War, as well as in the context of the last 2,000 years, which has seen virtually nonstop European combat), we see now how quickly peace can slip from our grasp and that with the fulfillment of Fatima may now come the era of the secrets of Medjugorje.

New Medjugorje mystery as large metal statue exudes fluid

A huge metal corpus of the Crucified Christ is exuding a watery unknown substance behind St. James Church in Medjugorje Bosnia-Hercegovina.

The statue, a recent addition to the famous grounds, was made in Slovenia of what appears to be heavy bronze. It's in a lot where vineyards once stood, with Mount Krizevac—or "Cross Mountain"—in the background.

The substance is coming from a side of the right knee where metal has been worn down or scraped in a natural way to form what could pass as a wound. It is from there, at the top of the small scraped area, that a substance moves in small, pulsing quantities until a drop is formed and it begins to methodically streak down the statue. First dozens but by Sunday hundreds of pilgrims were gathering around the knee to touch a substance that feels like a cross between water and oil and comes inexplicably from the metal. Can bronze "sweat"? Could it be a natural phenomenon? Could the statue—about 15 feet high—have been filled with water?

One of the seers went to see it Sunday, but so far there has been no comment from the parish on this new mystery at the place where the Blessed Mother began appearing precisely 20 years ago.

[*note*: John Blair, project manager for Jozef Custom Ironworks, a large firm in Bridgeport, tells *Spirit Daily* that the fact that a large bronze corpus of Christ at Medjugorje is filled at the bottom with concrete might increase the chance of humidity but that "it would be a stretch" to try to explain the flow of liquid on the filling.

"It doesn't make sense," said Blair, an expert on bronze. "It doesn't make sense that it would hold water that long. Absolutely not."

Blair was asked if when there's humidity bronze sweats to the point where something can exude from the metal itself. "That's a really curious question," he replied. "I've never seen it from humidity. However, when I apply a patina, when I flame it with a torch, it does sweat then. You do get moisture over the surface of the bronze. But I've never seen it from heat or humidity."

Blair said the only probable explanation at this point (and he has not examined the actual statue) is water somehow finding its way into the interior and then leaching out.]

Mysterious Medjugorje fluid fits wound on Shroud

We've been bringing you word of a "wound" that has exuded a strange liquid from a bronze statue of the Crucified Christ in Medjugorje. If supernatural, this is one of the most remarkable phenomena recorded at the world-famous site. The flow has stopped (at least temporarily), but it was witnessed throughout the week following the twentieth anniversary last June and was also reported last March and October.

Experts are puzzled over what would cause a watery-oily fluid to flow from an area of the right knee that has eroded and stained in such a way as to look like a wound.

But interesting is the fact that the mark can be seen, along with others, as corresponding to the Shroud of Turin—the famous linen said to bear an image of Christ. Professor Giovanni Battista of the University of Milan has identified heavy damage to the knees of the figure in the shroud—including a large contusion to the left knee in combination with excoriations with jagged edges in the region of the patella or kneecap, and further, smaller contusion wounds to the right knee.

This would agree with the "wound" on the Medjugorje corpus—if not in the exact same place, with the general idea of Christ falling, and most probably injuring the side of the damaged knees.

Evidence from other shroud experts bolsters the notion of right knee wounds as implied by the mysterious statue. "The body [in the shroud] is peppered with marks of a severe flogging estimated at between 60 and 120 lashes of a whip with two or three studs at the thong end," notes archeologist William Meacham. "Each contusion is about 3.7 cm long, and these are found on both sides of the body from the shoulders to the calves, with only the arms spared. Superimposed on the marks of flogging on the right shoulder and left scapular region are two broad excoriated areas, generally considered to have resulted from friction or pressure from a flat surface, as from carrying the crossbar or writhing on the cross. There are also contusions on both knees and cuts on the left kneecap, as from repeated falls."

Although the left knee is always identified on the shroud as the one with the most remarkable wounds, experts contacted by *Spirit Daily* confirmed the involvement of knees in Christ's suffering. As for the phenomenon itself—the oozing of a liquid from the metal—bronze experts have told us that it should not exude any liquid unless there is a hole that is somehow collecting rainwater, which then periodically escapes.

The statue is filled with concrete to the waist, but experts said to their knowledge this shouldn't have enhanced the potential of water emanating.

The possibility remains that humidity has caused the emanation, although the fact that the exudation has been as a single droplet in one specific area that looks like a wound has tended to argue against this explanation, as has the fact that the flow was reported on two months when temperatures were not sweltering. Other, smaller emanations may have existed on the statue—including, indeed, the right side of the left knee.

Are there other aspects of the statue that will conform with the shroud? Will it ooze again? And if so—*if* it is supernatural—is it a simple affirmation of Medjugorje, another in a long range of phenomena—or a sign that like Christ the Church is suffering falls on the way to Calvary?

[But after that, resurrection!]

Statue at Medjugorje said to be oozing again

We have confirmed a report that there is oozing again from a large bronze corpus of Christ behind St. James Church in Medjugorje.

Like last June—when the exudation was noticed around the time of anniversary celebrations—continuous droplets of a watery fluid have been coming from what looks like a point of erosion or "wound" on the side of the statue's right knee.

We don't know if it's supernatural. We'll wait for more information. But it is certainly strange—and because it involves an actual physical object, it is one of the most potentially interesting manifestations in the twenty years of phenomena.

The exudation, which brings to mind weeping Madonnas, occurs on a sporadic basis and was especially noticeable the first week of October, according to one witness, Savio C. Barros—a former government worker from Mississauga in Canada who watched the phenomenon on October 4 and 5 with dozens of others as crowds again began to form around the corpus.

"When I looked, I saw the water coming out of the side of the knee," said Barros. "I touched the water itself and so did a lot of people. Many people saw it. The drops were one after another, continuously falling. People were saying different things, different ways, but I felt it was very strange that the water was coming out that way."

Others have described it as watery drops that feel like a cross between saltwater and oil flowing from the 15-foot statue—and hundreds witnessed it last summer.

Why there would be such a steady accumulation of moisture in a specific part of the statue has confounded experts. A source in the parish has told us that it's filled with concrete from the feet to the waist, and bronze experts in the U.S. say they have never heard of bronze reacting in such away—except for an initial "sweating" of bronze when it is first fashioned and put to intense heat.

The drops have occurred in cooler weather—reported also last

March and also last October—and even in a hot humid environment bronze shouldn't react in that way, according to John Blair, project manager for Jozef Custom Ironworks, a large firm in Bridgeport, Connecticut.

Blair called the situation "absolutely" unusual" when asked if when there's humidity bronze sweats to the point where something can exude from the metal itself.

"That's a really curious question," he said when we first consulted him last summer—after seeing it ourselves. "I've never seen it from humidity. However, when I apply a patina, when I flame it with a torch, it does sweat then. You do get moisture over the surface of the bronze. But I've never seen it from heat or humidity."

Is it unusual for such metal to react in such a way from one particular part and occur every couple minutes?

"Oh, sure," replied Blair. "Absolutely. My only observation of bronze sweating is in the beginning of the patinization process, as we begin to heat the bronze. It does sweat for a minute there. But it's nothing like that—where it's actually dripping. There's a glaze over the surface and then you know your piece is beginning to warm up. As far as the thing crying or sweating like that, unless there's holes in it, with water getting in a source, and it's leaking like a roof would leak, no: it would have to be something at the miracle end of it."

There still may be a natural explanation. We'll wait and see what experts who can actually observe it have to say. But for the time being it's another mystery from the famous apparition site, and some even claim that substance has caused healing. The October report is the first since July 9, when a parish spokesperson said the drops had stopped.

When we stop criticizing others we're met by a wave of grace

The next time you feel like criticizing someone, stop. Hold off. Put it aside. And feel a wave of grace.

That's right: keeping our mouths shut opens the Kingdom of heaven. God loves silence. He loves when we contemplate. He loves when we suffer quietness instead of mouthing off and getting everybody's (and especially our own) nerves jangled.

It's a tough thing to do, like anything that brings God's favor. It takes discipline. It's a test. So treat it like that. For a few days, for a week, put it in your mind to approach every temptation to criticize as a challenge, and you'll be amazed at what happens. If you succeed in avoiding saying anything negative you'll start feeling great. You'll feel filled. Prayer will come easier—because when we don't criticize we're closer to God to begin with!

Of course, this is easier said than done. Criticizing others is a natural proclivity. We do it to try to elevate ourselves. It's a manifestation of pride. It's also a manifestation of envy. Putting down someone else makes us feel superior.

But the feeling is temporary. Whenever we talk against someone, it comes home to roost and if you watch events closely, you'll see yourself falling into the same type of behavior, or at least being tempted with the same behavior, that you have criticized others for.

Criticism is divisive. It degrades the one we attack. And we degrade ourselves. You'll note that the Pope rarely if ever criticizes a person by name. The same was true of Jesus. It was the matter of casting the first stone, and yet we live in a society that is obsessed with doing just that. Our radio shows are full of broadcasters whose entire claim to fame is downing others—and when we listen, when we enjoy someone besmirching another, when we like a constant spewing of negativity, we become participants and it comes back to bite us. There is a loss of grace.

So next time you feel like pointing out the negative in someone, first try to be that person's defense attorney. Ask yourself if you have ever done something similar. Strive to see the good parts of a personality, and focus on them. See all the reasons the person may have done what she or he did. That's what God does, and thank God for that!

For can you imagine what kind of shape we'd be in if God judged us like we judge others?

Are there really such things as "curses"?

Are there actually curses? Can someone affect you by what they say or think?

It's a controversial aspect of Christianity. Some say they see no biblical basis for it. Others argue that there are repeated references to just such a thing from *Genesis* through the New Testament—not only from God, Who is often mentioned in the way of cursing sinful men, but also the curses of others. In *Proverbs* it says that a curse without cause can not have an effect but implies that there is indeed such a thing and that it can come from others.

There are curses that result from black magic. There are curses that come from occult, pagan, or New Age objects. There are curses that hover over homes, neighborhoods, and lands. There are curses that haunt families through the generations.

We'll be discussing these various aspects in future articles. Today let's start at the foundation, with everyday ways that curses can operate. According to Carlos and Victoria Pantoja, who minister through St. Raphael Ministries in San Francisco, it's not just something that witches do near a caldron. Knowingly or unknowingly, we have all cursed others. When we dislike someone, and worst of all, when we hate a person, it's like throwing a spiritual dagger. And it can have physical results. In some cases people can take sick (think of the term *ill-will*), and often we find ourselves in frustrating bondages. No matter what we do, we can't succeed. We can't make ends meet. We can't finish a job. We can't succeed at school. We can't find good relationships. We can't reach peace in our families.

Most often it's just the suffering of life but there are occasions when it's because of ill will.

The fact that we can curse people without even knowing it is why we're called to constantly control not only what we say but what we *think*. "People don't understand consciously that they're cursing another person," says Carlos, mentioning the example of a relative who didn't want him to come to the U.S. and told him he would not amount to anything here—a "curse" that was only broken, says Carlos, when he asked for her forgiveness and requested that she break the hold this had on him.

When we call someone dumb or bad or ugly, we can be casting a real shadow on them.

"Words are power," warns Victoria. "Kids turn out like what they're parents describe them as."

Especially powerful is the curse that comes through jealousy. This dagger is sharper than others. Indeed, as it says in *Proverbs*, "Anger is relentless, and wrath overwhelming—but before jealousy who can stand?" (27:4)

When we're jealous of someone we are wishing them ill luck and as it says in the Bible, ill fortune can then come. "The spirit of jealousy is the spirit of the devil himself," asserts Victoria. "There was the jealousy of the devil in the Garden. He was jealous of Adam and Eve. That's the whole reason for his temptation."

Curses cause spiritual wounds, and demons can attach themselves to such hurts, according to the Pantojas. We all need to spiritually cleanse ourselves by regularly asking Christ to remove any negativity that may have come upon us and to let us recognize any way we can curse others.

For as Carlos and Victoria point out, in the end it's worse for the person who is hateful, disturbed, or jealous. "When you curse someone else, it comes back to you," says Carlos. "Jealousy affects the person who is jealous more than the person who the jealousy is directed at."

The antidote is love. When we love people, we are not wishing them ill will. Instead, we are sending *healing*. We should even bless those who curse us. It says that right in the Bible (*Matthew* 5:44). When we have love it's like a shield. We disarm a curse. It cannot alight upon us.

The day Danny died

(written September 21, 2001)

By Michael H. Brown

Today I'm heading off for the wake of one of the closest friends I've ever had. There won't be a body there. It's still somewhere in the wreckage of the World Trade Center. His name was Danny Smith and he worked in the southern tower for Euro-Brokers and the day he died something left, something deep inside of me diminished. In fact something diminished for the whole nation; we will never be quite the same; the tragedy has caused a watershed event spiritually.

From what we can piece together he'd started down the stairs after the fire hit the northern tower but then there was an all-clear and he headed back up. We may never know exactly how he died or even where he was. He worked on the 84th floor and was somewhere up there when that second plane struck. The last his wife Mary heard he'd called to tell her to let the kids know that he was all right. They're 14 and 11.

That was Danny, unafraid, thinking first of others, and at 6'6" larger than life. We met at Fordham University. We worked together in a deli in The Bronx and when it was robbed—when a gun was put on him—he never panicked. He never shook. Within days, he had shrugged it off. He taught me something about courage and also something about love. This was a huge guy who lifted weights and could scare anyone he wanted to scare but whose biggest attribute was his heart and also his generosity. Once when I was living in Manhattan he came to me and said he had just read about how hard it was to make it as an author and told me that he'd support me if I ever went broke.

I never forgot that, and I know that Big Dan (as we called him) would have given his life for his friends.

No greater love. That was Danny. He wasn't much for going to church, but like it says in Scripture, God forgives a lot of things to those who love a lot, and so somewhere out there in the beyond is

Danny and he's okay. He's in the Hands of God. I pray for his final entry into heaven and at the same time I pray his death wasn't in vain. I hope my buddy died for a cause. I hope people in this country have awakened to the real presence of evil and the need for purification. The day Danny died, this warning, this chastisement—whatever you want to call it—struck very deep. It made me realize how bad things can get. It made me know that heaven is on the move. It made me know we have to change.

God allows evil and victim-souls and draws good from it. It's that simple. It has happened through history. It will continue to happen. The Lord's had enough. We've gone way too far with the "feel-good" mentality. That's true both inside and outside the Church. We're supposed to be upbeat and we're supposed to maintain joy but we're not supposed to ignore wickedness.

We're supposed to *purge* evil. We're supposed to cast it out. Currently, it runs rampant. This country has gone on a wild spree of materialism and lust and now we see the smoldering ruins and somewhere in those ruins is my pal Danny.

Remember him today: Danny Smith. Northport, New York. Age, 47. The Mass is Saturday at 11 a.m. He had this smile you'd never forget and that was the last thing one co-worker saw—Danny smiling a smile of disbelief and staying calm and telling her to hit the exit. It wouldn't surprise me if he got caught up helping someone weaker than he was or letting everyone in front of him. I don't know what happened. I just know that it's autumn and the leaves fall and it's easy to get morbid but I won't do that. I won't do that because I know that with all his love, Danny was not only larger than life, but also larger than death.

From the Pope to seers, warnings about the United Nations

by Michael H. Brown

In recent years John Paul II and a slew of reputed seers have issued warnings about the United Nations and its potential effect on the world. Last week we reported on the connection between a major U.N. official and a New Age center in Colorado [see below]. In an insidious fashion it is trying to move the world toward global governance and while we caution people not to become overly conspiratorial or paranoid and while we appreciate many of the U.N.'s efforts—especially in exposing environmental problems—the spirit it is evoking is troubling.

We're troubled because the U.N. has demonstrated an anti-Christian approach, which is seen in its policies toward feminism and abortion. In 1994 the International Conference on Population and Development appeared in effect to legitimize abortion on demand and accept artificial contraception methods—pitting it directly against the Vatican, where John Paul II actually cried "We protest!" from his window overlooking St. Peter's Square one Sunday in April of that year.

When it comes to the U.N. the Pope has thundered like an Old Testament prophet!

"John Paul II had decided to declare his own state of war against the United Nations," wrote Carl Bernstein and Marco Politi in a biography of him. "He was furious. His closest friend in the Vatican, Cardinal Deskur, had never seen the Pope in such a rage. Usually John Paul II paid a visit every week to the ailing cardinal. Seated at the table where Deskur had arranged so many dinners to launch Bishop Wojtyla, John Paul II spoke freely. 'They are causing the shipwreck of humanity.' His condemnation referred to both the U.N. and the Western democracies."

I remember trying to pray in the lobby of the U.N. once and finding it all but impossible. It was like a spirit was holding me back. While waiting for a meeting, it was all I could do to finally say a Rosary.

This is because of secularism and even occultism. As one correspondent, Lee Penn, points out, world political and spiritual leaders held a hectic series of summit meetings at the U.N. last summer. "There were few discernible results—other than providing additional proof that the U.N., many non-Christian 'spiritual leaders,' and most of the organizations associated with the U.N. are hostile to traditional Christianity and support a government-regulated global economic system."

At other recent interfaith events, such as the 1999 Parliament of World Religions, and meetings of what is known as the United Religions Initiative since 1996, there has been significant participation, notes Penn, by neo-pagans, cultists, and New Agers.

The U.N. has sought to unite religions on eco-spirituality and earth-based religions. During the 1990s it began a program that included the mailing of suggestions for ecological sermons to *thousands* of churches around the world. At the U.N.'s Earth Summit in Rio in 1992 there was not only a tremendous New Age flavor but also the fact that a prayer known as the "Great Invocation" was used as an opening litany at the plenary session of non-governmental organizations—a prayer written by an occult group that once owned a publishing unit called "Lucifer Publishing."

We'll have more about all this in the future. But let's get to what visionaries say. I'll start with Ukrainian mystic Josyp Terelya—who on September 18, 1992, had an alleged revelation describing the U.N. as a *"dead skull with the voice of nations."*

"It is Satan himself who speaks through the false prophet of the organization of the United Nations, using the dead corpse of the organization of the United Nations to deceive mankind," Terelya claims he was told by the Virgin Mary.

This matches strikingly—startlingly—with what was reported by Zdenko "Jim" Singer, a Canadian man who began receiving apparitions in 1989. "Out of His mercy and grace, the Father has gifted you the Queen of Peace, yet nations prostitute themselves to this dead head which now lives again in that city by the ocean," Singer claims he was told by the Lord in 1993 (even though at the time he had not seen Terelya's message, which had not yet been published).

As always, we submit such messages without endorsement on other messages given by the seers and for your own discernment only. Please discern with prayer and caution. We also note that if it was Christian-based and less intent on domination, the U.N.—which has done many beneficial things—could become a great force for good.

Christmas is the time for generational healing

As we gather with our families this Christmas it's a good time to purge. All of us need to pray certain things away from or out of our families and God listens powerfully on the birthday of His Son. Thus, Christmas is a unique opportunity to dispense of family demons.

Perhaps this is meant literally. It's a controversial realm but there are a growing number of priests ministering what is known as "generational" or "family" healing. One of them is Father Robert DeGrandis, a St. Joseph priest who has written more than 25 books and has conducted healing in more than 30 countries (at least by the last count we saw). "There has been a growing recognition of inheritance that goes far beyond physical characteristics, to include the psychological make-up as well," he writes. "How often do we hear about anger or stubbornness running in a family? But if I am always angry, my father was always angry, and my grandfather was always angry, it had to start somewhere. Anger, somewhere in its source, *is unlove that never was healed.*"

In other words, just as there are physical and behavioral tendencies that we inherit, so are there tendencies in the *spirit*. We all know what was inherited from Adam and Eve, and we're all familiar with that part of Scripture that discusses "sins of the father" (*Exodus* 34:7).

Spirituality is passed down the generations in a way we can't see and yet in a way that according to Father DeGrandis and another priest, Father John H. Hampsch of Los Angeles, can have profound effects—even causing illness. "Old, unresolved and unforgiven hurts appear to be 'inherited,' or genetically encoded into the system and acted out in future generations," says Father DeGrandis in a book called *Intergenerational Healing*. "There are unresolved hurts so strong that they get into the bloodline and keep coming up to be resolved in future generations."

There are sins. There are hurts. There is unforgiveness. When something has happened in the past that has not been forgiven, this can haunt a family until it *is* forgiven. Strange as it may sound, we may need to offer up Masses for ancestors we don't even know and in our prayers—in our hearts—forgive them. Of course, it's most important to forgive those living. When a family strives to live together in unselfish love and to worship God together (as at Christmas), its members will know contentment and harmony, notes Father Hampsch—but if they're negligent, "they will experience God's judgment negatively by the presence of domestic strife, jealousy, infidelity, suspicion, unhappiness, marital discord, broken marriages, suspicion, arguments, recalcitrance in children, arguments, addictions, in-law conflicts."

These two priests, both well-educated (in the case of Father Hampsch, a former seminary professor and psychological consultant), claim there are even curses. "Just as the Lord's Spirit can touch people and set them free physically and psychologically, the evil spirit can also bind people at the time of the curse and into future generations," notes Father DeGrandis—who we caught up with recently and who is still actively ministering around the world.

There is often murder in a family's background, notes the priest, and also a great problem with occultism. When an ancestor dabbled with fortune-telling, mediumship, clairvoyance, and of course witchcraft, these spirits, like genes, are passed down the generations. This substantiates the sacrament of Baptism, for as soon as a child is born, it needs to be dedicated to Christ and delivered from anything demonic. Healing priests often suggest placing a chart of the family tree on the altar during a special Mass for the family. It takes persistent prayer, and we have to go to God for answers. "Only the Holy Spirit, Who searches the minds and hearts and discerns our deepest needs (*Romans* 8:27), can know what is ready to be healed," writes Father DeGrandis, whose books are among our most popular.

Often, those searching for a reason why something is plaguing their family will be surprised at how the Spirit shows them something in their ancestry (often occultism) of which they were not familiar. In this way, says Father DeGrandis, those who are strong-willed are delivered of the need to control and those who still have an abused child within them are healed and those who say no to the darkness of what they have inherited begin to find health, whether physically or emotionally.

If one part suffers, every part suffers, and this suffering can be stopped.

Are there too many accidents in your family? Is there ill fortune?

Go to Confession. Attend Mass. Offer the Rosary. Fast. Intercede for the Lord to forgive the sins of ancestors. "We are talking about 'blessing all that is within us' (*Psalm* 103:1) through forgiveness," says Father DeGrandis, "and thus hopefully changing the pattern of future generations."

Even one member of a family may be the instrument of God in the salvation of all others in the family tree or household, claim these two fascinating priests. What we need to do is pray to the Holy Spirit to enlighten us as to what a problem may be—really pray for illumination—and then take the matter to Jesus in the Eucharist. At Mass, many bondages can be broken, and the way to prepare for this is to go to Confession. It's also a good time to hunt through the household and discard any books or objects pertinent to lust, astrology, or matters of the occult (including novels).

Before Christmas, pray for guidance on how *you* can purge your own family. Ask the Holy Spirit what prayers to say. Ask God to remove hurts and curses. Plead the Blood of Christ. "In Jesus' Name and by His authority I come against this curse, etc. I call down the Precious Blood of Jesus and I break this curse on my family or person in the Name of Jesus," is one prayer Father DeGrandis suggests saying three times for each instance.

There are those who claim that even obesity or serious ailments like cancer haunt families in a way that can have a root that is spiritual. We see in Scripture how many times Jesus had to cast out a demon—a demon of muteness or some other ailment—before the illness left. Father Hampsch says generational spirits can cause alcoholism, psychological disorders, occultism, phobias, sexual sin, drug use, the spirits of control, anger, impatience, lust, and many forms of otherwise intractable physical illnesses. There may be simple behavioral causes in certain instances, but often there also seem to be spiritual holds—and it is up to us break them!

Spirits cause unseen problems and it's time to free our families. Pray together this Christmas, or at least pray for each family member when you gather, in whatever way is feasible. Use Holy water in your homes. Pray for deliverance. Pray for your entire blood line and forgive every single family member who has caused you hurt (as well as ancestors!) and you may be surprised at the sudden onset of happiness!

With deception rampant, the accent is on discernment

By Michael H. Brown

So often, we're met with the issue of discernment. It's important because we're the Mystical Body of Christ, and it was mysticism—miracles, and especially His Resurrection—that affirmed Christ as the Savior.

As a journalist, my job is often to go into gray areas and try to recover what otherwise may be lost. There are so *many* revelations that are imperfect, as all prophecy (except that from Christ) is imperfect (see *1 Corinthians* 13:9), and so we consider the fact that there are always problems because humans are involved.

Yet it is also crucial to be careful. The most well-intentioned can be deceived. We have all seen that occur. While the Pope is very open to mysticism—and has warmly greeted dozens of seers, at least at public sessions—in virtually every case *something* wrong can be spotted if one searches for the negative. This can even and perhaps especially occur with the most striking phenomena. We're concerned because while we report on such cases and always take an initially positive view (unless we have reason not to), we urge great caution. Back in the 16th century was a Franciscan nun in Cordova, Spain, who as the famous theologian the Very Reverend Adolphe Tanqueray said, "aided by the devil," simulated "all the mystical phenomena of ecstasy, levitation, stigmata, revelations, and prophecies reportedly fulfilled. Thinking herself at the point of death, she made a confession which she later retracted, was exorcised, and moved to another convent."

Even the most well-intentioned can be deceived, and from time to time we all are!

We are indeed all susceptible, and yet we are called as the Mystical Body to take the good out of a situation. Apparitions. Locutions. The discernment is always difficult. There has been controversy over everything from Lourdes (where demonic voices, trying to contaminate the revelation, came from the cave) to

Medjugorje. I see this too with near-death experiences. In one casewe've reported, a man seemed to have a feeling that he had existed in heaven before earth. This is contrary, at least on the surface, to Catholic teaching. But when I queried him at length, this person said that he does not actually believe he existed before conception, because he had no conscious recollection, but that he was trying to convey the feeling of sensing that he always existed in the Mind of God (which is more difficult to argue with). In eternity, there is no "before" or "after" and so there is really no pre-existence.

Whew! So difficult. But Scripture urges us to seek gifts of the Spirit—especially prophecy—and the supernatural is at the very foundation of our faith. We are the *mystical* body of Christ. We are *told* to prophesy—not to despise it. And so—through fasting and prayer—we continue. It's important. Crucial! It was when they demystified the Church that the pews emptied.

But this warning: there is tremendous deception out there right now and no matter how holy something or someone seems at first, only through humility and fasting and prayer—long prayer, many hours—will you discern it. We urge that you not visit any alleged mystic, even if such a mystic is a religious, and especially not allow the laying on of hands, without much previous prayer and fasting and Scripture reading.

Only prayer brings the Holy Spirit, and only the Holy Spirit knows the full truth.

When doors close, wait for God to make the decision

By Michael H. Brown

Does it ever happen to you that doors close? That no matter how hard you try to do something, it doesn't work? That there's no grace?

When that happens—when there are constant obstacles, when you're all thumbs, when nothing is going right—you have to stop, pray, and ask if it's what God wants.

Because when we try to do something that isn't right for us (at least at that particular point in time), there are bumps in the road. You all know what I mean: Just about every day we run into stretches where things don't go right, and sometimes this persists throughout the day and then we're made to wonder.

Now, don't get me wrong: there are days when we're simply tested more than others. Sometimes it nearly seems like there's a good day and then a tough day and then a good day and so on. There are also times when it's Satan putting up the roadblocks.

But often the problem and the reason for our frustration is that we're doing what *we* want to do instead of what God wants us to do, and He withdraws His grace. When that happens, not only is it a rough road but there is also an underlying tension.

It's called a "gut feeling," and it's important to listen to such "indicators." Pay attention. Whenever we feel unsettled it may because we're doing or contemplating or wanting something that God doesn't want for us—because in the end and even though we don't see it at the time it won't be good for us.

When that happens, don't force it. Stop. Pray. While there are times that the resistance comes from the devil, there's a difference between his resistance and the innate feeling of unsettlement. When the devil attacks and we're doing the Will of God, despite that attack we will have peace about it. We will feel calm. On the other hand, when we're rubbing the Holy Spirit the wrong way, we'll be unsettled.

When that happens, recite the Rosary. Pray. Cry from the heart to God. Go to Mass. It brings clarity. It pops new direction into our minds. It brings simplicity to decisions that we have over-complicated.

So stop stubbing your toes. Stop forging ahead when something doesn't feel like you *should* forge ahead. Listen to God instead of your own inclinations. He'll give you the right direction and in the end—if you're patient—He'll make the important decisions for you.

For your discernment:

Former nightclub king says he saw future during near-death experience

By Michael H. Brown

I just read an intriguing book over the weekend. It's called *The Fast Lane to Heaven*, and it's about Ned Dougherty, who once owned the hottest nightclub in the New York City area. The club was in the Hamptons on Long Island (home to the super-rich), and was called Club Marakesh. Ned had a second club in West Palm Beach, and lived the glamorous life: limos, models, celebrities, seaplanes, Dom Perignon champagne.

On July 2, 1984, something happened to him, something like a heart attack or a stroke, and Dougherty found himself collapsing on the sidewalk outside his club. He felt like he was "floating, suspended in a black, bottomless pit." In the distance he could hear voices. "I have no vitals! We're losing him!" said an emergency technician in an ambulance en route to the hospital. Dougherty was able to sit up in the spirit and rise above the ambulance—watching it speed off. As he was suspended in air he saw a "kaleidoscopic review" of his lifestyle and possessions, which then vaporized. Suddenly a mass of energy formed over him in the sky and shaped itself into a cylinder funneling upwards. He was drawn into another realm—a realm in which he saw deceased loved ones, a realm in which he was enveloped by the Light of God.

There was a "symphonic" music. There were buildings made out of no earthly material. There were spirits. Dougherty very capably recounts the experience of reviewing his life and understanding what it had been all about. It really makes for fascinating reading.

But what makes this account unusual is that Dougherty—hardly a devout Catholic (in fact a heavy drinker who had liked the life of a playboy)—had an experience in the afterlife with a "Lady of Light" who stood next to a large globe of the earth and began to speak to him about the future of the world.

According to Dougherty (and remember, this is in a book that came out in *March*), the "Lady of Light"—who he would later identify as the Virgin Mary—showed him events that would first happen in the Middle East and then Italy. "I was told that these events would be acts of 'aggression, terrorism, and war, performed by self-proclaimed radical groups, supposedly in the name of God," he wrote before the events of September 11. Dougherty flatly predicted that "terrorist attacks and acts of war and aggression will continue to plague the Middle East, Africa, and Europe." He was shown a future in which violence would spread from the Middle East to Europe, and then to the former Soviet Union and to the Far East—particularly China.

The greatest threat, he was shown, would come from China and a "two hundred million army" (see *Revelation 9:16*). "The Lady of Light specifically told me, 'Pray for the conversion of China,'" claims Dougherty. "'The conversion of China to God is necessary for the salvation of the world.'"

Naturally, such claims have to be discerned, although, for Ned, the fruits seemed good. He was delivered from the "fast lane" and all the drugs, sex, and booze that had come with it. He says the phenomena he has seen is similar to what he has since learned about apparitions at Zeitun, Egypt, where Mary was also called the Lady of Light. This is intense stuff and brings to mind Fatima—where the Virgin came nearly a hundred years ago and expressed an almost identical concern about a similar threat from Communist Russia.

But most remarkable was what Dougherty had been told about the U.S. "While acts of terrorism and war and political unrest plague the Eastern Hemisphere, the Western Hemisphere will be spared the worst of the terrorism," he was told. "However, a major terrorist attack may befall New York City or Washington, D.C., severely impacting the way we live in the United States."

Remember, this was recorded in a book released six months before the attack on the Pentagon and World Trade Center! We learn of all this just a week after running an article about another Long Island resident who, a week before September 11, was allegedly receiving apparitions of Therese the Little Flower with similar foreboding. Clearly, things are beginning to happen fast and furiously—especially around New York. Indeed, Dougherty later had visions of the Virgin at a shrine in Eastport, along with an experience with the Archangel Michael. We'll discuss this next. And we'll look at what else Dougherty prophesied.

For although he did not see terrorism destroying the United States, he claims to have foreseen other events that would. . .

Man who 'died' and came back says he saw dramatic future role for obscure shrine and disasters like tidal waves

By Michael H. Brown

We carried an article yesterday about Ned Dougherty, a New York-area nightclub owner who was radically transformed by a near-death experience [*see previous story*]. During that episode—in which his vital signs disappeared—he says he was taken to the hereafter and encountered a "Lady of Light" who showed him events in the world's, the nation's, and his own future.

We'll be getting into more of that tomorrow but first, his predictions about a shrine on Long Island. It's called "Our Lady of the Island" and is located near the Hamptons in Eastport. Dougherty says that after his death episode he began to have mystical experiences at this shrine operated by Montfort Missionaries with a striking 18-foot statue of the Madonna and Child.

Dougherty, the former owner of the posh Club Marakesh in the super-rich Hamptons (who "died" on July 2, 1984, from cardiac or respiratory failure), says in a book called *Fast Lane to Heaven* that during a trip to a heavenly realm and then in subsequent alleged visions he was shown future events that included multitudes flocking to this obscure shrine.

We are currently trying to discern all this. There are always many aspects to consider and always points of debate with "near-death" experiences. But we are taking it seriously because Dougherty seems like a very credible man and one of his prophecies—that terrorism would strike New York or Washington in such a way as to change our lives—has obviously materialized and was documented in his book last March.

The vision of the shrine, says this otherwise down-to-earth businessman—who was not devout before his episode—indicates future events at the shrine that will "foreshadow the End Times." He believes that the shrine will become "a safe place or haven for many people who would be drawn to the shrine during the End

Times."

We're not sure what to make of terms like the "end times" (as Ned emphasizes, much can be changed through prayer), but important is his report that manifestations are occurring at Our Lady of the Island. Indeed, the statue is located in such a way that when one faces it one is facing the precise area where TWA Flight 800—which some suspect was sabotaged by terrorists—crashed some years back. Dougherty says that on his first visit to the shrine, which he had previously been shown in vision as a clearing, he sensed the Virgin Mary near a large pine near the statue. There he says the Virgin reviewed scenes from his near-death episode and spoke to him about his mission.

At first skeptical ("I am by nature cynical and disbelieving," he says), confirmation came on December 8, 1994, when he went to the shrine to pray and meditate and saw flashes of light emanating from the pine tree at the top of the clearing.

"At first, it seemed as if the pine tree was enveloped by a flash fire, but then the flash of fire moved away from the tree and formed an oval shape six feet high, and it came down the hillside and onto the path directly in front of me," writes Dougherty in his book. "I stood mesmerized as I realized that the golden flame came from a celestial being."

According to the former businessman (now founder of a prolife charitable organization, *Mission of Angels*), the light slowly moved up a pathway and paused in front of him—brighter than the sun but not blinding him. She spoke to him only briefly about a request of his being granted and was gone—leaving Dougherty mesmerized and in a state of disbelief.

As the former nightclub owner looked for any other witnesses to confirm what he had seen, he says he observed "clouds of golden light" settle on the tops of the pine trees, turning the branches and needles a deep violet.

The lights seemed to move as if to guide him. When he reached the shrine's main road the apparitions allegedly ceased. He says that while in prayer he heard a voice telling him to go to Egypt—where he discovered tremendous similarities to the phenomena that had occurred during the 1960s in Zeitun, Egypt.

There, the Virgin, appearing above a Coptic Church—in apparitions approved by ecclesiastical officials—was likewise known as "Our Lady of Light"!

Indeed, hundreds of thousands had witnessed her at Zeitun—including many Muslims and even former Egyptian president Abdul Nasser.

At Zeitun lights that looked like doves appeared over the street, round and gold in color.

As in Doughtery's own visions, she had also appeared inside a luminous circle at Zeitun and was even photographed. At the church there a painting especially struck him. "The artist had captured what the photographers could not: a portrait of the Lady of Light as she had appeared at St. Mary's Church in Zeitun, and just as she had appeared to me at Our Lady of the Island Shrine in Eastport, New York, on the morning of December 8, 1994," he says.

Dougherty says that during his "death" the Lady of Light showed him a scene from a hilltop on the coastline of Long Island as rows of massive tidal waves descended on the coastline, inundating the land. "I was told the world could be saved, but not by its leaders, but by prayer groups throughout the world," Dougherty says in words strikingly similar to a Long Island woman who last week gave us the same message from alleged visitations of the Virgin and Therese the Little Flower. "I was told that the fate of mankind rested on our ability, individually and collectively, to change the direction of mankind in accordance with God's plan."

Man who saw Mary during 'near-death' warns of terror attack on Vatican

We've been running articles on Ned Dougherty, who once owned the famous Club Marakesh in a wealthy suburb of New York City but gave that up and is now a devout Catholic who runs a charitable group and volunteers at a Marian shrine on Long Island. Ned clinically "died" from respiratory or cardiac arrest on July 2, 1984, and during that episode allegedly had an experience with the hereafter and a heavenly entity he identifies as the Virgin Mary [*see previous story*].

"She became known to me as the Lady of Light, and she radiated an incredibly golden light far brighter and of a much greater magnitude than the light of any of the other angelic or spiritual beings," he wrote in a book called *Fast Lane to Heaven*. "Clearly, the Lady of Light held a very high place in the spiritual hierarchy of this heavenly realm."

We've covered some of this in previous stories. What we'd like to focus on now are alleged predictions from that experience—as well as revelations that Dougherty says he has received in the years since. As with any such revelation, there is bound to be controversy. We ourselves have many questions about near-death episodes, including the idea, contradictory to many schools of theology, that our souls are made in heaven before we are born. We must always be on guard against deception, and, unfortunately, as with secular publishers, many of those who publish such accounts also stray into dubious realms. We present it, as always, for your discernment. We do it because Dougherty has transformed his life and in his book—which came out last March—he foresaw the terrorist attack in striking language.

His prophecies also correctly foresaw episodes in his life. He says that during his afterlife experience he was shown a vision in which he was addressing researchers and medical doctors in a university auditorium. That materialized in 1995 when he addressed the North American Conference of the International Association for Near-Death Studies at the University of Hartford in Connecticut. He was shown himself at the bedside of sick people. This came to be when he entered a hospice-training program. He was shown a specific hilly area—and years later he came across just such land in Pennsylvania and ended up establishing something else that he says had been prophesied to him—a charitable pro-life foundation called *Mission of Angels.*

That doesn't mean we have to accept all subsequent revelations, but the Bible admonishes us not to reject prophecy, but rather to test it and keep what's good. We say this because some of the predictions are dramatic. Dougherty had predicted that "a major terrorist attack may befall New York City or Washington, D.C., severely impacting the way we live in the United States"—a prediction that has been fulfilled in only too obvious a fashion.

"The only thing I was unsure of was whether it was 'New York *or* Washington' or 'New York *and* Washington,'" he told *Spirit Daily.* "What I saw were buildings toppling over and people running in chaos and confusion. I lived for 17 years with those visions in my mind. I saw from the street level. In this vision I was on the street watching this toppling over without an understanding of which buildings they were. Every time I tried to go into Manhattan, I had difficulty breathing. It seemed like there was a negative cloud over that city for me."

What else had he been told? What else does he assert will happen?

As we reported, Dougherty sees aggression in the Middle East, China, Africa, and Europe, while the Western Hemisphere encounters natural disasters. He says that without prayer and a strong return to a pro-life society, there will be destruction.

"Freakish, erratic, and unseasonable weather patterns will create severe tidal flooding and erosion," Dougherty asserts in *Fast Lane to Heaven.* "There will be devastating tornadoes and wind storms; severe winter conditions with record snowfalls and freezing temperatures; record summer heat waves with severe drought; and an increase in destructive storms and hurricanes."

Dougherty is not talking about mere "signs of the times." He says he was shown visions of massive events and claims that he was shown that the banking and financial institutions could collapse "due in large part to the failure of the insurance companies as a result of natural disasters." In the end he sees the U.S. in "political, economic, and social chaos"—unless there is spiritual change. "I had a sense that the future would involve devastation on both coasts," he says. "It would destroy all of our military bases, which are all located in low-lying areas." In the wake of destruction, he says, "shadowy and publicly-unknown world figures will attempt to establish a 'new world order' by creating a worldwide government supposedly for the benefit of humanity."

He warns especially of geophysical disturbances in the eastern Atlantic—which we have previously reported when we excerpted *Sent To Earth*, a book about the return of ancient disasters.

He says the United States government "will fail to meet its financial obligations as a result of its staggering national debt and will collapse."

He said the Lady showed him the world shaking. He doesn't know if this was a geophysical or spiritual event, but it was dramatic and worldwide. He saw "massive earthquakes, volcanic eruptions, and huge tidal waves on both the east and west coasts of the United States, as well as around the world."

What we do right now will determine, he says, what happens next. If there is not a radical conversion—and a great proliferation of prayer groups—the events could affect a whole seacoast. He said he was shown visions of a terrific ocean surge in Manhattan, on Long Island, and in Florida (at a bridge he believes is the span between the mainland and Key Biscayne). He believes that in the future coastal and other low-lying or unstable areas will diminish in population while mountainous and other "stable" areas become more desirable. It's his further belief that the "critical period of transition" will be completed prior to the year 2034.

This struck home because there has long been the speculation that while events may occur throughout this century, major ones will be seen between now and 2040 based on the longevity of the seers at Medjugorje (who are currently in their thirties and who say that they will live to see the secrets). Dougherty believes that spiritually-minded people "will be drawn together to create self-supporting and self-sustaining communities" and will serve as the architect's for God's plan—which is at great odds with a world of abortion, immorality, and materialism. We might add that in all likelihood if these situations play out there will be smaller series of events within the larger scope of purification, and these may peak sooner.

Dougherty—whose visions came without any association with prophecy groups, and indeed before situations like Medjugorje were even widely known—stresses that right now the Lord is giving us the opportunity to change the course of events. "Although my future visions of a global nature seemed unbelievable even to me, I learned that many other near-death experiencers throughout the world were coming back from the Other Side with the same or similar visions and messages," he says, adding, however, that the wrong reaction right now (including the way we handle war) "could trigger natural disasters."

"I saw events in New York City that were not only from terrorism but also from natural disasters that may befall New York City in the future," he wrote many months ago in his book. "I saw that we're not facing geopolitical events but geophysical events, involving what I saw as a massive tidal wave, and I saw visions of this happening from different locations and one of them in particular was from the clearing of the shrine in Eastport *[see previous story*]. I lived with these visions for years, but until 1994 or 1995 I didn't feel the call to investigate further."

As for the Vatican, "I believe that a similar terrorist attack will occur in the future in Italy, specifically in Rome. I believe that a fanatical religious group on a much larger scale will conduct the attack although it will be directed against one world leader. The focus of the attack will be upon the Vatican and the papacy."

"None of these events need happen," Dougherty stresses. The Virgin told him that "the most powerful weapon in the human arsenal is through prayer—not through our political leaders or power brokers. It's really up to what we do from here. Simply the most important thing we can do now is pray. I was shown we would have the ability to change the world for the better. That's the way I prefer to see things."

As for September 11 and his visions of destruction in New York, he told *Spirit Daily*, "When it happened (September 11), it was very painful. I saw that as a wake-up call for us all. I view all the people lost as victim souls. On that day their lives had to be sacrificed for this wake-up call, but they were not sacrificed in vain."

Was John Paul just talking, or was he signaling a purification?

by Michael H. Brown

The word came Wednesday morning. It was from Rod Dreher, a columnist at *The New York Post*. Rod was in Rome to cover the historic induction of 44 new cardinals and was filing a story. "You'll be quite surprised, I think, by what John Paul said in his consistory homily today," Dreher said. "Read down toward the end of it, the stuff about John Paul telling the cardinals to read the 'signs of the times,' and noting that the Gospel has been preached to 'all corners of the earth'—this in a homily that weighed heavily on martyrdom."

According to Dreher, John Paul had urged the cardinals to draw closer to God in prayer so that they could engage a world where globalization and scientific change brings the potential for crisis.

"Noting that the new cardinals represent 27 countries," he wrote, "John Paul said he saw in this a sign that the Gospel has been 'spread now in all corners of the planet.'"

The Gospel preached to all corners? Signs of the times?

Unless just rhetorical, it was galvanizing language. I have not yet seen the entire text of his remarks (and will wait until I have for any final analysis), but the words seemed loaded. The preaching of the "good news" throughout the world is in *Matthew* 24—the passage called "the beginning of calamities."

In that passage Jesus speaks of wars, rumors of wars, a great increase in evil, cold-heartedness, famine, pestilence, "and earthquakes in many places"—which begins to sounds like something out of a modern newspaper.

The expression "signs of the times" comes from *Matthew* 16:3 in the same breath with which Christ spoke about "an evil, faithless age" and the "sign of Jonah"—a reference to the prophecy of Nineveh's destruction.

In *Revelation* 7:1-2 we find the "corners of the world" mentioned in the context of angels "given power to ravage the land and the sea."

Is this all one big coincidence? Is it a coincidence spoken at a time when there are rumors of war involving China or Iraq or the Holy Land, when there are storms—typhoons, floods—when quakes are registered in India and El Salvador and Mexico and Peru and the Philippines and dozens of other places?

We'll leave that to your own discernment. We can say this: the Pope's remarks come at a time when, in the words of Zenit News Service (on February 14), "never before, as in recent weeks, has the Pope quoted the Book of Apocalypse so much." It was a reference to an address last week at a general audience when John Paul commented that "nature itself, in fact, subjected as it is to lack of meaning, degradation and devastation caused by sin, thus participates in the joy of the deliverance brought about by Christ in the Holy Spirit."

That seemed like a reference to a stirring in nature—one the Vatican has previously mentioned in light of climate change brought about in part, according to the Vatican (and many scientists), by human abuse of God's creation.

The Pope also pointedly reminded the cardinals that red symbolized the willingness "of giving the supreme witness of blood"—something that is also a part of purification.

"The Church and the Spirit await and invoke that moment when Christ 'delivers the kingdom to God the Father, after destroying every rule and every authority and power,'" intoned the Pope. "At the end of this battle—sung in wonderful pages of the Apocalypse—Christ will fulfill the 'recapitulation' and those who will be united to Him will form the community of the redeemed, which `will not be wounded any longer by sin, stains, self-love, that destroy or wound the earthly community.'"

At the end of his address the Pope said these remarkable words:

"With her sight fixed on the day of light, the Church, beloved bride of the Lamb, raises the ardent invocation: 'Maranatha' (*Corinthians* 16:22), 'Come, Lord Jesus!' (*Apocalypse* 22:20)."

In the context of remarks to the cardinals that had to do with the preaching of the Gospel to all corners before a denouement, these other recent words bear close discernment. I don't want to read too much into things. I don't want to put words in the Pope's mouth. But the Pope has a mystical bent (some think he himself may have visions) and he seems to be signaling major events—most probably a *breakdown* of the modern way of life and a return to a time when, as he said on February 14, "God and man, man and woman, humanity and nature are in harmony, in dialogue, in communion."

The most effective defense against evil can be to avoid it to begin with

by Michael H. Brown

Last week I was flying back from the South on a packed flight when a tall heavyset man settled next to me. I was in the aisle seat. He was in the middle. He seemed troubled. He had no greeting. In short order he pulled out a magazine with a sexy cover and began to look at it.

I began to feel very uncomfortable and remembered a similar event that had happened to the author of a book I had read. He related how he was on a plane when passengers on both sides of him started reading racy magazines. "Lord," he prayed, "I can't cope with this today. Please chase evil far away." To his astonishment the man on his right suddenly swore and put his magazine away. The other noted that and put his magazine away too.

Since I was now in the same situation, I tried it myself. I prayed in the name of Jesus that this man would stop looking at the magazine. I was exhausted from a long day and didn't feel like facing this. I prayed and prayed and the man did nothing but open the magazine and keep looking at it. He was the last to have boarded the full plane, and we were ready to take off. I sighed to myself in resignation.

Then it happened—something that, in hundreds of flights, I had never seen. A flight attendant suddenly came to our row, looked at this man, and asked to see him privately, in the jetway. I had no idea what *that* could be all about, but a few minutes later the man came back to our row, reached in the overhead for his luggage, and left the plane. His last gesture was to reach over and take his magazine. He apparently had been on standby and at the last moment they bumped him to let an off-duty pilot take the flight!

My lesson: sometimes the best prayer is the one in which we simply ask God to let us *avoid* evil—the prayer that keeps us away from evil to begin with!

There are times when we have to confront evil but often we

can avoid it. That doesn't mean we cower. That doesn't mean we give up spiritual combat. As anyone will see by reading my book, *Prayer of the Warrior*, I believe we often have to take the forces of darkness head on. But there are times when the lion is best dealt with by avoiding it.

Yet too often we find ourselves in the midst of just such evil. Often we stumble into it through curiosity or by exercising jealousy, judgment, involving ourselves in disputes that are none of our business, or simply by being lax in fasting and prayer. You know what an evil sting feels like. The Bible calls them "fiery darts."

It can also happen after spiritual success: seeking to discourage us, the devil will come around to tempt us or do something to diminish our victory.

The higher we move into the spiritual realm, the greater is the danger of even a minor slip. That's why it's important not only to pray to beat evil, to combat it effectively, when we are called to combat, but often to avoid it entirely. As we move deeper into the spiritual realm of the miraculous, we need to pray, fast, and avoid unnecessary temptation. "Keep us out of the arena of evil, Lord!"

When we pray with faith, God offers His supernatural power to do just that.

If Bush wins, those who voted for him as pro-life can cite a miracle

If as expected George W. Bush becomes the 43rd president, those who prayed for him as the best hope of pro-life can cite evidence of divine intervention. First of all, odds are enormous that any candidate wins the electoral college while losing the general public vote. It hasn't happened in more than a century. But of course that's what appears likely to occur: if the count nationally was accurate, both Bush and Gore got 48 percent of the vote but Gore edged him out by about 200,000 votes.

That a race involving 100 million votes would come down to 200,000 (a quarter of a percent) is phenomenal.

And that the candidate who got the greatest number of popular votes would fall short of what he needed in electoral count by just four votes—267—is amazing.

More phenomenal, however, is what happened in the states: against all odds, Gore lost his home territory of Tennessee—something that virtually never happens—and then we come to Florida. Here six million votes were cast, and as we speak Bush is leading and was certified the winner by a nearly incomprehensible 932 votes, 1/64th of one percent!

Add to this the improbability that a Democrat would design a ballot (the infamous "butterfly")—largely blamed for taking votes away from Gore—and that a Democratically-controlled election board in Miami would at the last minute decide against a recount that many felt would give Gore the extra votes to win, and it becomes all the more astonishing.

The odds against all these eventualities are astronomical. And it doesn't stop with numbers. On December 8—Feast of the Immaculate Conception—the issue will be before the Florida Supreme Court—which could spell the end of the election—and many believe the final deadline is December 12, when the electoral college formalizes a final tally.

That's the feast day of Our Lady of Guadalupe—who is not only patroness of the Americas but also a symbol for the pro-life movement!

Cloning of human embryo is direct challenge to God

By Michael H. Brown

It happened on U.S. soil—not in Italy, not on some remote Caribbean island. On Sunday we got word that a firm in Worcester, Massachusetts, created the first cloned human embryo (or at least the first publicly announced) in an action that can only be described as in contravention of the true Creator.

This is extremely serious business—more serious than war, more serious than terrorists—and will have repercussions. Last August, when the federal government decided to allow limited research into human stem cells, we warned that the door to cloning had creaked open and that scientists would now try to barge through it. We had no idea that they would burst through with such an explosion. We had also warned that the stem-cell decision would be met by chastisement. Less than a month later was September 11.

Indeed, there were headlines on the very morning of the attack on how researchers were demanding greater freedom to create embryos. *"Scientists Urge Bigger Supply Of Stem Cells; Report Backs Cloning to Create New Lines,"* said *The New York Times* on September 11 just miles from what in a few minutes was to become known as "ground zero." And now we have actually done it—or at least the firm in Worcester, Advanced Cell Technologies, has done it—has snuck it in during the diversion of Osama Bin Laden—and there is great danger. This will bring events. This is directly challenging the authority of God.

In 1990 there was a prophecy that in four years (by 1994) mankind would be faced with a "great new evil," an evil that seemed to have beneficial effects, and that how we responded to this new evil would determine the extent of a chastisement.

We note not only that breakthroughs were made in cloning technology precisely four years after the 1990 prophecy but also that Advanced Cell Technology was created in 1994!

A "coincidence" it is that we have traveled through the Worcester area twice in the past three weeks, warning of abortion and cloning and the effects they will bring.

Those who argue that folks should not issue warnings because they may "scare" people might want to consider that this country may *need* to be scared—that it may need more than the see-no-evil feelgood attitude that has brought it to the brink of disaster. Apparently, America has not been scared enough. Since September 11, it has failed to look inwardly; it has gone back to business as usual; indeed, since September 11, in the U.S., more than 270,000 babies have been killed through abortion.

That's dozens of times as many as died at the World Trade Center. In fact every *day* we abort about as many as died on September 11, including by way of late-term techniques.

Yes, we need to root out the evil of terrorists; we need to root out Osama Bin Laden; but even more urgent is to root out the evil in ourselves.

The haunting prediction of a 19th century mystic

The words of Blessed Anna-Katarina Emmerick seem almost eerie. She was a well-known Augustinian nun and mystic in the 19th century. She bore the stigmata. Allegedly, she had the gift of prophecy. And on June 1, 1821, she described a vision in which she saw "nearly all the bishops of the world, but only a small number were perfectly sound. I also saw the Holy Father—God-fearing and prayerful. Nothing left to be desired in his appearance, but he was weakened by old age and by much suffering. His head was lolling from side to side, and it dropped onto his chest as if he were falling asleep. He often fainted and seemed to be dying. But when he was praying, he was often comforted by apparitions from Heaven. Then, his head was erect, but as soon as it dropped again onto his chest, I saw a number of people looking quickly right and left, that is, in the direction of the world."

The epidemic next time: what the CDC fears most

by Michael H. Brown

More than a year ago I visited the Centers for Disease Control in Atlanta and what I remember most vividly was standing just outside a sealed laboratory where the most dangerous microbes known to man are stored and examined. It was daunting: there through the glass I could glimpse the pipes filtering air, the "spacesuits," the shelves of test animals.

Inside were viruses that could cause a national emergency.

It was a "level-four" containment area, as dangerous as it gets. Among the viruses under study was ebola, which has been in the news this week because of concerns that a woman who arrived in Toronto from Africa may have contracted it.

Fortunately she didn't have it, but it reminds us of the diseases out there and their savage effects.

Mad-cow. HIV. And the feared viruses like ebola.

"Ebola attacks every organ and tissue in the human body except skeletal muscle and bone," wrote Richard Preston. "It is a perfect parasite because it transforms virtually every part of the body into a digested slime of virus particles. . . blood clots begin to appear. . . the body turns to mush. . . the skin bubbles into a sea of white blisters. . . spontaneous rips appear on the skin, and hemorrhagic blood pours from the rips. . . the skin goes soft and pulpy, and can tear off. . . your mouth bleeds, and you bleed around your teeth. . . ebola attacks the lining of the eyeball, and the eyeballs may fill up with blood."

It has killed a number of missionaries—including a nun whose blood was found on the floor, chair, and walls. There is that kind of convulsion and hemorrhage. And it's highly contagious. Were it not for the fact that it kills so swiftly—preventing a person from widespread contact with others—it would wipe out entire metropolitan areas.

Yet when I visited CDC I was told that this isn't the disease officials fear the most. Believe it or not, the greatest fear is a new strain of influenza. That *can* last long enough to spread, and in the era of air travel could be anywhere in the world in less than 72 hours.

"In the winter of 1997-1998 there was a virus, avian influenza, H5N1, which is found in poultry and had never been associated with humans," I was told by Dr. Joseph E. McDade, deputy director at CDC for the infectious disease center. "If that virus ever acquired the ability for rapid transmission from person to person, if that virus, which mutates very fast, had taken off, there was no underlying immunity anywhere in the world because nobody had ever been exposed to the particular virus strain and there was no vaccine available. The potential was enormous. We dodged a bullet. You can't think of a scenario more dangerous."

Indeed, from 1918 to 1920 a strain of flu killed between 20 and 40 million worldwide (including two of the seers from Fatima). Some believe the deadly flu started at Fort Riley, Kansas, after strange weather patterns that brought both cold and heat and dust storms that caused the skies to blacken.

I heard the same concern about flu from Pierre Rollin—who works in the level-four lab and has been to Africa during ebola outbreaks. It was certainly possible, he said, for the flu to hit a higher stride than even in 1918, and if it comes it may be one of the expected chastisements. Plague has been a part of God's purification since the time of Moses and we're in for purification. At LaSalette in France where the Blessed Virgin appeared in 1846 she allegedly warned about "infectious disease."

I stood for a long while staring up at the lab. So dangerous are the microbes, explained Dr. McDade, that there is negative pressure so air can't seep out. This is where "virus X" may one day find its way. In other sealed labs scientists in full double gear were incubating aviary virus.

Ebola? Mad-cow? Influenza? Or perhaps a new strain of HIV?

"Expect the unexpected," Dr. McDade said.

Famed mystic claims turmoil in Israel and natural upheavals are a "specific sign" of looming major event

Venezuelan mystic Maria Esperanza has been telling her family that the current upheavals in Israel as well as natural stirrings such as the volcanoes in places like the Philippines and Italy are "specific signs" that events are intensifying and in the next several years will join to precipitate a major occurrence of some type.

"She sees these as clear signs of an imminent event that will awaken consciences," her son-in-law, Carlos Marrero Bornn, told *Spirit Daily* Monday. "Something important will happen very soon. This is all a preparation for a great event that will be sent to show the real meaning of life."

Esperanza is associated with Betania, an apparition site near Caracas that has rare official Church approval, with full ecclesiastical recognition since 1987. Such sanction was also granted recently to a site in Africa where similar indications have been forecast. In Medjugorje, Bosnia-Hercegovina, where six seers have been granted secrets, it has been said only that events will begin to unfold within their lifetimes (they are now in their thirties).

For months Esperanza, now 73 and ailing, has indicated that the world will enter a "new stage" in the next several years, and has alluded to the year 2004. While references to specific years are always highly questionable, Esperanza has not described the year in apocalyptic terms—has emphasized that it has nothing to do with the end of the world—but rather claims it will be a stepped-up time of awakening, indicating something that seems more in the spiritual than worldly realm.

It's not clear if the year has anything to do with the natural disturbances she also sees as coming or with a special heavenly manifestation but according to Carlos she expects such events "to reach a climax and [converge] to one point and show people the truth."

"As we get closer, they are going to be clearer," he said. "Things are going to be more and more intense as we get closer to 2004." He said Maria has been gathering her family for daily Rosary and sharing.

Right now he said heaven is "collecting followers" for a time when "things will start to make more sense and many people will be awakened."

"There will be an influence in the whole world to show God's plan."

Esperanza links cloning to potential disasters

Venezuelan seer Maria Esperanza, widely viewed as one of the world's foremost mystics, warns that human cloning is a "mortal sin" and urged prayer to prevent what she sees as looming disasters if humankind doesn't grow closer to God.

It was her second major admonishment in the past year.

"That's a sin, a mortal sin," Maria replied when asked about cloning. "The only one who has that right is God. It's not going to have a good end, definitely. It's horrible. It is evil, the devil who is inspiring them. The devil now wants to confront God straight, 'man to man,' through human minds. It's grave. We must pray for this a lot. It will bring a lot of scandal and suffering to the world."

Esperanza, whose apparitions at Betania have been approved by the official Church, says the move toward cloning will cause great division and besides natural disasters will bring war. Just last fall the seer, a "spiritual daughter" of famed Italian priest Padre Pio, warned that the world was approaching a time of great military tension, with two nations (one large, one small) conspiring against the U.S.—*a prophecy followed almost immediately by news that the Russian leader was visiting Cuba and then by word that the Chinese were supplying arms to Iraq.*

According to Maria, such dangers will accompany disturbances in nature. She has long seen a build-up in such events, smaller events that will precipitate into ones that are much larger, until there is a reawakening. She has warned that the earth's core "is not in balance" and when asked about earthquakes said, "I feel one close to this place, this area. And a lot of water is involved—close to this area. But we can stop all that with prayer. With prayer from our hearts this may be stopped."

She is an old friend and we spoke with her, her husband Geo, and her family 30 miles west of New York City in Morristown, New Jersey. She looked tired with difficulty getting up from a chair but in her eyes was still an incredible sparkle. It wasn't clear if it would occur in the middle or at the end of such events, but Maria said God was going to lift our spiritual blinders, that through the Light of His grace mankind would soon begin to see the truth. She did not dwell on disasters. She said we are in a "time of trial" that will clear the way for a brighter future—and using words similar to those recently employed by the Pope, spoke about the coming of a "new earth" which will begin with an increase in God's grace—a heightening of our awareness—as God radiates His special if invisible light from heaven.

"I feel that here on earth, like a reflection of heaven, we will have beautiful things in the future that will resemble the things of heaven," Maria said. "Here on earth we are going to see beautiful cities that are going to be built in a resemblance of heaven, like the coming of God's kingdom—a new world. There will be like communities all over the world. We will live in communities. We are already beginning trials, a time of trials, and these trials will come to help people realize the importance of helping each other. People will realize that without their brothers, they cannot go on. It will start from the year 2004 on. It will be the beginning. Rivers of supernatural light are awaiting us—surprises, beautiful surprises. Each one of us will encounter ourselves, and beautiful ideas will come to our minds, beautiful talents, and more than anything else, we will achieve the simplicity of an innocent child. And that's the most important thing. We will be able to achieve the innocence of a child but with the maturity and knowledge, the wisdom, of an adult.

"It has to be that way," continued Maria, "because otherwise God can not enter in our souls and hearts. When this light comes it comes with supernatural light and God will allow us to feel His Presence deep in our hearts, the divine spark that will awaken our conscience, to help us realize that God is everything and we are nothing without Him. When we get this light we will be able to feel God in our hearts again. We will feel Him all the time with us."

"My children, I am with you day and night," she says she was told by Jesus. *"I live among you. And I will give you My light."*

"With this votive light, this continuous light, will come hope, strength, and the will to be able to do things in the right way. We must try to live each day with His presence on our minds and hearts.

If your brother wants to live in a different way, just let him walk his path. Never try to force. We must try to show the harmony and love of God in our behavior."

Maria and her family confirmed that she still has daily visions, which began in 1933 when she was five. Asked if she could tell if others were seeing Jesus or the Virgin Mary, Esperanza said that she could, and smiled when asked if she then thought the Pope has had visions. "Yes, but he will never tell," said Maria.

Mystic Maria Esperanza had warned of great disturbances with the United States

It was back in the 1990's that Venezuelan mystic, Maria Esperanza, warned about two towers in New York and evil plans. We thought back then it had to do with the truck bombing. But maybe there was more to it than that.

Earlier this year, we reported Esperanza's warning that foreign powers, including a small power, had plans on America, including on its own soil. "We are living very difficult times right now even though things look like they're somewhat under control, she told *Spirit Daily.* "We must be very, very alert. The United States must take care of itself a lot because there is much hatred toward the U.S. right now, so now *more than ever* the United states must be careful." Esperanza and others have long warned of terrorism on American soil as part of the beginning of chastisements. Many have discussed war within our own borders. They have said that our protection has been diminished through our own moral course.

Although in recent years America has avoided major casualties during disasters such as Hurricane Andrew, the Los Angeles earthquake of 1994, and the Mississippi flood, it is clear that now we are in a time of *human* loss. It is also clear that we are in a time of fasting. With prayer and fasting, according to Medjugorje we can even stop war. And now it is obvious that such measures are urgently needed.

Maria continued to *Spirit Daily* last winter, "There are two nations that have their eyes on the U.S. right now. They are not necessarily big nations. One is very smart and powerful and the other is less harmful and these two nations are in accordance and will be allies. They want somehow to upset the United States, to work inside and cause disturbances. They feel they can put the nation in jeopardy working not just from the outside but also from the inside. They feel they can be as powerful as the United States. They have people inside already. With a lot of prayer it can be stopped."

Mystic Maria Esperanza warns U.S. not to go to war

World-renowned mystic Maria Esperanza of Venezuela warned Friday that immediately going to war over Tuesday's event would be "the greatest mistake."

Speaking to *Spirit Daily,* the seer said, "If the United States goes to war right now, it will be the worst possible mistake, the greatest mistake, and would be nearly impossible to stop. The U.S. is smart and should wait patiently. War would be imprudent—don't attack."

Esperanza's words are closely watched because previous prophecies of hers have materialized. Last January, she warned that foreign powers—one large, one small—were working together to "provoke" America. She had said (and we have reported) that the provocation would be severe and would be both from outside and inside the U.S.—on it's own soil. At the time she had also counseled prudence. On August 25, we received the fax of a message Maria was given by Saint Peter. The message said that "a great event will be happening in 3 weeks or 3 months." The attack on New York occurred in the third week.

But instead of war, said Maria, the United States must turn to what she calls the four "pillars": prayer, meditation, penance, and the Eucharist. "With that you will be able," she said, "to win."

Esperanza urged recitation of fifteen decades of the Rosary and daily Mass. She emphasized the need for families to pray together.

If this happens, she said, the U.S. will be unharmed in the long run by the recent disasters.

"Definitely it's going to escalate but at the same time through prayer we can stop a big thing from happening," she said. "Right now the U.S. has to be very careful and prudent—go little by little."

"Prayer is what is going to influence the whole problem," she said. "From now until 2004, in this period, everything will be resolved. Halfway through 2004 it will look better, but until then we must be careful. God can work miracles."

Esperanza, who is connected with the Church-approved apparition site of Betania, Venezuela, said that the attacks in New York City and at the Pentagon were allowed by God as "an awakening of conscience" and to strengthen the U.S. spiritually. She said, "Faith will grow."

"Our Lord is crying out at us for conversions," she said. "This has been a lesson for the whole world. The faith of people in today's world is too superficial. We must have an open heart to the Lord and His grace, because God now is going to shake the whole world, not only in the U.S. Not a violent shaking but something that makes people aware of His Presence."

When asked if the current crisis was a result of recent decisions on human cloning and related research, she said that was a part of it but the events of September 11 were related to general immorality and spiritual shortcomings.

"I know the wound has been very big," she said, "but now we have to see the situation through God's eyes and ask for forgiveness, for courage, and for the will to pray and do penance and rid ourselves of pride." Maria said recent physical problems she has been suffering are related to the current crisis.

Seer who foresaw "disturbance" by foreign power in U.S. now turns concern to Pope

If we needed any more evidence that Maria Esperanza de Bianchini is a major historical mystic, we have received it during the past few weeks. Of course, we didn't really need such evidence. We've known that for a long time. But what occurred in recent days has been a strong confirmation. It was last December that we ran the following headline: "World-known mystic Maria Esperanza warns U.S. of foreign danger, sees the world 'saddened' in a short while, is concerned in particular with the Mid East, the Pope, and two nations."

That's what we ran last winter with her sanction. The article went on to say that a heaviness in her chest indicated something was on the way. "The United States has to be very careful," she had told *Spirit Daily*. "It has to act with a lot of prudence." As her son-in-law, Carlos Marrero Bornn, explained, "She feels in her heart that there is a certain big thing that is about to happen."

Maria, whose visions are associated with the apparition site of Betania near Caracas (in Venezuela)—one of the few such sites winning formal Church approval during the twentieth century—said that matters would unfold in the way of a series of events climaxed by a major situation. She said at the time that the next several years would be crucial, and that the U.S. had to be "very, very alert. The United States must take care of itself a lot because there is much hatred toward the U.S. right now, so now *more than ever* the United States must be careful. There are two nations that have their eyes on the U.S. right now. They are not necessarily big nations. One is very smart and powerful and the other is less [so] and these two nations are in accordance and will be allies. They want somehow to upset the United States, to work inside and cause disturbances. They feel they can put the nation in jeopardy working not just from the outside but also from the inside. . . They have people inside already. . ."

That's what she warned ten months ago. "As a sign, as an awakening of consciences, she sees a very big event," Carlos had said. "Something that will shake the world. She feels it is going to take a little more time—not too much time, but a little more...Not right now. A little further than now."

As we said, that was toward the end of last December. The timing was expressed in a way that appears totally accurate in retrospect. *An awakening of consciences.* She specifically warned about materialism—and of course when the event came it involved the very center of Western materialism.

But that wasn't all. Last March, while she was visiting northern New Jersey—within 30 miles of New York—she said she felt something was going to happen *in that area.* We thought she might be referring to an earthquake. She warned that evils like cloning would lead to events.

A couple months after that prediction, at the beginning of summer, Maria told her family that the upheavals in Israel as well as natural stirrings such as the volcanoes (in places like the Philippines and Italy) were "specific signs" that events were intensifying and that in the next several years will join to precipitate a major occurrence of some type. "She sees these as clear signs of an imminent event that will awaken consciences," Carlos had told us. "Something important will happen very soon. This is all a preparation for a great event that will be sent to show the real meaning of life."

On August 25, at 9:35 p.m. those close to Maria—who had returned to the New York area for a visit—recorded her as saying, "A great event will be happening in three weeks or three months. As the Holy Father's condition weakens, the event is for the whole world."

It was the third week after that prophecy that the attack in New York City occurred—and Maria was virtually at the scene, praying in the New York-New Jersey area.

Not only was there a gargantuan "disturbance" inside the U.S., but last Tuesday (September 25), the Pope began to fail as Maria worried. She had been telling family and friends that she was herself suffering in order to take some of the burden off him and hopefully help him maintain his pontificate during the tumultuous time.

In other words, as mystic are wont to do, she was taking on some of his suffering. She was stooped, often hunched over, and had great difficulty (and still does) walking. Incredible was how similar her own ailments were to those of John Paul II.

True to her words, the Pope seemed to be weakening. "His hands trembled, he slumped in his chair and aides rushed to his side to offer comfort halfway through a speech he could not finish," said *The Washington Post*. "Pope John Paul II's stop in Armenia on Tuesday, his fourth day of a foreign tour, offered a new test of the 81-year-old pontiff's frail health."

While some reports appeared a bit exaggerated (it was planned for him to cut short his speech), there was no doubt that *symptoms of his Parkinson's disease were showing.*

Incredibly, Maria, who had said many months ago that she was sharing in his suffering—and that she was intent on doing so because he was needed during the upcoming period of crises—herself suffered symptoms of what was diagnosed as a touch of Parkinson's!

Soon after the terrorist bombing, Maria expressed the urge to leave the area of New York and travel to Rome.

Let us make clear that Maria doesn't like to speak of these things. She is circumspect. She never draws attention to herself. She never accents her gifts. But she has granted permission to quote certain of her remarks and her message is crucial at this crucial hour. The message: pray for the Pope, because he's especially in need. Pray for the U.S. Pray for the world. Pray 15 decades of the Rosary each day and pray with the family!

Alas, her own frailty is such that she is now heading back to Venezuela. She'll do so with her husband Geo and their incredibly beautiful family. We've never seen a family like it, and here you see the real fruit. Such love. Such devotion. No one likes to be away from Maria once they have been around her. She leaves a terrific sense of joy, and so far there is no one we have seen quite like her!

Her concerns continue. She believes we will see difficult trials at least until the second part of 2004—when a light from heaven will shine. She sees another earth-shaking event, although this time not "violent." The world is entering a "new stage."

What that could be is anyone's guess. We present such material with the attitude she has: no fear, a calm demeanor, but prayer and vigilance. It is not useful to ignore reality. We must know what to pray about. Right now is a prophetic time—and prophecy is foremost. At the same time we must have balance and not obsess on the negative. Could it be that after all the struggle a great day of light is coming?

For now our only conclusion is that this is one incredible mystic. . .

Our love to you Maria! Bon voyage! Thanks!

Seer warns that U.S. is still at risk

World-known seer Maria Esperanza of Venezuela warned Thursday that the world is going through "convulsions" and that the United States remains acutely vulnerable to terrorism despite a relatively sedate period since September 11. "The risk is still there," she says. "You have to be alert all the time because there may be surprises. The United States must be very careful right now."

Her concern has not lessened since last fall, although she has hope that certain events can be averted. "There is a group of people who are trying to show the world that things are under control, but if we do not unite in prayer things will get worse," she told *Spirit Daily* Thursday night through an interpreter. "The people must be united because these are very difficult times. We are living in a very difficult time. Mankind is going too fast and is not stopping to meditate. There are those making decisions without really meditating, in their own way. They are not waiting for God. They are searching for their own truths. There is a group and I don't like them. There is a group that wants to de-stabilize the United States and break down its unity, but the grace of God is greater than anything, and the Holy Spirit is exerting His graces. The Holy Spirit is pouring His graces abundantly."

Asked whether the group or groups were political, the mystic—widely seen as the greatest since Padre Pio, whom she personally knew—did not elaborate and focused on what must be done to prevent what she sees as a series of upheavals.

It was striking language coming from the same mystic who, way back in 1992, foresaw "two huge towers with black smoke all around them" and who more recently—last winter, and then again in March and August—warned that something "big" was about to happen involving foreign interests *on American soil.*

So specific was the prophecy that she requested urgent prayer that time too, saying that the event would not be immediate but would occur "in a little while," which fit the subsequent time-frame of the following September. She had predicted that the provocation would be severe and would be both from outside and inside the U.S. She warned that at least two foreign powers—one large, one small—were working together to "provoke" America. At the time she had also counseled prudence. Then last March Maria specified that a rumbling of some sort would occur in the area of New York-New Jersey, and on August 25 said a "great event" would happen within "three weeks or three months" that would "shake the world"—and ended up being personally present in the New York City area the third week after the prophecy, on September 11.

For a year now Esperanza has indicated that the world will enter a "new stage" in the next several years. She had told her family that the upheavals in Israel as well as natural stirrings (such as recent volcanoes in places like the Philippines) were "specific signs" that events were intensifying and in the next several years would join to precipitate a major occurrence of some type.

Esperanza, who is associated with Betania (an apparition site near Caracas that has rare official Church approval, with full ecclesiastical recognition since 1987), and who has experienced visions of Jesus and the Virgin Mary, has also expressed great concern about the Pope and is said by her family to have assumed some of his sufferings—even developing a Parkinson-like syndrome uncannily similar to his. She is often extremely weak, has great difficulty walking, and we urge prayers for her as she faces what she herself describes as one of her most difficult times ever but also "another test in life, no more than that." She is currently under treatment by a neurologist, but thus far without great improvement in what has been a long agony.

"Prayer is the fundamental base in order to help mankind," says Maria urgently. "We must be alert to save our souls and deserve what God has planned for us. I leave these things in the Hands of the Lord. He knows. He knows what He is doing. I know my condition is delicate, but I will do my best until the last moment. That's what the Lord wants us to do."

Previously, Esperanza had specified that Mass and daily recitation of the Rosary's 15 decades are crucial. She has warned and continues to warn that abortion, genetic manipulation, and materialism will lead to both natural disasters and war. She is concerned that men with "egos" are muddying events when "the only way to see the truth is through humility. We have to be very humble, because pride is what is destroying the world, and so is materialism. We must be humble and generous."

Indeed, it is a time of darkness. It is a time of convulsions. It is a time during which the evil one has turned devices against all—bringing forth trials not just on the world stage, but within communities and families. It is a time when evil has whispered deceptions into ears, and has distorted truth at every turn, setting brother against sister and causing every form of personal suffering. Although Maria has mentioned a special grace for the year 2004, in the larger picture, she presents no specific frame of time. She says that after tribulation there will be a renewal and that when it comes—whenever that may be—the renewal will be both physical and spiritual. There will be a new time. She sees events leading to a "light"; and that, she says, will pave the way to what she describes mysteriously as "a new dawn of Jesus."

The remedy for frightening times is found in high Church

Christians of all stripes have been heading for the fundamentals of their faith and this is especially true of Catholics. Books on traditions of the Church are hot items, and so are stories of conversions.

This is encouraging because the Catholic faith has the most powerful weapon against evil in the form of the Eucharist—and there has never been a better time to use it. When we pray during Consecration, when we lift our hearts up as the priest lifts the Host, and when he lifts the cup filled with the Precious Blood, there is the potential for all the power in the universe.

We can break evil. We can lift our families out of a mire. We can pray for America.

It is all the more potent when coupled with a good Confession.

Those who doubt the Real presence need only know the history of eucharistic miracles. During the eighth century in Lanciano, Italy, a Communion Host suddenly changed into actual flesh while a doubting priest—no longer sure it was the Real Presence—was celebrating Mass. He was suddenly very certain.

During 1280 in Slavonice, Czechoslovakia, a herdsman spotted mysterious flames on a cluster of bushes. When he got there he saw a Communion Host in the middle of the fire. It was later identified as a Host that had been stolen from a local church and discarded in the area. The heat had not so much as scorched it.

In Dubna, Poland, during 1867, the devout saw soft rays glowing from a monstrance. Some claimed the manifestation was immediately followed by an image of Jesus in the Blessed Sacrament. This continued during the whole of a Forty Hour Devotion, witnessed both by believing Catholics and by schismatics who had stopped by out of curiosity.

In 1970, a red spot of blood developed on a Host in Stich, Germany. It wasn't quite as dramatic as the flesh at Lanciano, but once again it showed the Real Presence. And it was followed by dozens of similar Eucharistic miracles. In Betania, Venezuela, a priest encountered blood after he broke the large Host during Mass and the Bishop ordered it kept for special veneration.

In America—the Midwest—a priest claimed that during the course of several weeks in 1996 a Host kept for ablution turned, as at Lanciano, into something resembling flesh and blood. The emotion nearly overcame him.

In Upstate New York, at a shrine dedicated to Our Lady of Fatima, a medical doctor reported the sudden materialization of a Communion wafer in a chapel of the Blessed Sacrament.

These are only some of the recently claimed occurrences. Many are still in need of study but already we know that, transcending boundaries, the Holy Spirit seems to be saying the same thing everywhere: I have given you signs and wonders. I have given you apparitions and healings. Now, I am showing you the True Presence.

The time has come to take the lessons we have learned from many phenomena and employ them for personal protection. The time has come to join Christ's army in a more profound manner. The time has come to revisit the very cornerstones of the Catholic faith and better appreciate their power. The time has come to focus on our eternal destinations—and make sure that ours is the destination of Jesus, which means heaven.

This is the message that comes both from Eucharistic miracles, charismatic gifts, and the revelations from places such as Medjugorje.

One great fruit of Our Blessed Mother is Eucharistic Adoration. She is Our Lady of the Eucharist. She was the one who gave her own flesh and blood to Jesus. She's a part of the Eucharist. We should remember that at Fatima, Portugal, the apparitions began with the appearance of an angel who held a chalice with a Host mysteriously suspended above it.

The angel prostrated himself as blood fell into the cup. "Most Holy Trinity," he said, "Father, Son, and Holy Ghost, I adore You profoundly and I offer You the most precious Body, Blood, Soul, and Divinity of Jesus Christ, present in all the tabernacles of the world. . ."

At the conclusion of those famous apparitions thousands saw

the sun act very strangely and what looked like a "shield" or Communion Host move in front of the solar orb, so that they could stare at it.

The miracle of the sun—looking as it did like a radiant Host on October 13, 1917—was another sign telling us to get back to the Eucharist.

In all the legitimate apparitions since, the common theme has been: return to the basics of the Church. Revisit the historical gifts. Understand better the sacraments. Form union with Christ not so much through the spectacular as through deeper devotion.

For years I've written about apparitions of Our Blessed Mother. I've written about spiritual warfare. I've written of the evil in our era. I've written of prophecy. I've written of angels and current wonders. I can't think of more relevant topics for our special time. We're in a serious historical moment, and Mary is among us.

But when Our Blessed Mother arrives, it's always on behalf of her Son. It's always for Christ. She is the messenger of Jesus. She always points to Him. She says it's through the Eucharist and a Christian approach to life that we best come to terms with what the future has to offer. It's through the Eucharist that we understand the times in which we live. It's through Mass that we make sense of apparitions and other gifts of the Holy Spirit.

And it's through the Eucharist—through the Light of Jesus—that we dispel the current darkness. When Christ is present, evil can not remain. When Jesus is with us, so is the Trinity. When the Trinity is with us, our very Creator is at hand. And God is infinitely more powerful than Lucifer and all the fallen angels combined!

Only if we pray and honor the sacraments will we be able to fully lessen events that otherwise loom in the future.

In the Eucharist are the most powerful words since creation

When Christ is present, when Christ is with us, evil can not remain. When Jesus is with us, so is the Trinity. When the Trinity is with us, our very Creator is at hand. And God is infinitely more powerful than Lucifer and all the fallen angels.

While many of us struggle to find a way in which to lessen the illness and darkness of our world—to chase away evil spirits—such is already available to us through Jesus and the power He set loose at the Last Supper, which was the first Eucharist.

It was at the Last Supper that Jesus took the bread, broke it, and gave it to His disciples, saying, *"This is My body to be given for you. Do this as a remembrance of Me."* He did the same with the cup of wine. *"This cup is the new covenant in My Blood, which will be shed for you."*

They were the most powerful words since Creation. It was the denouement of Our Savior's very mission. It was a climax—a high point—of the ages. Christ was showing why He had come and the incredible nature of His rescue mission.

By sharing bread and wine, the disciples would be invoking the power of His entire mission. It was a covenant meal at Passover. They would be tapping into God's power. They would be touching His garment. No wonder the ritual would survive for centuries! No wonder miracles would be associated with the Eucharist!

When we take the Eucharist we are the bleeding woman touching the robe of Christ (*Matthew* 9:20) and feeling the healing power, and we are the wedding guests at Cana, seeing His first miracle, and we are sitting with Him as He speaks His last to the disciples.

Through the ages it has been proven that the Eucharist takes us into the New Testament. It gives us true insight.

Are you confused or scared about current times? Are you trying to make sense of what is going on around us?

If you feel the least bit scared, you need the Eucharist. You need its insight. You need the calmness of nearness to the Lord.

The Eucharist is where we should seek advice. The Eucharist is what guides us in uncharted territory. For hidden in it is the key to how we should live the current troubling times and what we can expect in the future. Hidden in the Eucharist is the way to humility and faith. Hidden in the Host is the key to love.

In the Eucharist, most importantly, are the keys to Heaven.

"The most important thing in the spiritual life is to ask for the Holy Spirit"

"Come Holy Spirit. Come Holy Spirit."

We can never repeat that enough. It's the most fundamental of prayers. You can even ask the Holy Spirit to tell you what you need and how to pray for it!

It is the Holy Spirit Who grants guidance, heals sickness, strengthens our bodies, and protects us against all untoward events. It's the Holy Spirit Who imbues Mass with Christ's Presence. When there are miracles or revelations, these are accomplished through the Holy Spirit. During Mass He is especially strong. He is especially willing to pervade our spirits.

And we should invite that. We should beg for His arrival. We should beg Him to pray through our minds and lips. Again, we should ask Him to reveal to us what it is we should be praying about.

He is the Spirit of Truth. He is the Spirit of prayerfulness.

When the priest gives us the opportunity to reflect upon our sins, we should ask the Holy Spirit to tell us what sins we most need to purge. We should ask Him to reach deep into our pasts and expunge any evil. We should ask the Holy Spirit to enlighten us as to what we need for spiritual development.

And we should cover ourselves with the whiteness of His protection.

Such is crucial in our time, when evil spirits (which we'll be discussing more this week) are more numerous than ever—when they continue to climb in a horde from the pit, when they antagonize and anger and divide us. We need special protection, and that protection is given by the Holy Spirit. He draws us to the Father. He draws us to Jesus. As part of the Holy Trinity, He has the power to grant us health (if such is the Will of God) and shield us from demonism.

At Mass we should ask the Holy Spirit to protect us and our loved ones from accidents and disease. We should ask for protection from any unfortunate events. We should ask the Spirit to send special angels and further empower those angels we have. We should ask Him to guide our every thought and action. We should ask for a long, healthy life, a holy death, and the sure route to heaven.

Nothing brings the Holy Spirit like the Eucharist, and with God, anything is possible. Anything can change. Anything can be accomplished. As the Virgin of Medjugorje said, *"The most important thing in the spiritual life is to ask for the gift of the Holy Spirit. When the Holy Spirit comes, then peace will be established. When that occurs, everything around you changes. Pray for the Holy Spirit for enlightenment. Ask the Holy Spirit to renew your souls, to renew the entire world. Raise your hands, yearn for Jesus because in His Resurrection He wants to fill you with graces."*

When that happens, when we have the Holy Spirit, then, according to Our Blessed Mother, we have everything.

Christmas mystery: how the power of God manifests in Christ as the Infant

A great mystery of our faith is the power of Christ as Infant. When we invoke Him under that stage of His life, there is an extraordinary, healing, and protective grace. Let's remember that it was with the Infant that Mary first appeared at Medjugorje in 1981, and also the Child Who on one famous occasion appeared to Sister Lucia dos Santos of Fatima. In 1925 Lucia received an apparition of the Virgin with the Child at which time the Child spoke, telling Lucia to have compassion on His mother's heart, which was pierced by the thorns of ingratitude.

Through history, Mary has often appeared—hundreds of times—with the Infant, and with Him comes tremendous force. From the Child is a unique power. Something very special touches the Heart of God when we seek His Son as the Infant, and this array of grace—this special power—is best invoked at Mass and especially at Christmas.

So precious is the Mass and invoking the Infant that saints would have eliminated everything in their lives *but* the Eucharist. They were tortured for it. They were martyred for it. During winter Francis de Sales crawled on an icy beam of wood to cross a stream that separated him from church.

Clearly, he understood what we should all understand: that Mass is the most powerful act in the universe. During Mass we are not only sitting with Christ during the Last Supper, but also revisiting all aspects and the very onset of His life.

Think about that. Think about the fact that Mass transports us into the time of Jesus. Mass replays every event in Jesus' life and for that matter every major event leading up to it. We get this through the Gospels. We get this through other Scriptural readings. And we get it through the precious Eucharistic rituals.

During Mass we relive the life of Christ—of his adulthood, of His *infancy*—with an intimacy unknown even to His disciples. We are with Him as God devised the plan of salvation. We are with Mary when His birth is announced. We relive the appearance of

Gabriel. We are with Him at His conception. We're with Him when His power touches Elizabeth from the womb of Mary. We're with Him at His birth. We're with Him as He is wrapped in swaddling clothes, and when the wise men visit, and we're with Him as visitors wonder at the majesty of this impoverished Infant. We're with Him when they flee to Egypt.

For during Mass, during the Eucharist, we are declaring ourselves a part of His mission. We're declaring a willingness to follow in His footsteps. We're acknowledging His great act of redemption.

That's the enormity of power available to you this week and every week. That's the gravity of the moment. That's the transcendental nature—the truly miraculous nature—of "Christ Mass."

It brings back Calvary. It keeps giving us His Blood. It defeats all sin.

This Christmas, wipe the slate clean; take your faults to the Infant; ask for His cleanness, His purity.

He'll give that to you. He'll forgive you. He'll let you turn over a new leaf. As St. Francis de Sales said, "In no action does Our Savior show Himself more loving or more tender than in this one, in which, as it were, He annihilates Himself and reduces Himself to food in order to penetrate our souls and unite Himself in the hearts of His faithful."

Darkness of any sort must lift when there is faith, humility, and the liturgy

By Michael H. Brown

During Mass God's power manifests in a living, life-giving, joyful light that serves as the antidote of darkness. It is the extreme *opposite* of evil.

That's how Christ appears: as Light, and at Mass we all get to see this. At Mass we're at a higher level than a visionary. If we go to Jesus with our hearts, His Light comes and no evil can defeat us.

About a year ago I was speaking with a woman whose family was involved in a famous, horrifying murder. Many bad things had been practiced in the house before the murder, and now, after the slayings (parents had been killed), there was that much more darkness. It was almost palpable. Even at mid-day, the room where the murders occurred always was dark—actually *dark*—with an eerie feeling.

That persisted until the family brought in a priest. When he said Mass, something remarkable occurred. "As he raised the host," said this woman, "I could see light come in. I could see the darkness actually rise like a curtain."

The Eucharist can erase even the most *potent* forms of evil. The next time something seems impossible, take it to Mass and watch how its grip on you disappears (or at least lessens). "Confession and Communion are worth as much as a strong exorcism," noted one person who was delivered from demons by Father Gabriel Amorth, the official Rome exorcist.

It's true of the entire Mass. Indeed, at the very entry, when we use Holy Water, we're renouncing sin, and demons hate this. The same goes for just about every aspect of the ritual. Devils flee from Scripture. They flee from the priest's blessings. They flee especially upon elevation of the Host.

With Mass, with the Host, the devil's pride is broken. In its place comes the humbleness of Jesus. With Mass comes His strength on the Cross. These are three deepest secrets of the Eucharist and they are the way we defeat Satan: faith, humility, and love.

Separate prophecies saw "cloud" over New York

Whether or not the crash of American Flight 587 in New York City was a mechanical failure or terrorists, it's obvious that the city is under some sort of evil cloud. We know that this sounds harsh, and it's not meant to. It's meant to marshal prayer. We have heard this term used in two recent prophecies—both documented *before* the events of September 11. One was the so-called *1990 prophecy* that we first reported last June 27 and which stated bluntly that "New York City is under an evil cloud and will be for 12 years." It warned that "the pride there will be broken," and the prophecy came to mind two months later when the World Trade Center (which many considered New York's pride and joy) came crumbling down.

Then last week we learned that in a book called *Fast Lane to Heaven*, Ned Dougherty, a New York area man, claimed he had a near-death experience and that during it a woman he identifies as the Virgin Mary (we are still discerning this), indicated a terrorist threat on New York. When we called him up, Ned startled us by using a similar term in stating that he had a vision of destruction in the city. "Every time I tried to go into Manhattan, I had difficulty breathing," he said. "It seemed like there was a *negative cloud* (our emphasis) over that city for me."

We are thus meant to pray for repentance and a lifting of this cloud. We must pray for New Yorkers. We must pray that folks there and everywhere realize the true reason for what is going on.

Again, it doesn't matter whether it's a terrorist or an accident. In a chastisement, events of all kinds occur for many different reasons. We are not meant to fear them, but neither are we meant to ignore them. As Scripture tells us, the *truth* sets us free. The 1990 prophecy said that before the major chastisements events will occur on a regional scale and will not usually be recognized as such, as we have seen since September 11. We found it eerie that in researching *Sent To Earth*, the three places we chose to visit in studying the possible scenarios for chastisement in New York were the World Trade Center, the New York City Emergency Management Center, and Rockaway Beach (although what we envisioned as most likely to happen was a hurricane). Two of the three were destroyed September 11, while Rockaway was where the jet hit.

And what is the truth of Flight 587?

Only time will tell. We hope and pray that the government is fully leveling with us. We say this because folks who have been in that Queens neighborhood for 50 years say in all that time there has been no similar mishap. There is always a first time, although we are concerned about whether the full truth has come out about the flight that blew up in 1996 just off Long Island (in fact, right near a shrine that Dougherty saw in a vision), and there was also the flight that crashed into the ocean off Nova Scotia in 1998. There was also the case of Egypt Air Flight 990 in 1999, whereby a co-pilot was heard chanting a Muslim prayer about death before the flight system was oddly disengaged.

Much more recently—in fact, since September 11—we have had a Russian flight from Israel down; a major mishap on an Italian airfield; a Greyhound bus driver stabbed as a foreigner took control of the wheel and crashed the vehicle; an attempted hijacking of a medical plane in New Mexico; the anthrax scares; the arrest of a foreigner with knives and Mace trying to board a plane in Chicago; and other situations that have been pooh-poohed as accidents or coincidence or copycats. The New York crash may indeed have been mechanical; there are indications the problem could have started in the engine.

Maybe, but let's always remember what the Bible says about truth and let's be truthful: we need to root both our *own* evil and the terrorists out. We need to clean house. And that doesn't mean sweeping anything—including deep spiritual problems—under the rug. The less evil there is, the less terrorism or accidents or whatever it can attract.

O, New York, city I loved, city of my youth, city where I once lived; city of goodness but also astonishing debauchery; city of materialism and sensuality and pride; city that had grown too irreverent; capital of worldliness; mecca of pro-choice: O great New York take a moral tally and forget the defiance and ask forgiveness before venting anger!

Ask forgiveness and the prayers we will all say—*must* say—will get you and us through this.

With prayer is the way out of every situation, even those that seem to have no exit

"*Dear children, today I wish to call you to pray, pray, pray,*" said a message in 1985 from Medjugorje. "*In prayer you shall perceive the greatest joy, and the way out of every situation that has no exit.*"

Those are dramatic words: situations that seem to have no exits. We've all experienced that: what seems frightening, or without a solution. So it is that we pray for the U.S. and its leaders—who find themselves in a tremendous predicament. On the one hand there is no doubt that they must stop the threat of terrorists. At this hour some form of military incursion into Afghanistan and perhaps other Muslims nations seems all but inevitable. It could be hard to find the terrorists, and at the same time such an action may provoke *jihad*—a "holy" war—that spreads across Islam. Here at home, any attack against Osama bin Ladin could lead to more acts of terrorism.

It's a situation that seems to have no exit and yet through prayer President Bush will be guided to make decisions that find a miraculous solution. In fact, *only* through prayer—not politics, not diplomacy, not ratiocination—will the exact right measures be found. This is also true in our lives: prayer offers surprising answers. When we're confronted with what seems impossible, we pray and with sudden clarity see the way out. You know how it is: Often we find ourselves in what seems like a bleak place. Often we can't imagine *how* to solve a problem. Often we find ourselves in situations that seem to have no good alternative.

It could be a financial crisis. It could be a problem with one's career. It could be a dilemma with children.

From time to time we all feel painted into a corner.

That's the time to pray. That's the time to drop everything and lift the heart upward. It's remarkable how solutions wing into our heads during prayer—answers that would otherwise allude us.

Is that to downplay the serious nature of our time? Not at all.

It's an exceedingly dangerous time, and we won't sugarcoat that. It's the "feelgood" attitude in modern New Age America—the attitude that we can't issue serious admonitions—that has led to a downward spiritual spiral. We need only turn to *Matthew* 24 to see the tone that Christ took.

But as we have said throughout this crisis, there is also no room for fear. Those who fear—who can't face a serious situation—need to pray. When they do they will see their fear dissipate like fog in the sunshine of morning. If you're afraid, if you feel scared, you need to increase your praying. With prayer comes faith and with faith there is no room for the slightest trepidation. While it's crucial to recognize the serious nature of what's going on, more crucial is the need to increase supplications. This is also true in our daily lives. The current crisis is not just political; the attack is also on a personal level. At the same time that America faces geopolitical evils, so do we face a rush of personal evil.

But once more this is stopped by prayer. With prayer, *anything* is possible. Do you have a spouse who is looking for a fight? A friend or co-worker who sends you fiery darts? A child who just won't come to God?

It is a time of great evil assault but we forget the words of *Ephesians*: draw the strength from the Lord and His mighty power. Put on the armor of God so that you may be able to stand firm against the tactics of the devil. Our battle is not against human foes but against the principalities and powers, the rulers of this world of darkness—the evil spirits who hover in regions above. Stand fast. Use truth as your belt, and justice as your breastplate. Use faith as your shield. Do we face serious times? You better believe it. But we must never forget the dramatic words of Medjugorje. "*Advance against satan by means of prayer,*" the Virgin said in 1985. "*Put on the armor for battle and with the Rosary in your hand, defeat him! May prayer reign in the whole world* (1989). *Through prayer you can prevent wars from happening; with prayer you can stop wars* (1982). *With prayer you can even suspend the laws of nature.*"

Exorcist in Rome says the Church has stripped itself of weapons against evil

Father Gabriele Amorth, the official exorcist in Rome, has warned that wanton consumerism, sexual promiscuity, the occult, abortion, and homosexuality have caused a tremendous outbreak of demonic activity at a time when the Church has stripped itself of weapons to fight it.

Amorth's remarks come in a bestselling book, *An Exorcist Tells His Story*, and parallel warnings from such places as Fatima—where seer Lucia dos Santos said we are facing a "decisive" battle with the devil—and Medjugorje, where just two weeks ago, on January 1, the Virgin told seer Marija Pavlovic that devotion is urgent at a time when "Satan is free from chains." The remarks also parallel comments by the Pope himself, who before he ascended to the throne of Peter once commented that we are in an "apocalyptic" battle between light and dark.

Indeed, it was just last summer that the Pope himself, along with Father Amorth, attempted to exorcise a 19-year-old girl who erupted into a demonic tirade during an audience at the Vatican [see original story].

In the rest of the Church, however, the practice of exorcism has largely disappeared except for extraordinary cases—and only after approval of psychologists or psychiatrists who rarely believe in demonic phenomena to begin with. Though Jesus admonished His follower to cast out devils—and did so Himself on numerous occasions—in many cities this charism has been all but lost.

"I must point out that too many churchmen are totally disinterested in these problems, and so they leave the faithful defenseless," writes Father Amorth. "I believe that taking the exorcisms out of the baptismal ritual was a grave mistake (and it seems that Paul VI shared my opinion). I believe that it was a mistake to have eliminated, without a suitable replacement, the prayer to St. Michael the Archangel that we used to recite after each Mass. I am convinced that allowing the ministry of exorcism to die is an unforgivable deficiency to be laid squarely at the door of the bishops. Every diocese should have at least one exorcist at the cathedral, and every large parish and sanctuary should have one as well. Today the exorcist is seen as a rarity, almost impossible to find. His activity, on the other hand, has an indispensable pastoral value, as valuable as that of the preacher, the confessor, and those who administer the other sacraments.

"The Catholic hierarchy must say a forceful *mea culpa*," continues Amorth. "I am personally acquainted with many Italian bishops; I know of only a few who have ever practiced or who have assisted during an exorcism or who are adequately aware of this problem, I do not hesitate to repeat what I have written elsewhere; if a bishop, when faced with a valid request for an exorcism—I am not talking about the request of some demented person—does not address the problem, either personally or by delegating the task to a qualified priest, he is guilty of a most serious sin of omission. As a result of this negligence, we now have lost what once was *the school*; in the past, a practicing exorcist would instruct a novice."

With eyes of faith we turn from victim to victor

Here's something that can change your life, or at least your attitude. It's a simple message: with the eyes of faith, we become victors and not victims and fulfill who we really are. That's quite a promise. No matter where you are, no matter how life has been treating you, there is always the opportunity to pull ourselves up by the bootstraps and turn what seems like a situation without an exit into victory.

What are the "eyes of faith"?

They're the eyes we use to see beyond earth. They are the eyes of the future. They are the eyes that can visualize negativity or bring up to a positive way that will materialize blessings.

God honors faith. That's throughout the Bible. And faith means seeing things with the firm conviction that God can take us any place, if it's in His plan; if it fits His will.

Has someone said something negative to you—or about you?

Shake it off. Dust it from your back like you would any grit. Learn this as a first step: the dispelling of negativity from others. While there are times when we are legitimately corrected, too often negativity is satan's way of binding us in discouragement.

And at its first appearance, we must take the time to reject it; we must immediately root it out!

The more we do that—the more we learn to brush off evil—the easier it becomes.

Next, we have to see ourselves in a positive light. *God does.* He loves you more than you love yourself, and sees your true potential—the power you have to become a glorious servant in eternity. He *knows* that beneath the exterior, under the skin of the earthly body—and often deep under the burdens of life—is a being of terrific beauty (waiting to burst out of the cocoon and fly skyward).

How do we gain that beauty? Here we get back to the eyes of faith. With those eyes we elevate our vision above present turmoil—beyond any problem—and see the best of outcomes. We see what we want to happen. We see who we *want* to be.

And if it's God's will that's the path we will then follow. When we elevate our eyes, when we look above those who harass us, when we see beyond earthly trials—no matter how severe—we are on the road of glory.

On the cross, it's what Christ saw. It's the heaven He had in mind even as He was crucified. It's the paradise He offered the thief.

Satan, on the other hand, wants us to lose hope, wants us to be discouraged, wants us to find ourselves so down that we don't think there's a way out of the hole! Often, our prayers are blocked until we first cast him away in the Name of Jesus.

So next time you feel down, shake off that feeling, settle down to prayer, and in the depths of prayer see yourselves and your situation in the best of light. See your problems dissolving—or working to your ultimate benefit. See Christ lifting you up.

Satan is only as powerful as you let him be. Christ is the ruler over all aspects of existence and He has more joy and peace waiting for you than you have ever experienced or ever imagined but is waiting for you to raise the eyes of faith—to look to the land of joy—and claim it.

The "bad" news that we must fast turns out to be the best news ever

The Holy Father is calling on us to fast Friday (December 14) due to the situation in the world—the "dark clouds" he sees gathering—and he's doing so because he knows just how powerful fasting is. The more you do it, the more powerful it becomes. And believe it or not, the more you fast the more you like it. At the end of a fast you really feel God's *power*. He loves when we deny the flesh and look towards heaven.

That's what fasting is: a statement that we choose the spirit over the flesh, and the longer we can deny ourselves, the better. It allows us to transcend the physical. At Medjugorje, the Virgin has constantly urged us to fast. It's in dozens of messages. *"The Devil tries to impose his power on you, but you must remain strong and persevere in your faith,"* the Virgin said in November of 1981. *"You must pray and fast. I will always be close to you."*

You must fast, that is, unless you are physically ill, in which case you can find an alternative. The times are dangerous and fasting is the strongest weapon against the devil. He is prince of this world and fasting takes us above it. When you see people who lose their way or drift into dark aspects of religion—who become critical, who do not love, who drift toward falsity—it is often because there is no fasting. When we fast we develop discipline and that discipline is transmitted to all spiritual aspects.

It helps us pray. It *magnifies* prayer. And it regulates our thoughts. With fasting we're able to control our habits, make breakthroughs to other people, loose bonds, tear down strongholds, fend off those who persecute, cleanse our pride, and bring loved ones back to the faith. It's incredible how during or just after a fast prayers are so often and powerfully answered. Fasting is *liberating*. It helps us discern. We are able to lift spiritual blinders and see farther and more clearly.

God honors our efforts. Simply avoiding a snack or single meal is a good way to start. But it should proceed further. Maybe some coffee and juice but the best fast is a day without a snack or meal, and the very best fast is bread and water.

If not that, then whatever possible way, the best effort possible. Give up something you really truly enjoy. Offer it to God. *"Without you I am not able to help the world,"* said an August 28, 1986, message from Medjugorje. *"Repeated prayers and fasting reduce punishments from God,"* added a November 6, 1982, message.

It was by heeding Jonah and doing penance—not just abstinence, but donning sackcloth and *fasting*—that the city of Nineveh, the New York of its day, avoided chastisement.

Pope John Paul II is now calling out to the world as a modern Jonah and is uncannily in line with Medjugorje. Indeed, we're told a close friend of the Pope believes the Pontiff himself has visions, and we don't doubt it. He has certainly harbored a soft spot for Medjugorje, and let us repeat her July 21, 1982, message: *"Through fasting and prayer, one can stop wars, one can suspend the laws of nature."*

That's pretty good news! In fact, about as good as it gets. When there is a problem in your family—when someone is troubled, when someone is ill, even desperately so—fasting for that person can lift the natural laws and evil coming against him or her and lead to healing. It is spiritual. It causes deliverance. Fasting is *potent* in dispelling the devil.

What could be better news than that?

With fasting, we have the opportunity (be it the Will of God) to reverse *anything*. Our prayers are maximized. Our souls are cleansed. We're with Jesus on the desert.

When you fast, go through the house and pray all the evil out and do the same through the day wherever you are.

This is how our country will be saved and how terrorism will be stopped and how our children—how future generations—will be rescued.

A Fatima timeline

1100s—a poor girl from a hamlet near Fatima sees a heavenly woman who tells her to go home and look in the kitchen, where the youngster finds desperately needed bread.

1380—a miraculous spring is found near Fatima at Aljubarrota and healings take place, approved by the local bishop.

1300s—a knight named Nuno and his men claim an apparition of angels over Fatima, including the Archangel Michael, who some later associate with the 1917 appearance of Mary.

1400s—deaf girl from the hamlet of Casal Santa Maria a mile and a half from Fatima is healed after an apparition of the Virgin over a cluster of ortiga bushes.

1915—an angel appears to several youngsters, including a seven-year-old peasant girl named Lucia Aborbora (later Lucia dos Santos) above a copse of trees 90 miles north of Lisbon. At first it looks like a cloud in human form.

1916—the angel returns and appears to Lucia and now two cousins, Jacinta and Francisco Marto, as they're tossing rocks in a valley. The angel identifies himself as the Angel of Peace. "It was a young man, about 14 or 15 years old, whiter than snow, transparent as crystal when the sun shines through it," Lucia later recalls.

1917—the Virgin appears to Lucia, Francisco, and Jacinta on May 13 and returns each month on the 13th with the exception of August, when the seers were forced away from the site by authorities.

1917—June 13, the secret is given to Jacinta, then seven years old and soon to succumb to a great epidemic of influenza.

1917—July 13, the secret is now also given to Lucia, who turns pale and shrieks, saying afterwards that the message was good news for some, bad for others.

1920s—Lucia enters convent. Jacinta and Francisco have succumbed to a worldwide flu epidemic that kills 20 to 40 million.

1938—Great sign prophesied at Fatima seen as aurora borealis startles Europe, followed by world war.

1943—Lucia takes ill at a convent in Tuy, Spain, and the bishop back in Leira, Portugal, which oversees Fatima, becomes concerned that she might die without revealing the secret. He orders her to write it down.

1944—after several months of struggling with the devil, Lucia is finally able to take down what she has remembered all these years. The secret is committed to a notebook. It is finally recorded. It is rumored that Lucia is visited by the Virgin as she struggles to write it.

1950s—the first two parts of the secret begin circulation in devotional literature. They forecast Communism, the end of World War One, and World War Two, which will cost more than 40 million lives, making many martyrs.

1960s—Sister Lucia says the third secret can be released at this time but advises against it, saying it is a matter for the Church hierarchy.

1981—Pope John Paul II is felled by a gunshot on May 13, the anniversary of the first apparition. It is rumored (but not confirmed) that at the last moment he bent to look at a Fatima medal a young woman was wearing in the crowd at St. Peter's Square and that this motion caused the bullet to barely miss his aorta. Whatever the case, he credits the Virgin with saving his life and sends the bullet to be placed in her statue at Fatima. During his convalescence at Policlinico Gemelli he sees the miracle of the sun over the Seven Hills of Rome and asks for the complete Fatima dossier, which he reads fervently.

1984—on March 25, heeding the request at Fatima, John Paul II consecrates the world and implicitly Fatima to Mary's Immaculate

Heart, an action Sister Lucia later confirms as having been accepted by heaven and an action she claims prevented a nuclear war that would otherwise have happened the next year.

1985—Mikhail Gorbachev rises to power in the Soviet Union; Lech Walesa, under the guidance of John Paul II, leads Solidarity in Poland; and Communism begins to miraculously crumble—which Lucia says is the "triumph of Mary's Immaculate Heart."

2000—on May 13, during the beatification of Francisco and Jacinta, part of the third secret is revealed. It predicts the assassination attempt against John Paul.

2000—full text of secret revealed.

Faustina prophecy of cross in the sky found to link to miracle found in fourth century

A famous Catholic prophecy that the sky will turn dark and there will materialize a great luminous cross appears connected with a hidden event that occurred in the fourth century.

The prophecy by Saint Faustina of Poland, recorded in her diary, conveyed these alleged words from Jesus in the 1930s: *"Before I come as a just judge, I am coming first as the King of Mercy. Before the day of justice arrives, there will be given to people a sign in the heavens of this sort: All light in the heavens will be extinguished, and there will be great darkness over the whole earth. Then the sign of the cross will be seen in the sky, and from the openings where the hands and feet of the Savior were nailed will come forth great lights which will light up the earth for a period of time. This will take place shortly before the last day."*

That prophecy connects with an event recorded over Jerusalem in the fourth century by Saint Cyril of Jerusalem, a doctor of the Church. In a letter to the Emperor Constantius, he wrote, "On the nones of May, about the third hour, a great luminous cross appeared in the heavens, just over Golgotha, reaching as far as the holy mount of Olivet, seen, not by one or two persons, but clearly and evidently by the whole city. This was not, as might be thought, a fancy-bred and transient appearance: but it continued several hours together, visible to our eyes and brighter than the sun. The whole city, penetrated alike with awe and with joy at this portent, ran immediately to the church, all with one voice giving praise to our Lord Jesus Christ, the only Son of God."

The "nones" would be May 7 and when related to hours of the day in the ancient Church meant the fifth of seven canonical hours and came at the ninth hour of the day or at about 3 p.m.—which Saint Faustina was to proclaim as the "hour of mercy" almost 1,600 years later!

Prayer brings protection against fear and other fiery darts of the devil

If you are in any form of fear, cast it out. That's right. Get rid of it. That sounds easier said than done—and sometimes it is. We're in a tense time. No one would deny that. But we don't take enough time to calm down. Here's a simple but powerful truth: with sufficient prayer, all fear leaves.

And so we see that when there is too much fear, there is a spiritual lacking. There is an imbalance. All of us go through this, because few of us pray as much as the Bible recommends, which is without ceasing (*1 Thessalonians* 5:17). When God is always on our lips and minds fear vanishes.

That's because prayer brings faith and faith brings the positive. Faith brings protection. No matter what it is we fear—illness, terrorism, the boss at work—prayer offers a buffer. *Prayer* is the best medicine. As it says in *Ephesians* (6:16), faith should be held up as a shield against the fiery darts of the evil one, which are then extinguished.

When you're going into a situation that you fear or that may bring a fiery dart, say a prayer. Say it with FAITH. This will reduce the "zingers." You know how it is: every so often the devil sends you a sting. It can be in something someone does. It can be in what someone says. It can be in an e-mail!

As soon as the sting comes, stop what you are doing and pray until the anger or fear or rejection in you passes. Then you know you have the shield, and every time you do this, the shield will strengthen. It will become more effective. Soon, it will be impenetrable. The mistake we make is wallowing in any form of negativity. If someone insults you or hurts you, say little about it. Talking can magnify the sting. Only pray. When we pray instead of dwelling on it, it leaves much sooner.

The same is true of fear. Fear is a great device of the devil, who likes to make himself look bigger than he really is; it is a great device of intimidation; it must be cast out. When you feel fear come, settle yourself into prayer and specifically command the *spirit of fear* away. "I command you, spirit of fear, by the power of God, in the Name of Jesus, to leave me and my surroundings and go to the foot of the cross to be disposed of according to the will of the Father. Never to return. Sealed against."

Try that next time fear comes. Try that next time a thought or news item or anything causes trepidation. Try it enough and the spirit of fear will become afraid of *you* and (if you pray enough) will never return.

Move afoot for recognition of American apparition that calls for U.S. to lead world spiritually at "urgent"

[First printed spring of 2001]

A major move is afoot for official Church recognition of a revelation that occurred in the United States—and that if successful would be the first such approval in U.S. history.

Already the case, which occurred in Ohio to a cloistered nun, is the closest the U.S. has come to an apparition with official sanction.

The revelations included locutions from Jesus, St. Joseph, and apparitions of the Virgin Mary as "Our Lady of America" to a cloistered nun, Sister Mildred Mary Neuzil, of the Contemplative Sisters of the Indwelling Trinity in Fostoria, Ohio. Sister Neuzil, now deceased, said she was asked to have a statue of the Virgin Mary constructed and placed after a solemn procession in the National Shrine of the Immaculate Conception in Washington, D.C.—and that if this happened the U.S. would turn back toward morality and the shrine would become a place of "wonders."

A request to do this is being sent to all cardinals and bishops in the U.S., along with a letter that has been sent to the Pope's personal secretary, Monsignor Stanislaw Dziwisz, requesting not only construction of the statue but a solemn consecration of the U.S. in order to avoid "catastrophe."

The letter asks the official Church "to honor her as Our Lady of America and to unite all the bishops of the United States in consecrating America to the Immaculate Heart of Mary for the protection of our nation and for the sanctification of so many souls."

It's not clear what route the process will take. Because Sister Mildred experienced apparitions of the Virgin not just in the Cincinnati area but also in two other dioceses through her life (in Indiana and Toledo), those proposing the cause are seeking Vatican aid and the naming of a national theologian to investigate. Attention will also be directed on the cardinal who oversees the National

Shrine.

While miraculous statues are recognized in the U.S.—most notably Our Lady of Prompt Succor in New Orleans and *La Conquistadora* in Santa Fe—never has an American apparition gained full approval—which involves a bishop's declaration and in many cases the commissioning of art depicting the apparition, along with a medal and often erection of a chapel, basilica, or church dedicated to Mary under the title.

A late archbishop, Paul F. Leibold of Cincinnati, had already taken the extraordinary step of ordering a medal fashioned after the apparition—in itself a form of sanction that hearkens to the famous "miraculous medal" apparitions in Paris. In addition, it has been revealed that before dying Archbishop Leibold had two large plaques depicting Our Lady of America made, hanging one in the chancery—and edging all the closer to full ecclesiastical approval. The archbishop also approved release of Sister Mildred's messages, granted them an official imprimatur, and in an extraordinary show of unity served as the seer's spiritual director from 1940 to 1972.

No apparitions have been fully sanctioned in the U.S. since its foundation but the Ohio case appears to have that chance. According to Sister Joseph Therese, a spokesman for the Contemplative Sisters, the archbishop was "about ready to do a great big statue of Our Lady of America, but then he passed away."

Already there have been at least three other statues constructed, and one of them, weighing 300 pounds, was carried by young Californians during Youth Day in Denver in 1993—in line with the Virgin's request to Sister Mildred that particular interest be focused on the nation's youth, who the nun said "are to be the leaders of this movement of renewal on the face of the earth."

Another statue has circulated to various parts of the world, including China.

Sister Mildred died on January 10, 2000 at the age of 83—but not before leaving a small booklet of messages and detailed correspondences with the archbishop. Born in Brooklyn, she professed as a religious in 1933 and began to encounter mystical experiences in 1938.

Only ten years later, in 1948, did she bring them to the attention of her confessor as they grew increasingly pressing and vivid—with special warnings for the United States. In May of 1958 Sister Mildred entered a cloister. By that time she had been receiving messages about a special devotion to Our Lady of America—a devotion that the Contemplative Sisters, as well as private groups in California and New Jersey, are now earnestly seeking to establish.

It was through this devotion—and placement of the statue in Washington—that Sister Mildred said she was told the U.S. would assume a place of special spiritual as opposed to just political leadership and avoid what Sister Mildred repeatedly warned were coming events. Interestingly, the apparitions of Mary began in 1956 on eve of the Feast of the North American Martyrs—the first martyrs canonized in connection with America.

"The main thing was sanctification of the family, the youth, and that the Blessed Mother wants to be honored in the National Shrine," says Sister Joseph. "And right now letters have gone out to the cardinals, archbishops, and the Holy Father's secretary."

According to Sister Joseph the letter to Monsignor Dziwisz was sent May 1 and will be followed up by a visit to Rome by a New Jersey couple supporting the cause. The letter mentions the Pope's reported desire to visit America at least one more time and suggests this be done in connection with Our Lady of America and a special consecration of the U.S.—an act the letter writers argue might be of even more importance than the consecration of Russia requested during the famous apparitions at Fatima, Portugal.

The letter also makes the request that American bishops read the messages, construct the statue of Our Lady of America, and place it at the shrine following the "solemn procession"—after which the messages say the shrine will become a place of major pilgrimage.

In the revelations, Mary reportedly said if this was done the shrine would become "a place of wonders." Such miracles would be more at the level of spiritual conversion, the Virgin indicated.

"Tell the bishops of the United States, my loyal sons, of my desires and how I wish them to be carried out," Mary told Sister Mildred, who saw Mary with a white veil reaching almost to her waist and a mantle and robe of pure white with no decoration. An

oblong brooch or clasp held the ends of the mantle together at the top. It was all gold, as was the high and brilliant crown she wore. Her hair and eyes seemed medium brown, said Sister Mildred. Her feet were bare, but not always visible—sometimes covered by the moving clouds on which she stood. Often she smiled and revealed a heart encircled by roses that sent forth flames of fire. "*I am Our Lady of America,*" said the Virgin. "*I desire that my children honor me, especially by the purity of their lives.*"

At times light twinkled from Mary's hair, wrote the nun, and seemed to radiate from within her.

It was in this aspect that the medal was struck by the archbishop. On the back is the Coat of Arms of the Christian Family with a symbol of the divine indwelling. "I was told that as long as it bore the form of a shield, the medal itself could be of any shape desired," Sister Mildred had noted. "Around the image of Our Lady, as she appeared September 26, 1956, these words are to be engraved: 'By thy Holy and Immaculate Conception, O Mary, deliver us from evil.' Those who wear the medal with great faith and fervent devotion to Our Lady will receive the grace of intense purity of heart and the particular love of the Holy Virgin and her Divine Son. Sinners will receive in life, so in death, this blessed medal will be as a shield to protect them against the evil spirits, and St. Michael himself will be at their side to allay their fears at the final hour."

According to Sister Mildred, "America, the United States in particular, is being given the tremendous, yet privileged, opportunity to lead all nations in a spiritual renewal never before so necessary, so important."

From the youth must come a flow of great love, said Sister Mildred.

And if it doesn't—*as we'll explore on Monday, when we look at the rest of her messages*—there would be what the Virgin allegedly called a "purification."

The astonishing messages from a U.S. apparition: "I come to you, O children of America, as a last resort"

Last week we reported on apparitions experienced by a humble nun, Sister Mildred Mary Ephrem Neuzil, in a convent at Fostoria, Ohio—a series of events that are now moving toward recognition and have come closer than any known U.S. apparition to official approval.

The revelations are more circumspect than many such prophecies but are astonishing nonetheless.

They were given to Sister Mildred from 1938 to 2000 and the approved ones were granted an imprimatur by Archbishop Paul F. Leibold of Cincinnati—who served as Sister Mildred's spiritual director and commemorated the apparitions with two plaques and a medal.

Sister Mildred claimed communication with Christ, the Virgin Mary, Saint Joseph, and angels. The focus of the messages is the need for purity and sanctification of families if America—which Sister Mildred said is supposed to spiritually lead the world—is to avoid "a terrible purification."

That the U.S. should be singled out for a spiritual and not just economic or political role in the world is a dramatic development—and that such an apparition is rising at this moment appears to be another sign of the times.

Sister Mildred quoted Jesus as saying, "My father is angry. If My children will not listen to My Heart, which is a voice of mercy and instruction, punishment will come swiftly and none shall be able to stay it. The pleadings of My Heart have held back the divine justice about to descend on an ungrateful and sinful generation."

"Woe to parents who set a bad example to their children," continue the messages. "Terrible will be their judgment. I will demand a strict account of every soul entrusted to their care. Woe to parents who teach their children how to gain materially in this world and neglect to prepare them for the next! Woe to children who disobey and show disrespect towards their parents."

In addition to purity—and sanctification of children—what was most lacking in the world, the nun quoted Jesus as saying, was faith. "There are so few souls that believe in Me and My love. They profess their belief and their love, but they do not live this belief. Their hearts are cold, for without faith there can be no love."

It was in 1956, eve of the Feast of the North American Martyrs, that the Virgin began her apparitions. When she appeared, said Sister Mildred, it was to say that miracles "greater than those granted at Lourdes and Fatima would be granted here in America, the United States in particular, if we do as she desires.

What the Virgin desired was the moral leadership of a nation that had been consecrated to her and was now straying. "I wish it to be the country dedicated to my purity," said Mary in a dramatic revelation of America's role in a spiritual territory that has long been dominated by foreign apparitions. "I desire, through my children of America, to further the cause of faith and purity among peoples and nations. I come to you, O children of America, as a last resort. I plead with you to listen to my voice. Cleanse your souls in the precious Blood of my Son. Live in His heart, and take me in that I may teach you to live in great purity of heart which is so pleasing to God. Be my army of chaste soldiers, ready to fight to the death to preserve the purity of your souls. I am the Immaculate one, patroness of your land. Be my faithful children as I have been your faithful mother."

There was drama in every aspect of the messages—though it is only now that they are beginning to receive wide circulation (and their cause proposed to America's bishops). At times the Virgin stood on a globe, her right foot on a crescent or quarter moon—as depicted at Guadalupe. On at least one occasion Sister Mildred described a white rose on each of the Virgin's feet (as at Lourdes) and above her head was a scroll on which was written in gold letters, *"All the glory of the king's daughter is within."*

Nothing is accomplished in life without pain, the Virgin told Sister Neuzil—who, as we will explore in future articles, had much to suffer—as had the Virgin. When she was portrayed with a sword in her heart, said Mary, it was because of the "grief plunged therein by my children who refuse to let me teach them the true way." She expressed special grief over priests who rejected her appearances while promising grace to those who showed their respect. Her wonders, she said, would be more spiritual than physical.

"When a picture or statue of myself as Our Lady of America is placed in the home and honored there, then will my Son bless His people with peace," said the Virgin—who specifically requested such a statue be placed in the National Shrine of the Immaculate Conception in Washington after a solemn procession." I desire to make the whole of America my shrine by making every heart accessible to the love of my Son."

The Virgin emphasized the importance of the mission and according to Sister Mildred asked that it be expressed to Church authorities—who would be charged with establishing a new devotion in America. Although the nun shunned attention and remained hidden in a cloister, she expressed confidence that the message would come out at the proper time. "On February 23, 1959, Our Lady came to me and admonished me to work on the 'message' as soon as possible so that it might be placed in the hands of the bishops who would be responsible for its fulfillment," wrote Sister Neuzil. "In a very serious manner Our Lady warned me that I must not delay any longer to do this, as the time is *now*."

"My Son's patience will not last forever," the nun quoted Mary as saying. "Help me hold back His anger, which is about to descend on sinful and ungrateful men. Suffering and anguish, such as never before experienced, is about to overtake mankind."

Unless there was penance, said Mary, God would visit men "with punishments hitherto unknown to them."

"My dear children," said Mary. "Either you will do as I desire and reform your lives, or God Himself will need to cleanse you in the fires of untold punishment. You must be prepared to receive His great gift of peace. If you will not prepare yourselves, God will Himself be forced to do so in His justice and mercy."

"Oh, the pride of souls!" Sister Mildred quoted Mary as lamenting. "How they resist my grace. O my priests, my religious, what would I not do for you if you would only let me! I come daily laden with graces, which you daily refuse. How long will I bear with you, O my chosen ones? How long will you spurn my approaches?"

There was a bright future if America would take up penance, if it would take up Christ, if it would unite with Mary as its mother. If not, "the punishment will be long and for many forever."

"If my desires are not fulfilled much suffering will come to this land," the Virgin said. "My faithful one, if my warnings are taken seriously and enough of my children strive constantly and faithfully to renew and reform themselves in their inward and outward lives, then there will be no nuclear war. What happens to the world depends upon those who live in it. There must be much more good than evil prevailing in order to prevent the holocaust that is so near approaching. Yet I tell you, my daughter, even should such a destruction happen because there were not enough souls who took my warning seriously, there will remain a remnant—untouched by the chaos who, having been faithful in following me and spreading my warnings, will gradually inhabit the earth again with their dedicated and holy lives."

Mary said her Immaculate Heart is "the channel through which the graces of the Sacred Heart are given to men" and warned that "the false peace of this world lures them and in the end will destroy them."

In the revelations, the Virgin allegedly referred to herself as a "co-redemptrix of the human race"—as did St. Joseph, her earthly spouse, who was also said to have appeared to Sister Mildred.

The revelation from Joseph, if authentic, could well be the most important associated with this hidden saint and may indicate an era in which he will take a much larger role. It is the first time we know of that he too is described as a "co-redemptor" and seems to place that title in a new context.

"My heart suffered with the hearts of Jesus and Mary," said Joseph in 1956. "Mine was a silent suffering, for it was my special vocation to hide and shield, as long as God willed, the Virgin Mother and Son from the malice and hatred of men. The most painful of my sorrows was that I knew beforehand of their passion, yet would not be there to console them. Their future suffering was ever present to me and became my daily cross. I became, in union with my holy spouse, co-redemptor of the human race. Through compassion for the *sufferings of Jesus and Mary* I cooperated, *as no other*, in the salvation of the world."

Joseph allegedly added that "immediately after my conception, I was, through the future merits of Jesus and because of my exceptional role of future virgin-father, cleansed from the stain of original sin. I was from that moment confirmed in grace and never had the slightest stain on my soul. This is my unique privilege among men.

"Mine was perfect obedience to the Divine Will, as it was shown and made known to me by me by the Jewish law and religion," Joseph allegedly said. "To be careless in this is most displeasing to God and will be severely punished in the next world. Let fathers also imitate my great purity of life and deep respect I held for my Immaculate spouse. Let them be an example to their children and fellow men, never willfully doing anything that would cause scandal among God's people.

"I desire souls to come to my heart that they may learn true union with the Divine Will," said Joseph.

The saint was said to have also appeared above a globe with clouds swirling about it, his hands similar to those of a priest during Mass, his eyes looking up as if in ecstasy. "Jesus and Mary desire that my pure heart, so long hidden and unknown, be now honored in a special way," said Joseph, who told Sister Mildred that he had been appointed the Pope's special protector and asked for a new devotion. "Let my children honor my most pure heart in a special manner on the First Wednesday of the month by reciting the joyful mysteries of the Rosary in memory of my life with Jesus and Mary and the love I bore them, the sorrow I suffered with them. Let them receive holy Communion in union with the love with which I received the Savior for the first time and each time I held Him in my arms."

As always, we warn that these apparitions must be discerned. As always, there are debatable aspects. Only those messages up to 1963—the year of the imprimatur—should be considered officially authorized, although those up to 1972 were known by the archbishop, who died that year of an aneurism. By 1980, the Virgin was warning Sister Mildred that the danger was "imminent" and that there was "no time to lose." The message was to be conveyed to the faithful, said Mary, "as the time is shorter than ever." There was an urgency about Our Lady, said Sister Neuzil, that left "no doubts as to the closeness of the terrible purification that is about to fall upon all nations."

Yet the nun's emphasis in her last years, say those who knew her, was on how these events could be *prevented.* She herself was a constantly cheerful soul with a good sense of humor despite terrible physical suffering. "She said that if the world would listen and do what God asked, everything would be fine," one of her close friends, Sister Joseph Therese, told *Spirit Daily*. "But if they didn't, something eventually was going to happen. With all the abortion and that, God isn't going to take that. She was concerned about the whole world and America leading the world. The impurity of the youth—she was very concerned about that."

"It is the United States that is to lead the world to peace, the peace of Christ, the peace that He brought with Him from heaven," she quoted the Virgin as saying. "Dear children, unless the United States accepts and carries out faithfully the mandate given to it by heaven to lead the world to peace, there will come upon it and all nations a great havoc of war and incredible suffering. If, however, the United States is faithful to this mandate from heaven and yet fails in the pursuit of peace because the rest of the world will not accept or cooperate, then the United States will not be burdened with the punishment about to fall."

"It is the darkest hour," said another approved message. "But if men will come to me, my Immaculate heart will make it bright again with the mercy which my Son will rain down through my hands. Help me save those who will not save themselves. Help me bring once again the sunshine of God's peace upon the world."

Asking that a prayer to the Immaculate Conception—patroness of the U.S.—be recited once a day, Sister Mildred said it "is evident that the forces of evil are enveloping the world. Their hatred, however, is now particularly focused on the United States because of the Divine Mandate given to it to lead the world to peace."

"Weep, then, dear children, weep with your mother over the sins of men," said Mary. "Intercede with me before the throne of mercy, for sin is overwhelming the world and punishment is not far away."

Next: the incredible mysticism of Sister Mildred

American mystic: The life of Sister Mildred

It was in bustling Brooklyn, back in 1916, that a young girl of Austrian parents was born. Named Mildred Mary Neuzil, she was to enter religious life at the tender age of 13 and profess as a religious in 1933. She died just a year ago—on January 10, 2000, at 83—and while she had strictly maintained a hidden life until then, disdaining even the propagation of her picture, and keeping her mysticism private, she is now becoming known as the seer in an apparition under the title "Our Lady of America" that if authenticated by the official Church would be the first such recognition in American history.

It's still a ways from total approval, but the groundwork is in place. First is the fact that Sister Mildred's messages were granted an imprimatur by Archbishop Paul F. Leibold of Cincinnati (whose archdiocese oversaw the city where Sister Mildred's mother house was located at the time and who was her spiritual director for 32 years).

More importantly—and constituting a form of official approval already—the archbishop had a medal struck and fashioned two plaques commemorating the apparitions to Sister Mildred, whose experiences spanned from 1938 until her death.

Though the archbishop, now deceased, did not issue a formal declaration declaring the apparitions "worthy of belief" (which constitutes final approval), he "probably would have done that had he not died in 1972," his former secretary, Father Francis Lammeier, told *The Cincinnati Enquirer*.

There is now a move afoot to gain the approval of American bishops, with the route not yet fully clear. Sister Mildred experienced her apparitions in a total of five dioceses: besides Fostoria, Ohio, where she was before she died in 2000—and which is technically in the Toledo diocese—she also had apparitions in Colorado, Arizona, Missouri, and Indiana (where she first met the future archbishop, who then oversaw her). There is also jurisdiction for Cincinnati because it had authority over her order's central house and was where Archbishop Leibold hung the plaque in the chancery.

At her death she belonged to the Contemplative Sister of the Indwelling Trinity in Fostoria (see below for address), and her experiences dated back to the 1930s.

At first, say those who knew her, Sister Mildred—"Millie" to fellow sisters—thought nothing of hearing from heavenly entities. She thought it was something that happened to all professed religious. She didn't mention it to her confessor until 1948. It was then that those close to her—and only those closest to her—began to learn that she had locutions and apparitions of Jesus, the Virgin Mary, and St. Joseph, as well as angels.

Among the more dramatic revelations: that America has been chosen by God to spiritually lead the world; that the key to avoiding chastisements would be purity of heart; that both the Virgin Mary and St. Joseph were to be considered co-redemptors (*cooperators* with Christ); that the youth were to be especially focused on in the United States; that a statue of Mary should be placed in the National Shrine of the Immaculate Conception in Washington, D.C. (a cause we urge all readers to help); and that the "Angel of Peace" who appeared to her was the Archangel Michael.

The messages Sister Mildred received were granted an imprimatur in 1963 and almost certainly had the archbishop's guidance until his death in 1972. According to Audrey Frank, a California woman who is spearheading a drive to have a basilica dedicated to the apparition on the West Coast, Archbishop Leibold corresponded at great length with Sister Millie and died with a copy of a letter from her in his hands.

"She suffered a great deal," says Mrs. Frank, who lives in the Sacramento area and took personal care of Sister Mildred in her waning months. "She had arthritis so bad she was hunched at a 45-degree angle. We couldn't believe she could even feed herself, the way her hands were gnarled. When we took her to have her cataracts removed so she could read her prayer list, they had to put her upside-down, on her head, to operate. Whenever anything associated with Our Lady of America was to occur, she was asked to suffer and she always accepted and something happened to her.

One time she broke her hip."

If there is one word those who knew her use to describe her it is simplicity. "She was so simple and ordinary, just very, very humble, and a wonderful sense of humor," says Sister Joseph Therese, a close friend of Sister Mildred's and spokesman for Our Lady of America Center in Fostoria, which is handling the cause. "Whoever came into her presence, she would immediately make them feel at home. She had something about her. There was this great peace. She was spiritual director to a bishop and several priests."

Mrs. Frank, who organized an effort to have a statue of Our Lady of America at World Youth Day in Denver, says Sister Mildred insisted on anonymity so the apparition would not become a "passing fancy." This was also on the advice of Archbishop Leibold, who said he wanted the apparition to set down its roots firmly before it was public—and who it is said promised Sister Millie in an apparition after his death that he would get the statue of Our Lady of America into the National Shrine of the Immaculate Conception in accordance with Mary's repeated requests.

It was said that the Virgin was always apparent to her in her last days, along with the archbishop (who had appeared to her every day for a year) and a dove signifying the Holy Spirit. In addition to the apparitions it's believed that Sister Mildred may have had interior stigmata. "We often wonder about that, whether she had the interior one," says Sister Joseph. "The past four or five years before she died, she suffered something terrible—she really, really suffered, and her hands were so disfigured. We never saw hands like her hands. Her hands and her side. She had terrible, terrible pain, and she never complained, she just suffered it all."

It was discovered in her letters to the archbishop that the nun also bilocated and had done so at least once to Lourdes, France.

Lourdes was her favorite apparition, and she was also close to Fatima and LaSalette, another apparition in France. Regarding Medjugorje, the current major site in Bosnia-Hercegovina, Sister Mildred commented only that if it was leading people to prayer and closeness to God that it was okay by her. She was cautious and said the devil occasionally appeared in masquerade as an angel or the Blessed Virgin—causing her always to test the spirits.

Her success in doing so was a testimony to her suffering and humility. She fled those who flattered her.

"There was a tremendous radiance and humility that were just outstanding," says another who knew her, Anita Marovich of New Jersey. "A tremendous peace and warmth and sense of presence and trust. She was utterly open to the will of God, a very holy person, but very human."

"Whenever you were with her, you felt a peace," adds Sister Joseph. "You truly felt a very deep, deep peace, and there was one lady in particular who when she touched Millie was healed. But the miracles were more interior miracles. She was just a simple humble soul, with a sense of humor, very simple and very cheerful."

Her job was tending to domestic chores. A year before her death Sister Millie claimed she was told by the Virgin that all apparitions from the beginning of time were leading up to the "divine indwelling."

She died believing that America would turn around.

"She said that if the world would listen and do what God asked, everything would be fine," says Sister Joseph. "But if they didn't, something eventually was going to happen. With all the abortion and that, God isn't going to take that. She was concerned about the whole world and America leading the world. The impurity of the youth—she was very concerned about that."

Ohio nun suffered intensely but was set on mission of statue to the end

Sister Mildred Mary Neuzil, the Ohio nun whose apparitions have suddenly risen as a national cause in the U.S. [see previous stories below], was determined to the end of her days on the mission of installing "Our Lady of America," a statue fashioned after her visions, in the National Shrine of the Immaculate Conception in Washington and bore tremendous mystical suffering for that cause, according to a nun who was with her in her final days.

It was just before World Youth Day in Denver in 1993—when a statue of Our Lady of America was first carried in public procession—that Sister Millie (as friends knew her) suddenly began an intense suffering that remained with her until her death at 83 a year ago.

The Virgin appeared to the nun as patroness of America from 1956 to 2000—granting messages that met with the formal approval of her spiritual director, Archbishop Paul F. Leibold of Cincinnati. Other messages from Jesus and angels dated back to 1938.

Among the messages was a request in 1956 by the Virgin for the U.S. to spiritually lead the world and to have the likeness of the apparitions placed in the nation's shrine—a request that her fellow sisters and supporters are now ardently seeking to fulfill.

It has been a long road, and it was an especially rough one for the seer. Each time the cause progressed, say those who knew her, Sister Mildred was given intense sufferings—whether strokes, a heart attack, severe arthritis, or a broken hip, which she endured with no complaint.

Toward the end, her part of the mission seemed complete.

"Right before she had one stroke, she was sitting in her chair and she said to me, 'The Blessed Mother told me now that she will take over,'" recalls Sister Joseph Therese of the Contemplative Sisters in Fostoria, Ohio. "That was August or September of 1999. Then her suffering became very, very, very intense after that. But her suffering really started before World Youth Day, really bad. The more progress, the more suffering. The devil told her, 'you give this up and you'll be fine.' He used to actually punch her around. He beat her up."

In one case just before World Youth Day friends spotted her being thrown about the inside of a truck the sisters used and couldn't get to her until she was bruised by what was described as an assault of the evil one. Witnesses said the truck could be seen rocking from the force of the attack (reminiscent of similar attacks on Padre Pio).

But the saintly nun never relented and continued to offer her suffering for the cause that started more than sixty years before. Toward the end she had "many" strokes, according to Sister Joseph, as well as asthma, the heart attack, and arthritis so severe she was hunched at a 45-degree angle.

"I was with her" at the end, says Sister Joseph. "When she came back from the hospital about a week before she died, I remember she looked at me and said, 'I see the light now. I see the light'—meaning she was going to be going. She had a tube. We had to feed her through a tube. But she died very, very peacefully. She was very contented and you could tell she was in prayer and that God was there. So many times I'd walk in and she'd say, 'Oh, the Blessed Mother is standing right there.'"

Thus did Sister Mildred Neuzil die early in the morning of January 10, 2000, leaving the mission of establishing Our Lady of America to her friends, relatives, and fellow sisters—a cause that, with a medal struck, a plaque ordered by an archbishop, and an imprimatur, has come the closest an American apparition ever has to full canonical recognition.

But the key remaining request of the Virgin—installment of the statue—remains unfinished business.

"We corresponded a lot about the statue and how Our Lady requested it and I had this feeling I was meant to help get the statue into the national shrine, so I was trying to work towards that," says Sister Monica Schrott, a Carmelite nun in Latrobe, Pennsylvania who met Sister Mildred during a psychology course in 1968. "That was one of the wishes of Our Lady and it was stated that when Our Lady's wishes are carried out, then the prayers will be answered for the nation and the world."

In the revelations the Virgin told Sister Mildred to "tell the bishops of the United States, my loyal sons, of my desires and how I wish them to be carried out. Through him who is head over you, make known the longings of my Immaculate Heart to establish the reign of my Divine Son in the hearts of men and thus save them from the scourge of heaven, both now and hereafter."

While Archbishop Leibold had fulfilled most of the requests and even hung the plaque of Our Lady of America in the chancery, he died suddenly of an aneurism before he could construct the official statue. The archbishop's former secretary, Father Francis Lammeier, confirms that the archbishop was "very close" to the apparitions and had "no doubt" about their authenticity after serving as Sister Mildred's spiritual director for 32 years.

It's unclear what if any diocese now has jurisdiction. At the time Sister Mildred's mother house was in Dayton—which falls in the Cincinnati diocese—but actually lived in Fostoria, which is under the bishop of Toledo. The nun also experienced some of the apparitions in other states, and so the matter is believed to be one in need of a national theologian, a committee of bishops, the rector of the national shrine, or the Vatican.

Whatever the case, the fact remains that messages from the Virgin granted an authorization by an archbishop who had served as the nun's spiritual director for three decades have not yet met their completion and are now the subject of efforts by a growing number of laymen across America. As we have reported previously, those who knew Sister Neuzil unanimously describe her as a suffering soul who sought to avoid publicity of any kind but ardently sought to have the requests met.

"She was very personable, very unassuming, never was out to draw attention to herself, and very kind," says a niece, Elaine Neuzil Bratrsovsky. "She didn't like fussing [over her]. Her experiences were to draw people to Our Lord and Blessed Mother. She never went around openly talking about it. If I asked her something about it she would respond. She had a deep love for the Trinity, the indwelling Christ, a deep love for Our Lady and concern for people being drawn back to the Christian lifestyle of the Holy Family."

According to Sister Monica, Sister Neuzil sent her a handwritten account of the apparitions but asked that it be destroyed after she read it. Sister Monica obeyed that wish, but copied it by her own hand before discarding the original papers. "I went along with her because there was a friendship between us and I knew she wasn't able to trick somebody," says the Carmelite nun. "She was so open and simple that she wouldn't be pulling anything over anybody. I thought she was incapable of deceiving anybody. She really had these visions. When we first contacted each other I didn't know anything of it. But then she sent me a medal of Our Lady of America and a little leaflet that went with it and then I wrote back and asked her a question about it. That's when she wrote about it in her own handwriting but asked me to destroy it afterwards because she wanted her identity hidden."

Sister Neuzil's sister, Grace, recalls that Mildred had always wanted to be a nun from an early age on. "Her parents were reluctant to have her leave home and enter the convent at the tender age of thirteen, but after speaking with the sisters, Mildred's parents finally gave permission with the understanding that Mildred would always be free to come back home, should she so desire," says Mrs. Bratrsovsky. "Sister Mildred adhered to her vocation throughout her life remaining completely dedicated to her Divine Spouse. She was a natural contemplative. She was creative and artistic. She had a beautiful singing voice. She also was an avid reader."

A professional writer who helped Sister Millie with a novena comments that "sister's wonderful warmth and down-to-earth humility were, perhaps, even more extraordinary than the apparitions."

Another nun from Massachusetts who corresponded with Sister Neuzil described her as "a very, very holy person "who once commented that she was surprised at the level of suffering but happily accepted it. Indeed, so stricken with arthritis was Sister Mildred at the end of her life that her back had to be broken to rest her flat in the coffin...

American apparition already past first stage of Church

Father Johann G. Roten, one of the world's foremost experts on Marian apparitions, told *Spirit Daily* Monday that revelations to a nun in Fostoria, Ohio, reached what he described as the "first stage" of Church approval.

This was constituted, he said, when the archbishop, Paul F. Leibold of Cincinnati, had a medal struck and a plaque commemorating the apparitions constructed.

There are two degrees of official recognition, said Father Roten. The second degree would be an explicit declaration—something that did not occur with the Fostoria apparitions. It is the first time, however, that an American apparition has passed the first stage, according to the expert.

"There is the first degree in which the spiritual happening is recognized, the expression of faith," said Father Roten, who works at the Marian Library in Dayton Ohio—the world's largest such library. "Then there is the second stage, recognition of the phenomena itself. A plaque would not qualify as that type of recognition but could qualify with the conditions of the first degree, and a medal too. It is a very tangible sign that the bishop is not against the apparition."

Throughout history approval of a vision, apparition, or miracle has been seen as indicated if the bishop with direct jurisdiction over the vicinity sanctions a painting or other rendering of the event; builds a chapel, church, or basilica at the spot of the occurrence; or issues a formal proclamation—a set of actions that has cast the Ohio apparitions in a new light with word that Archbishop Leibold had authorized both a medal and a relief to commemorate apparitions to Sister Mildred Mary Ephrem Neuzil. It the first known time that an American apparition with messages has been thus sanctioned by the official Church.

While the ultimate approval—construction of a church, issuance of a formal proclamation, and a visit by the Pope—has not occurred, the Ohio revelations are already at the level of hundreds of such historic instances in Europe.

The tradition dates back to the Virgin's first appearance to James the Apostle around A.D. 40 at Saragossa, Spain and has also been in evidence at ancient sites in both Le Puy, France, where Mary appeared in A.D. 47, and Ein Karim in Palestine, where miracles were associated during the first century with a drinking well rumored to have been used by Mary on her way to visit Elizabeth.

While in recent times the highest level of approval has been seen in the way of a Church declaration, for most of history approval has been indicated by the simple concurrence of the bishop that a miracle had occurred—something that Archbishop Paul F. Leibold, as prelate of Cincinnati at the time of the Ohio apparitions, had clearly indicated. Indeed, he had served as the spiritual director to the seer, Sister Mildred Mary Ephrem Neuzil, for 32 years and according to his secretary believed totally in the revelation and depending on what procedure he believed was appropriate may well have added an official statement on authenticity in addition to an imprimatur that he granted on January 23, 1963, to Sister Mildred's messages.

Those messages were also given a *nihil obstat* by Daniel Pilarczyk—then a priest but now current *archbishop of Cincinnati.*

A *nihil obstat* indicates that there are "no problems" or in a more technical interpretation of the Latin "nothing to hinder" release of a Catholic writing. It is an attestation by a Church censor that a book contains nothing damaging to faith or morals.

The matter of Sister Neuzil is now considered by some close to the cause of fulfilling final requests in the messages as in the hands of a national theologian they seek to have named or a group of bishops who they hope will have a statue based on the apparition placed at the National Shrine of the Immaculate Conception in Washington. In the approved messages the Virgin had asked Sister Mildred to have the medal struck and while Archbishop Leibold had accomplished that, he had succumbed to an aneurism before he was able to complete a statue. He died with a letter from Sister Mildred in his hands.

After the archbishop's death a terrible dispute arose between two factions of sisters, and a small group that included Sister

Mildred broke off from the mother house—the Order of the Precious Blood, leading to years of turmoil that could well muddy the waters of a further approval. Accusing the order of turning too liberal and taking away the contemplative life, the smaller group moved to Fostoria and remade vows to a chaplain but the new order was not formally recognized by the diocese in Toledo, where Fostoria is located.

While that has cast a shadow on revelations that occurred after the archbishop's death in 1972, the main issue remains the requests that had Archbishop Leibold's official endorsement—to dedicate a statue to the Virgin Mary's purity and install it in Washington.

The issuance by the archbishop of a medal is similar to what occurred in France during the "Miraculous Medal" apparitions in 1830 to St. Catherine Laboure, who began experiencing mystical events at 22—the precise age at which Sister Mildred had her first experiences. It was one of several startling parallels between the French and American apparitions. As in the Ohio case, where St. Joseph appeared, the Miraculous Medal involved Joseph when the Virgin appeared in a chapel on Rue du Bac in Paris near a picture of St. Joseph, and her dress was radiant white as in the alleged American apparition. In both cases a globe was at the bottom of the Virgin's feet and at one point, as in the case of St. Catherine Labore, the Virgin also held a globe—though in Sister Mildred's case the Virgin cried as she did so and the tears fell on the globe, according to a vision on September 27, 1956.

Where in the Miraculous Medal case there was the inscription, *"O Mary, conceived without sin, pray for us who have recourse to thee,"* in the approved part of the Fostoria revelations the Virgin taught Sister Mildred the little prayer, *"By thy Holy and Immaculate Conception, O Mary, deliver us from evil."*

And where the Miraculous Medal shows a heart pierced by a sword, so does the Fostoria case include a vision of a heart pierced by a sword. Where in the case of Fostoria Archbishop Leibold had a medal struck, with the Miraculous Medal it was Archbishop de Quelen of Paris.

The stunning links between "Our Lady of America" and other apparitions

The apparition we have been investigating from a nun in Ohio continues to present hidden details connecting it with major international revelations.

It starts with the fact that the seer, Sister Mildred Mary Ephrem Neuzil, was professed as a religious in 1933—the same year Saint Faustina Kowalska, known as the seer of "divine mercy," took her perpetual vows.

Saint Faustina propagated God's mercy at the same time as warning about His judgment—as is also evidenced in the American apparition. If that's not enough of an association, there is the fact that Sister Neuzil's mystical experiences began in 1938—the year of Saint Faustina's death and the end of the divine mercy revelations.

There is also a connection to Fatima: 1938 was the year of an extraordinary aurora borealis or "northern lights" that is now considered the "great sign" prophesied by the seers of Fatima.

And then there is the content of the messages. On December 20, 1959, Sister Neuzil said the Virgin came pleading for "penance, penance"—words also mentioned verbatim in the famous *third secret of Fatima.* Indeed, one of Sister Neuzil's major apparitions occurred on October 13, 1956—anniversary of the "spinning sun" at Fatima.

And so too was penance, or actually "penitence," a major message at the historic apparitions in France at Lourdes. There the Virgin began to appear on February 11—the same day that, exactly a hundred years later (on February 11, 1958) that Sister Neuzil heard the Virgin describe herself as the mother of sacred humanity!

Sister Neuzil received yet another of her major messages from the Virgin on August 5, 1957—the anniversary of *Our Lady of the Snow* in Rome (where, in A.D. 357, the Virgin requested construction of a church that is now known as the Basilica of Mary Major).

Meanwhile Sister Neuzil quoted the Immaculate Virgin as telling her that the mission was purity "among peoples and nations." This is precisely how Mary would later come—in 1976—at a Church-sanctioned site in *Betania, Venezuela,* where she identified herself as *"Mary, reconciler of all peoples and nations"*!

We have already noted that Sister Neuzil was the same age as Saint Catherine Laboure when the French seer first experienced mystical events and that like the *"Miraculous Medal"* (which is what Saint Catherine's apparitions were called), Sister Neuzil saw Mary with a globe and in a radiant white dress—which also brings to mind Knock, Ireland (during which Saint Joseph, as at Fostoria, also appeared!).

In Ohio the Virgin bore white lilies—as at a famous English site called *Walsingham!*

And the crown Sister Neuzil described as setting on the head of the Virgin is mindful not only of Knock but also of a Church-sanctioned apparition at *LaSalette, France* (where, as we will see in coming days, there was a great similarity between prophecies).

Statuette of Our Lady of America was transmitted to Vatican envoy

In 1972, shortly after the death of Cincinnati Archbishop Paul F. Leibold, a statuette of Our Lady of America was transmitted to the apostolic nunciature in Washington—further indicating formal diocesan recognition of revelations granted to Ohio nun Mildred Mary Ephrem Neuzil in what appears to be the first such ecclesiastical approval in American history.

On August 13, 1972, the chancery in Cincinnati noted in a letter to Sister Mildred that Monsignor Conrad Boffa, a close friend of Cincinnati Archbishop Paul F. Leibold and also of the delegate, had fixed the base of a statue that apparently had been broken and "then forwarded it to the Apostolic Delegate."

It was apparently one of two statues that Sister Neuzil had sent, showing the Madonna in white with a prominent crown. "I am most grateful for your kindness and generosity in sending the two statues to me and allowing me to make the choice as to the one that would be given to the Apostolic Delegate," wrote Father Francis Lammeier, the archbishop's secretary. "Indeed, I am most grateful and I am sure the Archbishop from his place in heaven is also pleased."

That action joined two others—the striking of a medal and the construction of reliefs based on Our Lady of America—in forming what experts say is a major aspect of formal approval.

Archbishop Leibold had died just two months before. He had also granted the messages from Our Lady of America an imprimatur and served as the seer's spiritual director. We'll have more on him tomorrow. The letter from Father Lammeier states that records of the apparitions were carefully moved from an archives house to the secretary's office. "It will be guarded securely here," states the letter—indicating concern for the safekeeping of papers that substantiate the archbishop's strong support of Sister Neuzil, who later came under strong attack, and details of apparitions that called for not only the striking of a medal and design of an image but also construction of a statue to be placed in the National Shrine of the

Immaculate Conception. Indeed, records sent to *Spirit Daily* indicate that Monsignor William F. McDonough, director of the shrine, visited Sister Mildred two years before the archbishop's death.

"I cannot tell you how much I enjoyed my trip to New Riegel [Ohio, where the nun's cloister was at the time]," said a June 29, 1970, letter from McDonough. "I have written to Archbishop Leibold and told him of my visit with you and of my opinions."

The director was so interested in the situation that he requested the seer write or personally visit if there were further messages. "I am not asking for a sign, but if there is a message that I should know, I would ask you to write to me or visit me at the National Shrine," he said. "The Archbishop thought that you could visit Washington without any great problem."

Thirty years later, however, the statue has still not been installed at the shrine. Several lay people, led by Sister Joseph Therese of the Our Lady of America Center (a tiny outpost in Fostoria, Ohio), are attempting to have the requests fulfilled and are in need of support. If the requests are met, promised the Virgin, there would be graces granted to America in the same way that graces have been granted at Lourdes. The site of Sister Mildred's first apparition near Rome City, Ohio, is already said to carry a strong feeling of grace, but the final request for the national statue is considered crucial.

In "last message" Ohio revelation issued strong warning to priests on obedience to Rome

In what was once described as the "last official message," Our Lady of America warned on attitudes—especially pride—in the Church.

In appearing to an Ohio nun named *Sister Mildred Mary Ephrem Neuzil,* the Virgin often demonstrated her deep affection and concern for priests. One example came in 1957. "My dear daughter, sweet child, write my words carefully, because they are of the utmost importance," the Virgin said in an apparition that had the authorization of the archbishop. "I address them to my beloved sons, the priests, dedicated to the most intense and extraordinary imitation of my Son in the perfect carrying on of His Eternal Priesthood.

"Beloved sons, so cherished and greatly blessed among the sons of men, be careful to uphold the sanctity and dignity of your calling. Let the faithful see in you the favored and especially loved imitators of the Son of God. Be modest in your dress and speech as becomes those of so exalted a vocation. The apparel and manners of a man of the world are not for you, who, though living in the world, must not take on its ways.

"It is through you that the grace of the Sacraments is given to souls. Strive then to make yourselves more worthy receptacles to receive these graces and transmit them in turn to the souls under your care."

Indeed, it was the bishops and priests who were a chief concern of the Virgin's. She warned that purity of heart would be essential to discernment. She warned that times were so insidious that evil was passed off for good.

Only strict spiritual discipline, she said, would offset the "false spirit."

"Dear sons, I ask you to practice self-denial and penance in a special manner, because it is you who must lead my children in the way of peace. Yet this peace will come only by way of the sword, the flaming sword of love. If, therefore, you love my Son and wish to honor me, heed my admonition and be the first to give the example of a life of penance and self-denial. Thus, by sanctification from within you, you will become a bright and burning light to the faithful, who look to you for help and guidance.

"I am pleased, dearly beloved sons, by the honor and love you have until now accorded me. Will you now go further and honor me yet more by taking my words to your hearts and doing what I ask?"

This was just before Second Vatican Council, which would lead to worrisome modernistic trends in the Church. Indeed, Sister Neuzil's own cloister would become embroiled in a horrible split when the Mother House decided to do away with the cloister, which then went its own way.

That was still twenty years away, but by 1959 the messages from both Mary and Jesus had grown a bit stiffer. "Oh, the pride of souls!" said one reviewed and authorized for release by Cincinnati Archbishop Paul F. Leibold, who edited the first booklet on Our Lady of America. "How they resist My grace! O My priests, My religious, what would I not do for you if you would only let Me! I come daily laden with graces, which you daily refuse.

"What am I to say, my best beloved? How long will you resist My love? It is from you I expect everything, and you give Me but the husks of your affections.

"How long will I bear with you, O My chosen ones? How long will you spurn My approaches?

"My little white dove, it was this ingratitude on the part of My priests and My religious that caused Me so much sorrow in My passion.

"Oh, how they resist My grace! How they fight against My love!"

But in 1960—as America entered its most dangerous decade—the Virgin came with a hopeful prophecy. "I place my confidence in my faithful sons, the Bishops, who will not fail to take up my cause and make it bear much fruit for sanctification among so many and countless souls."

Sister Mildred was instructed to specifically take the message to Archbishop Leibold, who granted an imprimatur to the prayer of Our Lady of America and even had a statue, medal, and relief of the apparition made at the chancery's expense. Among the requests was that a statue representing Our Lady of America be installed in the National Shrine of the Immaculate Conception to bring back purity to America—a nation the Virgin says has been commissioned to spiritually rescue the world. Thus far the request has not been met.

By 1982, the messages to priests had become stern and urgent. While one was described in a letter to a nun-friend in Massachusetts as the "last" formal communication, there were actually subsequent messages. As it happened, Sister Mildred received visions until her own death on January 10, 2000 and it's said that the Virgin as well as angels, St. Michael, a mystical dove, and Archbishop Leibold (who died in 1972) were constant presences to her.

But the 1982 message was unmatched for drama.

Warned the first authorized apparition of the Virgin in the U.S.: "Beloved daughter, sweet child, there are those in high places in the Church who disobey and refuse respect to my Son's Vicar on earth. These betray the teachings inspired by the Divine Spirit sent by my Son to be with the Church till the end of time. There are those who teach false doctrines and those who repudiate the holy sacraments. They are filled with intellectual pride, and so, refusing to follow my humble Son, they are being destroyed, together with those who misguidedly follow them down the path of error and falsehood. Pray for these poor ones who do not realize the misery and wretchedness they are in and to which they have and are still leading others."

Archbishop behind "Our Lady of America" seen as exceptional and pious man dedicated to apparition

He was seen by all as an extraordinary man. He was known for his great holiness. He appears to be the first American bishop to have approved an apparition. His name was Paul F. Leibold—archbishop of Cincinnati—and he may have been as important to what has become known as the "Our Lady of America" revelation as the seer herself.

As we have previously reported, Archbishop Leibold served as the spiritual director for Sister Mildred Mary Ephrem Neuzil, the visionary, for 32 years, first as a priest, then as a vicar general, an auxiliary bishop, a bishop in Indiana, and finally archbishop of Ohio's most powerful diocese.

Through those years he maintained a regular and often close communication with Sister Neuzil, and according to those close to the situation, he visited Sister Mildred and helped her plan a statue of Our Lady of America right up to his death in 1972 at the tender age of 57.

Indeed, as a bishop Leibold edited the very book of messages on Our Lady of America, made major suggestions for its organization, and even wrote the introduction, according to those close to the situation—besides lending it his imprimatur, which appeared at the very front of a message book, to prayers generated by the apparition. According to his former secretary, he had absolutely "no reservation" about the authenticity of the alleged revelation, and even struck a medal for it and made a relief to commemorate it, although he never issued a formal proclamation.

That may have been because there wasn't time. There was a genetic weakness in his family for aneurisms, and Archbishop Leibold succumbed to a "cerebral-vascular incident" on June 1, 1972, after attending graduation ceremonies at Xavier University.

But he will not soon be forgotten.

So respected and beloved was Archbishop Leibold that his funeral was broadcast across southern Ohio. There were 700 priests in the pews, and 44 priests concelebrated his funeral—including Most Reverend Luigi Raimondi, the Pope's apostolic delegate to the U.S., and four cardinals.

Those who couldn't cram into the cathedral held their own Masses or prayer services.

"There have been few prelates in the American hierarchy who possessed all the qualifications of a bishop in as eminent a degree as did Archbishop Leibold," noted retired Cincinnati archbishop Karl J. Alter (who served as Leibold's predecessor and who according to Father Lammeier was almost certainly consulted when Leibold was making some of his determinations about Our Lady of America).

But the main player in the apparition was Archbishop Leibold, and indeed, even after three decades, his name still evokes great reverence. Archbishop Philip Hannan of New Orleans has noted that the Cincinnati prelate was a truly exceptional bishop, and while Leibold's sharp mind and bureaucratic skills are often noted, most point with greatest emphasis to his piety and humility.

This was a bishop who believed in direct communication with heaven. This was a bishop open to the mystical. And this was a bishop who quietly left America its first official apparition.

We're still taking a wait-and-see attitude and plan further investigation but continue to be extremely impressed by the situation surrounding Our Lady of America while it was under the guidance of the archbishop.

Born in Dayton, Ohio—home of the world's largest Marian library—Leibold once commented that growing up he "couldn't really recall thinking of anything else, but the priesthood." He attended seminary in the U.S., was ordained on May 18, 1940, and studied canon law at the Angelicum in Rome, where he earned a doctorate. He became a chancellor of the Cincinnati diocese in 1948 and was consecrated a bishop in 1958—three years before lending his imprimatur to the design for the medal and five years before helping Sister Mildred with her book of messages—messages that are now much in demand as details of the situation continue to surface.

In 1966 Leibold was named bishop of Evansville, Indiana (in

the state, ironically, where Sister Mildred had her first apparitions). He served there for just three years before returning to Cincinnati as archbishop (which made him the "metropolitan" or first-ranking bishop of Ohio's six dioceses). While Cincinnati's archbishop he gained national attention when he publicly branded Leonard Bernstein's "Mass" as objectionable—the first prelate to do so. During his tenure as auxiliary bishop he conducted a campaign against the opening of a Playboy Club.

In short, the bishop who was so intimately involved with establishing Our Lady of America was not only the first known to have such an involvement with a U.S. apparition but was an unusually courageous, pious, and high-ranking prelate. That such a man lent his imprimatur to the situation and served as personal spiritual director to the seer up to his death will carry great weight as officials now consider a key request by the Virgin: to install a statue representing Our Lady of America at the National Shrine of the Immaculate Conception.

The Reverend John Cavanaugh, another colleague of the late archbishop, recalled being surprised by the level-headed Leibold's enthusiasm for Sister Mildred's visions. Despite the Church's "great hesitancy" about such private revelations, Leibold was convinced of their authenticity, said Cavanaugh in an interview with *The Cincinnati Enquirer*.

While great controversy and attack against Sister Neuzil's cloister followed the archbishop's death (as controversy often surrounds such situations), during his last years Leibold had served as an even hand on an apparition of tremendous potential importance. He and Sister Mildred were close friends who wrote many spiritual letters to each other. There was clearly a mystical element: according to Audrey Frank of Sacramento, who has been working for Our Lady of America's cause, Sister Mildred predicted many events in Leibold's life. "When he was just a priest she had prophesied that Leibold would be a bishop, and then that he would be an archbishop," says Mrs. Frank. "He not only supported her messages but wrote and edited part of it. They wrote letter after letter, and he always corresponded with Sister Mildred on feast days and anniversaries."

According to Sister Joseph Therese, the lone nun remaining from Sister Mildred's cloister (which was split from the Order of Precious Blood when the head of the cloister got in a dispute with the Mother House over continuing the cloister), there were private visits to the cloister by Archbishop Leibold right to the end. "He was sitting downstairs and they were planning," says Sister Joseph. "He was going to get a big statue of Our Lady of America built and put it right in the front grounds of the cloister. I think he was getting it built in Centerville, Ohio. He may have been the one who made two plaques [of Our Lady of America] for Bishop Leibold. They were in constant writing and she would visit him even when he was bishop in Indiana and she would go to Cincinnati."

According to accounts Sister Mildred may have sensed the prelate's approaching death. A week before he died, according to Mrs. Frank, Sister Mildred visited Archbishop Leibold, tweaked his hair, and said, "Remember, you're not going to leave me alone on this [the cause of Our Lady of America.]" He told her, 'Don't worry, I will, even if I have to help from heaven.'"

"He was very prayerful, a humble man, recollected," recalls Father Francis Lammeier, his former secretary. "He did have a very strict scheduled prayer life. He got up early in the morning and prayed and meditated before his daily Mass."

According to Lammeier, Archbishop Leibold had a devotion to both the Blessed Mother and Sacred Heart and had once visited Lourdes. One of his two brothers became a monsignor. Rising through the ranks during Vatican II, Leibold was known as a progressive bishop who sought more involvement of the laity but was concerned about how the Council's work would be interpreted. According to both Sister Joseph and Mrs. Frank, the archbishop began appearing in apparition to Sister Mildred on November 11, 1997 as her own death approached—coming each day precisely at 1 p.m. It was a period of great suffering for Sister Mildred. The nun—herself described as tremendously devout and humble—was not only suffering from heart problems, severe arthritis, asthma, cataracts, and other maladies, but had watched in sorrow as a split developed between her cloister, led by a Sister Florecita, and the Mother House (which was tending away from the contemplative

"Our Lady of America" appears to be first approved medal connected to alleged U.S. apparition

It was on May 1, 1961, that Paul F. Leibold, auxiliary bishop of Cincinnati, soon to be bishop of Evansville, Indiana, and then Cincinnati's archbishop, issued what may one day be viewed as a momentous imprimatur. His approval was signed on a sketching for a new medal derived from alleged apparitions of the Blessed Mother to nun Sister Mildred Mary Ephrem Neuzil, to whom Mary came, according to Sister Neuzil, as "Our Lady of America." According to Sister Neuzil (whose apparitions began near Rome City, Indiana, and later continued in Ohio), the medal was requested in 1958 as a "shield against evil."

That request was made in messages granted an imprimatur by Bishop Leibold, although there has not yet been a declaration on the apparitions themselves.

"I was told that as long as it bore the form of a shield, the medal itself could be of any shape desired," the nun wrote. "Around the image of Our Lady, as she appeared September 26, 1956 [when she first came as Our Lady of America], these words were to be engraved: 'By thy Holy and Immaculate Conception, O Mary, deliver us from evil.' Those who wear the medal with great faith and fervent devotion to Our Lady will receive the grace of intense purity of heart and the particular love of the Holy Virgin and her Divine Son. Sinners will receive the grace of repentance and the spiritual strength to live as true children of Mary. As in life, so in death, this blessed medal will be as a shield to protect them against the evil spirits, and St. Michael himself will be at their side to allay their fears at the final hour."

The medal was struck by Bishop Leibold. While a picture of the Virgin is on the front, on the reverse side is a coat of arms representing the Christian family. At the center is a shield of the Precious Blood, through which sanctifying grace is granted to fallen man. Sanctification of the family through imitation of the Holy Family is represented by a cross at the top of the shield and two lilies, and on each of those is depicted a burning heart. A flaming sword (also present in the third secret of Fatima) is there as a symbol of divine love, and the shield is surrounded by the beads of a rosary. On the shield the "Divine Indwelling" is represented by the eye of God in a triangle (long a Christian symbol on cathedrals and other religious situations before non-Christians, including some occultists like the Masons, tried to adopt it as a symbol), and there is a scroll above which reads, "Gloria Patri et Filio et Spiritu Sancto" and one below says, "Jesu, Maria, Joseph."

"The coat of arms Our Lady had inspired some years previously," wrote Sister Neuzil. "I did not know at the time for what purpose it was to be used, and Our Lady did not enlighten me on it until much later."

The first medals were made by Cyril Daleiden & Sons of Chicago. "Dear Mr. Daleiden," wrote Bishop Leibold on December 20, 1965, "kindly send 5,000 of the medals of Our Lady of America to Sister Mary Ephrem. . . But send the *bill to me*" [the bishop's own emphasis].

To our knowledge it is the first time a medal has been struck by a high-ranking diocesan official based on an apparition of Mary claimed in the United States.

As we said, it's always wise to hold a new devotion in prayer—and *fasting*—before any involvement with it, but this may be what America indeed does need (if it is properly blessed). And so we pray: *Dear God, that You grant us discernment, that You guide us in all sacramentals, that if it is Your Will You anoint this medal in a way that purges evil and purges all evil from it. We pray Lord that the paganism of our country be converted into Christianity and that as in times of old, holiness be returned to our families and pagan territory turned Christian. We pray Lord that You bring goodness to this nation through devotion to Your authentic mother and we implore through Christ that our nation be returned to Your all-powerful and all-good and eternal embrace.*

Archangel Michael was hidden force in apparition

A hidden aspect of the initially-approved apparitions reported in Indiana and then Ohio by a nun named Sister Mildred Mary Neuzil [*see previous stories*] was the appearance of the Archangel Michael. In fact, the great angel appeared to the nun two years before what she described as the first official visits of the Virgin Mary.

Such facts are coming to light as details about the experiences of this extraordinary nun continue to surface in a nation that has never had a Church-sanctioned apparition.

It was in the autumn of 1954, according to Sister Neuzil's records, that Michael first came to her. "I do not remember the exact date, as I did not intend on ever saying anything about it," she later wrote in a small booklet of messages granted an official imprimatur. "I was sitting in the room next to the kitchen with the intention of saying some of my prayers. Almost at the very moment I began to pray, I saw an angel."

The being was resplendent—dressed in a garment that was plain but perfectly and radiantly white. "I am the Angel of Peace," he said. "I come to those whose hearts are attuned to the Voice of God. To such as these I remain a perpetual light through blinding darkness. I was sent by Him Who said, 'I am the Light of the world.'"

It was later made known to Sister Mildred that the angel was Michael.

"Write!" the angel allegedly said on May 8, 1957. "I am Michael, Angel Captain of the Lord of Hosts. I come to announce the coming of the kingdom, the kingdom of peace. The time is at hand. Repent, bestir yourselves, O sons of men, repent and make ready your hearts that the King may establish His Kingdom within you. Do not delay, or the time of grace will pass and with it the peace you seek."

It was time, Michael told the humble nun, to stop all hesitation and make the message known. The world was darkening. America was ready to plunge into an era of great moral decline. There was lust. There was materialism. There was terrific danger. The country was about to see *Leave It To Beaver*—the Cleavers—replaced by the Manson family.

In 1958 the Archangel Michael appeared again, holding an immense flaming torch and asking the nun, who was in a cloister, to carry it through the world in a spiritual way. That was February 11, the anniversary of Lourdes. Michael came the next night in the same manner. It was just after this that Sister Neuzil ("Millie" to friends") was instructed to design a medal that would ward off evil—a medal and a set of messages that have found themselves in sudden circulation since the nun's holy and all but anonymous death.

Danger indeed! At the time of Sister Neuzil's apparitions the Sixties were on the horizon, and they would bring a tremendous spirit of rebellion—evil that would rise during the following decades in the way of irreligion, sexual perversion, and abortion, in the way of man-as-god and scientism.

In 1980 (during apparitions that were not included in those which had received an imprimatur) the Blessed Mother, coming as "Our Lady of America," told the nun that "Michael and the whole army of Blessed Spirits will give their assistance at all times," according to Sister Mildred. "As the Queen of Angels she has loving command over them and they accomplish whatever she wishes."

And what she wished, said Sister Mildred, was for America—by now reaping the results of the Sixties—to revert back to God, to purify itself, to sanctify the family. The mission of the U.S., said Our Lady of America, was to lead the world *spiritually* in the same way that it had led the world economically, technologically, and militarily.

And it would do so with the help of Michael.

For the rest of the nun's life, say those who knew her, the archangel was an almost constant presence. She talked about him "all the time," says Sister Joseph Therese, a close friend who now directs the tiny Our Lady of America Center, which has been struggling to make the messages known. "She mentioned him a whole lot. When she was in bed or sitting in a chair before she died she was always talking about St. Michael."

Sister Neuzil said her heavenly visitor referred to her as "my little Joan of Arc," and indeed Michael has been a key player in events throughout history. He is the one who threw Lucifer from heaven. Some believe he was in the fire in the "burning bush." We know from *Jude* that he contended with Satan over Moses' body. He came to Italy in the early Christian centuries to aid a bishop who was under the assault of Neapolitans. "I am Michael the Archangel, who ever stands before the Lord," he told an astonished man in A.D. 404 on Monte Gargano in Italy. Some believe he authored *Psalm* 85. He is known even in Islamic writing as "Mika'il." He saved Europe from the Turks, and France through Joan of Arc.

Now, according to the records of an American nun, he is on the scene in the United States—not so much to save it from external enemies as to save it from itself.

Alleged American seer described "trip" to netherworld

It was on February 24, 1958, as Sister Mildred Neuzil, a nun in New Riegel, Ohio, who experienced the "Our Lady of America" apparitions, was composing herself to sleep when she underwent what she described as "a strange and horrifying" experience. It was similar to visions given to other seers at places like Fatima and Medjugorje. This is how she recounted it:

"As I was not yet asleep I do not think it could have been a dream. It came suddenly without sign or warning and as such, left an indelible impression on my mind and heart.

"I found myself on a lonely road, one of course I had never seen or been on at any time. Before me was a large structure, something similar to a gigantic cathedral or castle. It was huge, somber, and forbidden. I was obliged to walk toward it though something inside me held me back in a kind of dread. Then at my side on the right I felt the strong presence of St. Michael.

"He did not speak, but just having him there made me feel safe. We continued our journey and at last came to what appeared to be the front entrance to the strange building. As we drew nearer, the two great doors which had qualities, so it seemed, of some sort of glasswork, opened of themselves.

"I saw no one. The interior revealed an odd, indescribable darkness, pervaded by a weird sort of light which was not really light. We entered, and without looking back I knew that the doors had closed inexorably behind us and that we would never leave the same way we had entered.

"When I said that the light was not really light I meant it was more like the distant glow of a raging fire. What appeared to be openings in this vast and horrible place looked more like huge windows, painted a vivid red solid and impenetrable, like an unbreakable wall of fire. Yet they did not have the usual accompaniments of fire, like flames or smoke, just, as I said before, a solid red like stained-glass windows of some sort. I felt the frightening certainty of where we were.

"Just the same I could not help asking my companion, 'What is this place?' Gravely, solemnly, he replied, *'This is hell.'* He said this in a way that I will never forget. I wondered that, except for the red openings, there was no appearance of fire anywhere. Answering these unvoiced thoughts, my companion explained, *'The fire is in the souls of the lost, not an outward but an inward fire that never dies.'*

"I did not see these lost souls but I knew that they were all about us and I thought of the horror that was theirs and that it would never end.

"The silence was appalling. It was the silence of death without hope. As we continued our journey there was not a breath of a sound. The intense and penetrating silence or rather stillness was terrifying beyond description. Yet that very silence screamed with the undying voice of despair—nothing, nothing, nothing—lost, lost, lost—forever, forever, forever. I was filled with the most terrible fear that I would never get out of this dreadful place. And oh how I missed the light. When explaining then to my companion, 'But there is no light,' he had answered, '*How can there be light where God is not.*' I kept begging St. Michael not to leave me. Never have I experienced such fear, such horror.

"As we walked on we came to what appeared to be a large body of water. It looked like an enormous circular pool. It all but overflowed with some sort of dark substance. What that was I do not know but it was not water. I did not touch it to make certain but knew in my mind that it was not water. I was too terror-stricken to investigate further. Lying about this pool, in a rather scattered manner were, what appeared to be dead objects of some sort. We did not go close enough for me to see just what they were.

"I cannot imagine anything worse or more horrible than what I felt and saw in this place. I was told, at least so I understood it, that this was the least part of eternal punishment. What then must the rest be like? I understood that no one could experience the full sight of hell and live. When we left this we came upon another aspect of eternal punishment which made a deep impression on me. On what appeared to be a rather wide ledge on the side of a mountain I saw many, many people going back and forth, back and forth, searching, searching. They were surrounded, engulfed in flames of fire. They seemed themselves to be a part of the fire as though it came from within them. My companion then explained to me that these were they who had no time for God while they lived upon earth. Now they were condemned to spend an eternity seeking Him Whom they would never find. An endless search without hope. What a torture this must be! Oh the justice of God!

"On the morning of February 20, 1958, during Holy Mass, the thought of the lost ones, especially the chosen, grieved me. Then Our Lord appearing to me at that moment spoke these words to me: *'Beloved, spouse, I condemn no one. If a soul is condemned it has condemned itself.'* And I knew in my heart that this was so, though my eyes filled with tears. . ."

Nun in apparition described huge angels sent to protect

It was an angel. Actually, it was two angels. According to Sister Mildred Mary Ephrem Neuzil (the nun who experienced the Our Lady of America apparitions), her mystical experiences once included the encounter with two mighty angels whose task—in light of recent events—was dramatic.

They had come, they told her, as guardians, as protectors, and as defenders of the U.S.

That was according to a vision the nun allegedly had in August of 1981—the same summer that the Virgin began to appear half a world away in Medjugorje, and with the same message: seek peace or there will be destruction. Seek goodness. Seek purity.

"If the people of this Land carry out faithfully the instructions and pleadings of the Lord Jesus and the Virgin Mother then they will be following me to the hour of peace," said one of the angels—described as immensely tall, carrying a flaming sword, and enveloped in a light whiter than white. "With this sword of the Divine white flame of Love and the lightning bolts of His infinite Justice God will strike down His enemies and heal the repentant sinner," promised the huge angel. "This Nation and all who follow in the pursuit of peace will know the protection of God and the destruction of those who fight and seek to destroy them through the evil powers of the infernal spirits of darkness and hate."

It was an astonishing promise: that if the U.S. led the world back to holiness and honored its consecration to the Immaculate Conception, it would be protected. If it protected the youth, if it avoided the material, and if it led the peoples to purity—and if it installed a statue of Our Lady of America, representing purity, in the National Shrine of the Immaculate Conception—the sword of God would come against its enemies.

If not, warned Our Lady of America, there would be what she described way back then as "the fires of untold punishment."

The countenance of the angels—bearing flaming swords—was startlingly similar to the image revealed two decades later in the *third secret of Fatima;* in that vision was what Fatima seer Lucia dos Santos has described as "an Angel with a flaming sword in his left hand; flashing, it gave out flames that looked as though they would set the world on fire."

That was Fatima. The second angel Sister Mildred saw in the U.S. was equally brilliant. He held shafts of light and told the nun, "With these shafts of light God seeks out and binds with eternal chains the evil powers and those who have sold themselves to these enemies of God and His people."

Of course, America has yet to return to purity, its materialism is flagrant, and its youth are in disarray. Meanwhile, within the Church, the request to install a statue at the national shrine has not yet been fulfilled—although the apparition reached a stage of initial ecclesiastical approval when a medal was struck, a plaque constructed, and a statuette was made by Archbishop Paul F. Leibold to specifically commemorate the apparition.

Petitions are now being circulated to the nation's bishops and the laity are urged to help spread them to dioceses across the troubled nation.

Sister Mildred, who died January 10, 2001, at the age of 83, described the angels as magnificent beyond words. "Both these blessed spirits seemed to be composed of light," she wrote. "I could barely see any form. Their garments were of a dazzling whiteness, their voices were not like any other ever heard, not audible except to the inner hearing which is indescribable.

"I was further informed that these two mighty spirits fight together side by side aided by an army of their companion spirits."

As far as the Virgin, her messages continued through the 1990s but one of the last (at least as recorded in a booklet) came in 1984. "From this final message, I received the very strong impression that Our Lady was telling us that she had done everything she could do to help and warn us. Now it was up to us. Whatever happens we will have brought on ourselves so whatever we decide and do now is our responsibility. . ."

St. Joseph rises from obscurity in messages from American apparition

St. Joseph, long a hidden and under-appreciated saint, has risen to sudden prominence by way of apparitions to Sister Mildred Mary Neuzil—the Ohio mystic who died last year and whose apparitions, already partially approved, are now being set before Church officials for further action. [*see previous story*]

The move to grant them wider recognition is in its very early stage but as details emerge they have had an "explosive" effect, according to those involved in the cause—and among the details is the role of Joseph, faithful husband of Mary and father on earth of the Savior Himself.

On March 11, 1958, the Virgin reportedly told Sister Mildred that Joseph was coming to speak to her because he has "an important part to play in bringing peace to the world."

When Joseph appeared, said Sister Neuzil, he described himself as the "virgin-father" whose stain from original sin was cleansed immediately after his conception "through the future merits of Jesus."

"My heart suffered with the hearts of Jesus and Mary," said the saint. "Mine was a silent suffering, for it was my special vocation to hide and shield, as long as God willed, the Virgin Mother and Son from the malice and hatred of men. The most painful part of my sorrows was that I knew beforehand of their passion, yet would not be there to console them."

In one vision Sister Mildred saw Joseph "suspended, as it were, a short distance above what had the appearance of a large globe with clouds moving about it. His head was slightly raised, the eyes gazing upward as if in ecstasy. The hands were in a position similar to that of the priest during the celebration of Holy Mass, only they extended upward somewhat more." His hair seemed dark brown, said Sister Mildred, and he had a small beard. He was clothed in a white robe that reached to his ankles. Over this he wore a cloak, according to a pamphlet issued by the Our Lady of America Center in Fostoria, Ohio.

If sanctioned the apparitions of Joseph would rank among the most powerful in Church history. In recent times he has been associated with just one major apparition, that of Knock, Ireland, and with lesser apparitions such as one on the side of a church in Pidkamin, Ukraine.

But in those appearances he was silent; to Sister Mildred (whose messages were granted an imprimatur) he spoke.

He came as a teacher of purity, said Sister Mildred, and through him God had "blessed all fatherhood."

"Fatherhood is from God," Joseph said to the nun, "and it must take once again its rightful place among men. The Holy Trinity desires thus to honor me that in my unique fatherhood all fatherhood might be blessed."

In another vision Sister Mildred, whose spiritual director was Archbishop Paul F. Leibold of Cincinnati, said she saw Joseph's "pure heart" on a cross of brown color. "It appeared to me that at the top of the heart, in the midst of the flames pouring out, was a pure white lily," wrote the nun, who said the saint desired a day set aside to honor his fatherhood. "In honoring in a special way my fatherhood, you also honor Jesus and Mary," he told Sister Neuzil, adding that he too was a "co-operator" or "co-redemptor." "The Divine Trinity has placed into our keeping the peace of the world."

Sister Mildred said St. Joseph's cloak at times seemed brown, at other times purple, with a belt and sandals that looked the color of gold. Though his appearance seemed quite youthful, the nun said he gave the impression of "great strength" and "rare maturity."

"The lines of his face appeared strong and purposeful, softened somewhat by a gentle serenity," said Sister Mildred in a booklet available through the Fostoria center. "I also saw his most pure heart at this time. Moreover, I saw the Holy Spirit in the form of a dove hovering above his head."

The nun added that two angels were at his side, each with a small, satin-covered pillow, one bearing a gold scepter, the other a gold crown.

"Then I heard these words: 'Thus should be honored whom the King desires to honor,'" said Sister Mildred.

According to the revelations Joseph had been given special powers of protection over the Pope and Church, as well as individual households, and requested that his heart be honored in a special way each first Wednesday of the month through recitation of the Rosary's joyful mysteries and Communion. "Let them receive Holy Communion in union with the love with which I received the Savior for the first time and each time I held Him in my arms," said Joseph on March 30, 1958—thus setting the stage for possible creation of a new devotion in the same manner that Fatima began the devotion of First Saturdays. He promised that those dedicated to this new devotion "will be consoled by my presence at their death, and I myself will conduct them safely into the presence of Jesus and Mary."

"Jesus and Mary desire that my pure heart, so long hidden and unknown, be now honored in a special way," said the apparition. "Their future suffering was ever present to me and became my daily cross," Joseph said in October 1956. "My spiritual fatherhood extends to all God's children, and together with my Virgin Spouse I watch over them with great love and solicitude. Through me the Heavenly Father has blessed all fatherhood, and through me He continues and will continue to do so till the end of time."

Did George Washington really have an apparition?

For decades—actually now centuries—rumors have swirled that George Washington, the father of our country, experienced an apparition of an angelic female and possibly the Virgin Mary herself during the harsh trial at Valley Forge.

Whether the vision was authentic and if so whether the figure he supposedly saw in it was Mary are two matters that will probably never be answered.

There are, however, some intriguing hints—and at the very least Washington (known to offer up his suffering and to have a woman "say the beads" for him) was far more spiritual than most of our history teachers taught.

Most tantalizing was a report in volume 4, number 12 of an old nineteenth-century veterans publication known as the *National Tribune*. Now known as *Stars and Stripes*, the publication quoted a man named Anthony Sherman as describing a vision that allegedly occurred in 1777.

It was said that as the chilly wind murmured through leafless trees, Washington, who was known to wander alone praying, spent nearly the entire afternoon in his quarters, allowing no interruptions. "When he came out, I noticed that his face was a shade paler than usual, and there seemed to be something on his mind of more than ordinary importance," claimed Sherman, who reputedly fought alongside Washington.

Returning just after dusk, he dispatched an orderly to the quarters of the officer who was presently in attendance. After a preliminary conversation of about half an hour, Washington, gazing upon his companion with that strange look of dignity which he alone could command, said to the latter: "I do not know whether it is owing to the anxiety of my mind, or what, but this afternoon as I was sitting at this table engaged in preparing a dispatch, something seemed to disturb me. Looking up, I beheld standing opposite me a singularly beautiful female. So astonished was I, for I had given strict order not to be disturbed, that it was some moments before I found language to inquire into the cause of her presence. A second, third, and even a fourth time did I repeat my question, but received no answer from my mysterious visitor except a slight raising of her eyes. By this time I felt strange sensations spreading through me. I would have risen but the riveted gaze of the being before me rendered volition impossible. I assayed once more to address her, but my tongue had become useless. Even thought itself had become paralyzed. A new influence, mysterious, potent, irresistible, took possession of me. All I could do was to gaze steadily, vacantly at my unknown visitant."

While there is plenty of room for skepticism (it was claimed Sherman remembered all this at the age of ninety-nine), there is no doubt that such a legend was in print by 1880 if not before.

"Gradually the surrounding atmosphere seemed as though becoming filled with sensations, and luminous," Washington was quoted as saying. "Everything about me seemed to ratify, the mysterious visitor herself becoming more airy and yet more distinct to my sight than before, I now began to feel as one dying, or rather to experience the sensations which I have sometimes imagined accompany dissolution. I did not think, I did not reason, I did not move; all were alike impossible."

It was then that Washington was said to have heard a voice, "Son of the Republic, look and learn," said the apparitional woman, extending an arm eastward.

It was claimed Washington then beheld a white vapor that gradually dissipated, revealing "all the countries of the world," and saw a cloud rise from Europe and America, a cloud that moved westward. . .

God has choice blessings for you

God has blessings for you, blessings you don't even know are there, blessings you may not even have requested. Our Lord is a giving God and He has all *kinds* of blessings in store for you. He has happiness. He has contentment. He has security.

Those are gifts He may have wrapped for you and it may be time to claim them. We're not talking about material things (although they may figure into it). We're talking about grace. The Lord has abundant graces assigned to each of you, and when you get to heaven, you'll see the extent of them. He may be ready to give you gifts of joy, patience, prayer, love, friends, insights, peace, and well-being. There's no telling *what* he has wrapped for you, and the point is to realize them now—to claim them—so there won't be regrets later, in the afterlife, when you'll be able to see the entire plan for your life.

What a promise this is! The Lord wants you to live life to the fullest and if you follow His precepts—clearly marked out in the New Testament—you will find what you have yearned for (albeit not always in the way you have yearned for it). The Lord wants us to have life and live abundantly and He wants us to live in the joy of knowing that earth is but a trial and that beyond that is His Kingdom.

He grants blessings in the same way that there are holiday gifts. Often He grants us what we request, but just as often He catches us off-guard. He surprises us. Often, He gives us things we *didn't* ask for. There are big gifts. There are small gifts. There are gifts that seem minor until we mature enough to appreciate them. Suddenly we turn a corner, and *there it is*: something from the Lord that sets us right and changes us in a way that's like manna from the sky and makes life all the better!

That's how generous God is. He's always looking to make us happy, but like any parent He doesn't give us things that are not good for us. When we die, we'll see the *many* things we sought that would have caused us damage. It will be remarkable to see God's plan for our lives laid out in ways we couldn't grasp while we were wearing earthly blinders.

We're His children, and He's the ultimate parent, which means He is also strict. He wants us to develop in the right way. He wants us to seek heaven. And so He sends what will give us the best opportunity to attain not just happiness on earth but happiness forever. To claim His blessings means having *faith*. We have to *know* He answers prayers—and then suddenly we see in quick succession how quickly (if it's in His will) He answers. As we increase in holiness we increase in faith; as we come closer to perfection we attain more of what in holiness we request.

There's no telling what He has in store for you. It could be a spouse, it could be a new job, it could be solving a problem with a son or daughter or friend. It could be the opportunity of suffering.

The Lord surprises with His goodness as well as His generosity. Only Christ would make His birthday a day in which *others* receive gifts! He may well be ready to give you what you have sought for so long, but is waiting for you to learn a final lesson in patience or prayer or humility. He may be waiting for you to turn your life completely over to Him.

Be holy. Know that there are blessings around the corner. Have faith! That potent combination will loose many blessings and lift you in a way that'll exceed even your favorite Christmas.

God designed it so that our greatest joy is closeness to Him

God designed the world so that our greatest joy is closeness to Him. No matter what you seek in life, no matter how much money you have, no matter your luxury, you'll never get greater pleasure than simply lifting your heart to Him.

Think about that: the basic act of worship is the source of highest gladness. And it's free! When we seek God—when we love Him, when we *adore* Him—He draws us above all physical circumstances.

No matter what you may be going through (pain, depression, worries), if you praise God He will bring you to joy.

That's because praise brings us close to Him, and there is no joy like the joy of knowing the Lord. He sends graces that can completely defy our circumstances. He brings joy where, by the standards of the world, there should be depression. There are those in poverty. There are those who are lonely. There are those with cancer. In God they find happiness.

The opposite is true of those who ignore God and thus set themselves at a distance. Take a look around and you'll see many of the rich with grim looks. No matter what they accomplish on earth, if they don't have a closeness to God, they never find true gladness. Meanwhile those who love the Lord have the glow of well-being.

To draw close we must love Him and seek to do His will, to be what he planned for us to be. We must seek Him in everything. Then comes a joy that's indescribable. You can buy a yacht or a Mercedes—you can marry well, you can be the most powerful person on earth—but if you don't have God you have not experienced true happiness. You have missed out on that transcendental elation—that ineffable joy that put a smile on the faces of so many saints who to the world seemed poverty-stricken. Remember that smile on the face of Mother Teresa!

When we pray, we draw close to God, and He grants us feelings that can not be attained elsewhere. God is joy and when you draw nearer to Him you draw nearer to joy. It's that simple. There's nothing you can do that will bring as much happiness. And closeness comes through praise. Adore God through the day. Do it from the heart. Love Him. Praise Him over and over—ten times, a hundred times. *Praise You Jesus, praise You Christ.*

That's what will bring you joy because the Lord is joy personified.

Was there miraculous intervention?

It was like a lightning bolt from the blue: on Wednesday a Democratic election board decided—with no warning—that it was not going to recount ballots in Miami after all. Despite a ruling by the state supreme court that such a count would be considered in a final tally—and despite hopes that, as Florida's most populous county, Miami alone might grant Gore enough votes for a victory—the *Democrats* on the canvassing board voted to stop such a count and go with the results they had already tabulated.

Democrats voting for something that heavily favored the Republican!

It ran against logic and common sense. It was a reversal that would have seemed unrealistic in a movie.

But there it was in black and white: "In yet another surprise twist in the Florida presidential balloting, Miami-Dade County officials today called off their manual recount of 654,000 votes and abandoned an alternative plan for a limited recount, saying they could not meet the Sunday deadline set by the Florida Supreme Court," reported the *Washington Post*, while the *New York Post* called it all "stunning."

Although they had started a recount, the Miami board was not going to proceed, and now Al Gore, who just 14 hours before looked ready to claim victory, was on the verge of defeat.

In the fantastic ups and downs of this dramatic election, it was a moment of highest drama. The hand counts were in heavily Democratic areas, which means that when extra votes are discovered, they will most likely favor Al Gore. To make the odds all the greater, those on the election canvassing boards were overwhelmingly Democrat. Any close calls were bound to benefit Gore and place Bush in all the more jeopardy. All the vice president needs is less than a thousand votes (at least before military ballots are fully considered) to pass Bush and claim the state's decisive electoral votes and possibly the presidency.

But the opposite happened, and it was so momentous and unlikely that many wondered if it was divine intervention. I wonder myself. This election isn't over yet. We don't know who will win.

More importantly, we can't speak for God. We don't know His plans. He loves both candidates equally.

And both candidates, like all us humans, have flaws. Both Bush and Gore favor abortions in certain circumstances (such as rape or a life-threatening situations), and both support the death penalty. Bush has said that America is not yet ready to overturn Roe versus Wade, and that their stance on abortion would not be the litmus test for those he appoints to the Supreme Court.

But Bush is much more pro-life than Gore and has made it clear that he would put the brakes on abortion. This has led to an outpouring of prayers for him from many who are desperate to rid the nation of the scourge of abortion and the immorality that has haunted us during the past decade.

Across the United States, internet sites are loaded with invocations, there has been fasting, there are prayer chains, Masses have been said, Protestants have been holding prayer vigils, and millions of those devoted to the Virgin Mary have been praying a special "Lepanto Rosary" (recalling a time when prayer miraculously stemmed a Muslim invasion of Europe) and passing around novenas.

I don't know the end result, and once more, I'm not implying who God favors. But with that many prayers for the pro-life cause, it seems likely that they are having some kind of effect and played a role in the remarkable events of this week and if continued will affect the final tally.

Did Guadalupe strike again?

Tuesday was the feast day of Our Lady of Guadalupe—a day when millions congregate at her shrine—and thousands of U.S. Catholics (and even some non-Catholics) had been invoking her to settle the election.

What has happened is incredible. The odds that the pro-life candidate, Bush, would win the electoral college while losing the general popular count are astronomical, and so is the fact that an election of 100 million would come down to a few hundred in Florida (at one point last Friday 154)— and then nine people in the Supreme Court.

That's 1/100,000th of one percent.

And the final decision came on her feast day.

That's the true use of the word "incredible."

Moreover, an image of the Virgin had appeared in a building in Clearwater, Florida, as if to presage major events, and it resembled the Guadalupe Virgin. Just recently another *appeared in Bush's home state* of Texas—and a mural of her miraculously survived *a fire last week,* as if to make sure we got the point!

We don't like taking sides in politics (God respects both candidates, as do we) but we want the pro-life view, and the decision Tuesday night had special meaning. Guadalupe is also consider patroness of the unborn—a weapon against abortion—and her miraculous image at Guadalupe, which materialized inexplicably on an Indian's cloak on December 12, 1531, hints in the way she is attired that in the image she was represented as being in an early stage of pregnancy.

A copy of an image that preceded Guadalupe (at an earlier miraculous site called Guadalupe in *Spain*) was taken on board a crucial flagship during the Battle of Lepanto (when Christians were praying to fend off an invasion of Europe by Muslims), and the Christian triumph in that battle led Pope Pius V to name the day "Our Lady of Victory."

If Bush ends up getting rid of abortion, it will be another example of her many victories and couldn't come at a more crucial time in history.

A trip to "ground zero" and a reminder of perpetual

By Michael H. Brown (October 17)

I took a trip to "ground zero" yesterday. I took the trip because I wanted to get a spiritual fix on the event and because I wanted to say good-bye to a close friend who is buried somewhere under the South Tower and because I just wanted to see for myself that these structures I had grown up with—that I had watched built in college, that I had used as a constant directional beacon when I lived in Manhattan—were really gone.

So I went to New York and I looked up at where the planes had hit, where the face of satan had formed in smoke on September 11, where there had been that incredible fireball that killed my friend and I saw the empty space where once there had been two of the world's tallest buildings.

Now there was only blue sky and the roll of clouds. All around, it was surreal. Except for construction rigs or emergency vehicles, there was no traffic. There was an eerie silence. On the Chase Bank at Broadway and Fulton were the many flyers of missing loved ones and pictures of Jesus and a tabloid story about the Virgin at Lourdes. *"It's time for America to pray,"* was the heading on one flyer from Love Chain Ministries, and across the way and just up a block or two was the old church *you have read about,* the chapel of St. Paul that somehow didn't collapse while buildings all around shook and shattered or turned into blackened skeletal remnants.

In the background was the lilt from a street violinist playing "America the Beautiful." It was like a funeral dirge. It *was* a dirge. I was there to say good-bye to my old friend Dan Smith—I needed closure on that—and I needed to see what had transpired in what I know was a warning from God. "The world is shaking," said another poster, and this is exactly the verbiage Maria Esperanza (the seer from Venezuela) had used when months ago she prophesied an event that would "shake the world."

It is one of a number of events that will occur as we move from a period of warning to a period of purification. We'll discuss that in coming days.

Near City Hall, at the Church of St. Andrew, I went to Mass for the victims and for Danny and for a city that better learn that this was more than just the act of a terrorist—for a *country* that better realize this. In the church, a beautiful building appointed in wood, was a precious statue of Our Lady of Fatima near a larger one of Jesus as the Sacred Heart reaching out.

There were about fifty people at Mass and afterward there was a healing service to dispel the terror and the uncertainty and in front of City Hall on the way out I happened to spot a pamphlet blowing in a gust of litter.

It had the Madonna and Child.

When I picked it up I saw that it was from the Perpetual Help Center in The Bronx.

There on the street. In the litter. Even there. Calling out.

Behold, O Mother of my God, my only hope, behold at your feet a miserable sinner who asks for mercy. . .

Down a few blocks, the smoke was still rising, the water still poured on the smoldering wreckage (and on the graves of 5,000), the cranes moving debris that in one case formed an incredible cross.

They'll pick up the pieces. This is a massive city. It will build where there is now rubble. But if it shows defiance—if it goes back to what it was, if it embraces its old way of disdain for all that is spiritual (and this goes too for the country)—then what happened on September 11 will be looked back at one day as only the opening shot.

Top expert says human cloning would lead to deformities and death

Dr. H. D. Griffin, assistant director at the Scottish institute that cloned Dolly the sheep, told *Spirit Daily* that attempts to clone humans are unconscionable and will lead in many cases to deformities, fetal death, and shortened life spans if indeed cloned humans are born.

"Where animals have been cloned, the success rate—the number of reconstructed embryos that make it to a live birth—is around one to two percent, and so the process is very inefficient," said Dr. Griffin of the Roslin Institute near Edinburg. "That's the published record. I think you could be sure that there are many experiments that have been tried that have been unsuccessful and therefore don't enter into the statistics. One to two percent is on average what you might expect in cloning of animals."

Dr. Griffin pointed out that a recent attempt to clone a gaur, a rare ox, in Iowa ended in failure when the animal died two days after birth.

So the chances of cloning a human child are low, and the chances that the child would die late in pregnancy or soon after birth seem quite high," said Dr. Griffin, whose company genetically engineers animals for potential agricultural use. "Nobody working in this field knowing the high incidence of failures and the fact that fetuses die late and *sometimes are abnormal* [our emphasis] would ever contemplate attempting to clone a human child."

Griffin scoffed at scientists who have vowed to clone the first full-bodied human by 2002.

"So far research groups around the world have been successful at cloning cattle, sheep, mice, goats, and pigs, but it's not been an easy technology for others to pick up and for example in mice only three groups worldwide have reported the ability to clone mice," he claimed. "Equally competent research groups have attempted to clone rabbits, rats, and monkeys, and have so far been unsuccessful, so there's no guarantee that's it's going to be easy to do in humans. The reprogramming of an adult cell is quite a remarkable feat. Nobody knows how's it's done. It's remarkable that it happens at all. And making it an efficient process where there's high success rate is going to be exceedingly difficult in animals and at the present stage of the technology just on safety grounds it would be wholly irresponsible for anyone to try and clone a child using these techniques."

Is human cloning going on in secret? Is it true, as rumor has it, that a man who lost a boy to disease more than a year ago plans to fly with a scientist to an in vitro fertilization laboratory in Asia to attempt a clone?

"I have no particular inside knowledge or way of finding out, and it's not the sort of information we'd be privy to," claimed Griffin, adding that it was "impossible to say" when the first human might be cloned.

Other attempts at human cloning have been reported, including one by *a bizarre cult* that wants to reproduce a 10-month-old girl who died last February. The project is being carried out in a secret laboratory in Nevada and has been funded in part with $450,000 given by the parents to Clonaid, the name the organization used to register in the Bahamas.

They have announced that they will use the Dolly technology from Scotland, but Dr. Griffin, overseeing operation at the lab where the Dolly technology was developed, says that such claims as well *as those of a team* composed of an American embryologist, Panos Zavos, and Italian scientist Severino Antinori are preposterous. "I think the enthusiasm is partly related to a desire for publicity," said Griffin. "I know no one who has experience successfully cloning animals who believes this technology should be used in human beings."

Can we thus rest assured? Is it still a long ways off? Or is there something to the rumors?

Stay tuned....

"It's going on," says Father Joseph C. Howard, who works with the *American Life League.* "There's no question. It has been. I don't know that a human has been gestated or born from a clone, but there's no question that it's been attempted and begun."

An interview with the priest involved in the case behind *The Exorcist*

We tracked down Father Walter H. Halloran, a Jesuit who assisted in the famous exorcism that served as the model for the blockbuster movie, *The Exorcist.* Now living in San Diego, where he is assistant pastor at St. Martin of Tours Church, Father Halloran still vividly remembers the case, which took place in 1949 and involved a young boy named Rob (not a girl) from the Washington-Baltimore area, with the final exorcism conducted in St. Louis, where the boy had relatives. Father Halloran assisted the main exorcist, Father William S. Bowdern of St. Francis Xavier Church in St. Louis. Father Halloran says the boy was 11. Others say 13. But everyone agrees on one thing: it was hair-raising. Here's our short talk:

SD: Father, how many times were you present in the exorcism sessions?

Fr. Halloran: I suppose every night for three weeks.

SD: Did you have any insight into the origin of the problem?

Fr. H: In a way he was a victim to the frame of mind of the aunt (who was into spiritualism).

SD: What happened at the end? We're told the Archangel Michael manifested.

Fr. H: I was taken off five days before the conclusion, but from what I understand there was a very loud sound, a *boom*—sort of like a sonic boom—and then the boy opened his eyes and said St. Michael came and that it was over. At the same time this took place there were about six or seven priests over in the college church saying their office and there was a huge boom over there and the whole church was completely lit up. Father Bowdern, who was doing the exorcism, and the boy were at the rectory. There was a very, very bright light that lit up the whole church.

SD: What was the most striking physical phenomena that you witnessed yourself during the exorcisms?

Fr. H: I think the markings on the boy's body. I didn't think there was any way they could have been self-induced, the marks, the scratches, the words, the numbers and that sort of thing that appeared [in blood red]. When the evil spirit took over the child, there seemed to be nothing he could do about it. There were a couple of times when something very dangerous might have happened and he had no recollection whatsoever of anything that took place when he was in one of these sieges. And that affected me, the power that someone or something has over someone.

SD: Was there any particular prayer that the evil spirit seemed to react to the most?

Fr. H: Yes. It was more elements or words or phrases in each prayer. Whenever the Blessed Mother's name would be invoked or mentioned, the child would get very, very agitated and when Our Lord's name—Christ, Our Lord, or Jesus—when that was said, and the same thing with Michael the Archangel. And then he'd become very, very agitated with holy water. With some of the prayers you sprinkle the person with holy water and he'd become wild, physically wild, flying around and that sort of thing.

SD: Flailing around with his hands, that sort of thing?

Fr. H: Yeah.

SD: Did you see the *Exorcist* movie?

Fr. H: I saw it right after it came out. I went with Father Bowdern and I thought it was a typical Hollywood, glitzy thing, real bizarre, trying to bring people to be fearful or to scream. I was disappointed with it. I thought it was a mess. And Father Bowdern did too. He gave sort of a running negative commentary throughout the whole movie. I thought the two of us were going to be thrown out of the theatre.

SD: So there was no neck craning around?

Fr. H: No. It was just ridiculous, and the gross one where the little girl is masturbating with a crucifix. It just didn't happen, that's all, and the huge amount of green vomit: Nonsense.

SD: There was some spitting, though, wasn't there?

Fr. H: Yeah, there was spitting, and when I think back on it, it amazes me, his accuracy. He'd spit right in your eye from about eight feet away.

SD: I understand at one point you saved the boy's life. He was ready to go over a cliff, wasn't he?

Fr. H: Yeah. I took him out to the retreat house in St. Louis, a very pretty place, to get out of the hospital and get some fresh air, and he didn't know anything about the Stations of the Cross and so I asked if he wanted to learn and he's says, oh sure. He was an affable little kid. Not many 11-year-olds would say they were interested in finding out about the Stations of the Cross, but he was. And I explained what each one signified and we got to the 12th station and I said, this commemorates Christ dying on the cross and with that he took off and ran toward the edge of a bluff that dropped down about 150, 200 feet down to the tracks and I hollered at him and nothing happened so I ran and for once in my life I made a decent tackle.

SD: Did you have any manifestation afterward, or was that the end of it? Did you come under demonic attack afterwards?

Fr. H: No, I never did.

SD: Did you fast during that whole thing?

Fr. H: On and off I did.

SD: Bread and water?

Fr. H: No, things like just taking a cup of coffee and a piece of toast and skipping a meal and at that time we were still practicing abstinence during Lent.

SD: Did Father Bowdern fast?

Fr. H: He did quite a bit, and sometimes he would go off because he was getting worn out [the exorcism lasted six weeks].

SD: How old were you?

Fr. H: About 28.

SD: Anything else that sticks out in your mind when you think back about Rob?

Fr. H: Well, when they baptized him—it was a conditional baptism, because he had been baptized a Lutheran as a baby—when they went through the ceremony again, on the way down to the church from his uncle's home, he kept grabbing the steering wheel of the car. He had the car up on the boulevard and some close calls of hitting or being hit by other cars. Then when they were giving him first Holy Communion, and I was present for this, he really fought that, he was flailing around and he'd open his mouth and then as soon as Father Bowdern came close with a Host, he'd swing at him. And I was supposed to be holding him all this time. But he'd relax and I'd relax a little bit and then he'd get an arm free and [the voice would] keep yelling, "No! He will not receive" or—and his eyes were closed!—he'd take a swing at Father Bowdern in the groin and say, "How's that for a nutcracker?" And then it must have been 15 or 20 minutes of this carrying on and he relaxed and received Holy Communion.

SD: Did you fear for your life.

Fr. H: No, not really. But I wondered why me, what purpose I was there for. There was one time he asked us to stop and took his pajama top off and he was covered with these marks, scratches, and he said they hurt. It was Holy Thursday and I was telling him about Holy Thursday and he started writhing around in pain and he said, look, I can't stand this. He seemed more affected when I said things like "the Blessed Sacrament" or mentioned the ordination of priests and things like that.

SD: What a confirmation of the power of our faith, and the powers that struggle with each other on this earth.

Fr. H: Yes. That's what affected me most, and I guess that's why I was so disappointed with the movies.

SD: Do you think it was Satan or a demon?

Fr. H: During the rite when it was asked its name the only answer I can remember that was given was "legion," which reminds us of the swineherd running into the lake.

Halloween: it's time to come against the devil's Christmas

by Michael H. Brown

A few years ago, I began putting plastic rosaries in with candy for the trick-or-treaters. That made me feel good. In my own little way I thought I was reclaiming some land. I thought I was taking some turf back from the devil. After all, Halloween is supposed to be "all hallows' eve," the vigil for a celebration of our *hallowed saints.*

No more. Now, it's the devil's Christmas. Look around. There are orange porch lights, trees decorated with ghouls, and lawn figurines (witches, vampires, and assorted monsters). A couple years ago when I was speaking in Catskill, New York, a woman told me that at a house nearby was a "nativity" scene with demons instead of Jesus, Mary, and Joseph.

This is not just kid's stuff. It's serious business. Halloween is an old flashback to pagan idolatry, and while Christianity replaced it with a holiday to honor the saints (in the eighth century), the devil has reassumed it in this spiritual tug-of-war.

I realize the danger of seeing a devil under every rock. There's no use getting paranoid. For most, Halloween is just an excuse to have a little fun, and in the right way, it can be fun.

But the bottom line is that Halloween as now presented is based on the occult and it's woefully unwise for our society to become immersed in that or in anything that involves spells, witches, or wizards, including Harry Potter (whose movie, ironically, is coming out now). The fact is that pagans, druids, and witches recognize eight feasts during the year, and Halloween (or *Samhain*, eve of witchcraft's "new year") is the most popular. It's one of the high feast days of both witchcraft and satanism. The Celts believed that during Samhain the veil separating the living from the dead was at its thinnest. They believed that on the evening of October 31, evil spirits and the souls of the dead passed through the barrier and entered the world of the living. Occultists consider Halloween to be one of the most powerful times to cast a spell.

Look at the ghoulish faces on TV. Look at the macabre celebration of the dead. Where Christ and God and the Holy Spirit focus on *life*, the devil focuses on death. Where Catholics pray for the deceased, especially purgatorial souls, Halloween tries to bring spirits from the hellfire.

And aligning oneself with that may not be as harmless as you think. When we invoke an energy (when we honor it with a statue or image), we invite it in. Just as a holy statue brings Jesus and the Blessed mother, so can a dark one bring demons.

Am I saying that dressing as a demon will cause a child to become possessed?

I'm not saying that. But it comes with a clear element of danger. And even if it didn't, do we want our kids to treat the devil as a game? Do we want them to revel in death, in tombstones, in darkness?

"God says, 'Don't imitate evil!'" (*Deuteronomy* 18:9-11). Think about it: would Jesus enjoy kids dressed up as evil spirits? As Freddie Kruegers? Would He want to see our little ones resembling His nemesis?

Bring back All Hallows' Eve. Bring back the "holy day" by dressing your kids as saints or angels. Take back evil territory just as Christ and His Blessed mother conquered pagan strongholds. And pray for the souls in purgatory!

As for trick-or-treat: get out some rosaries or medals or Bible tracts to go along with the Hersheys and Nestles.

If you want to be happy, be who God meant you to be

If you want to be happy, be who God meant you to be. Don't be what your friends think you should be. Don't do what everyone wants you to do. Don't shoot for Hollywood.

Shoot for happiness.

And that means doing what gives you peace. It means doing what brings you closer to Jesus. It means doing what God—and not everyone else—meant you to do and expected you to be.

You cannot fulfill the mission God has given you unless you are *yourself,* the way He intended you to be.

God intends some of us to be mailmen and some congressmen and some housewives and in the end He judges on how well we did what He set for us to do, how we handled our missions. Too often, we orient everything to what others will think when we shouldn't care about that. We should care about what heaven thinks. And that judgment is different than the way things are viewed from here (where physical allurements confuse those who seek to materialism).

When we are ourselves, we are closest to God because God made us and when we allow Him to orient us, when we allow Him to materialize our plans—when we *let go*—we have His happiness. What joy to simply walk the path that He set! What a joy to ignore the competition of a world that is blinded by the flesh! What a joy to rise above the judgments of those obsessed with attaining things that in the end they can't keep.

When we die, God will judge in great part on how close we ended our lives to what He intended as well as how much we loved. Were we terrific, spiritual housewives, great fathers, spiritual mailmen who spread His example, who worked in the places He had positioned us—or did we try to attain things because we aimed for societal stature? Were we good at housework, plumbing, rearing children—or did we force ourselves into "prestigious" occupations that were never designated for us? Did we preach His word or were we afraid of what others might think?

One of the wisest things we can realize is that whatever role God assigned us is as important as any other in the scheme of eternity. We're all equal. And we have to put God's desires above all others. This is key: not caring how we are viewed by others and instead seeking the happiness that God grants those who carry forth the mission He has designated.

Doing that means looking in the mirror and not worrying about how others view us but asking *Him* what we should be.

Happiness in life relies on a good self-image, and for that we go to Christ

Like anything else, a poor self-image can be healed by Jesus. That's the message of a priest named Father Robert DeGrandis. No matter what you think of yourself, and no matter what others have heaped upon you, God can remove it. He can restore you to the way He intended, and let you see yourself as He sees you. God heals us when we pray, and casts off what may have been heaped upon us during our lives, from the time we were children.

This is the subject of a little pamphlet by Father DeGrandis (along with Betty Tapscott) called *Healing of Self-Image,* and it brings up things we may never have considered. It gets to the root of problems (problems that have plagued us all our lives because they have not been properly addressed). Do you ever feel inferior? Are you uncomfortable with your self-view? Do you harbor childhood hurts?

"Whatever situation you are in—if you are ignored by rebellious children, put down by an overly demanding boss, humiliated by an unhappy and frustrated superior or director— then the foundation of your self-image may develop cracks and eventually may crumble," the priest warns.

When feelings of inferiority, grief, rejection, fear, failure, timidity, unworthiness, and hopelessness arrive, we need to realize that this is coming from the enemy and cast them out in the Name of Jesus, Who has the special task of deliverance. This is important as soon as such thoughts arrive, before they can take root. One by one, such feelings should be immediately addressed (in prayer) and dispelled.

At the same time, we must be careful not to reflect negatively on others, especially our children. We must be careful not to negatively label them. "It is very damaging to a child's self-image if he feels he can never really please his parents or teachers or if the goals are always being raised higher and higher to such an extent that they cannot be reached," note the authors. "Children should never be compared to each other. We need to accept them, each one, just the way they are."

And we have to accept ourselves. *Not our evil tendencies. Not our sinfulness.* But the way God made us. That means a self-image centered on Jesus and it means praising God—Who fulfills the way we feel at the same time that He takes our focus off ourselves. "We are wonderful, we are beautiful, we are the work of His hands, of His Redemption," says Father DeGrandis.

He is the One Who heals. He is the One Who casts negativity out. It is Jesus Who no matter *how* we view ourselves—and no matter what others may cast upon us—will repair our self-images, and will do that to the extent that we respect, love, and forgive others.

Reports of unusual healings continue at "church of icons"

The priests at a Greek Orthodox church in the New York suburb of Hempstead, Long Island, report that miraculous healings are continuing years after icons of the Virgin began shedding tears in the area. The phenomena involved three icons that were brought to St. Paul's Church: Our Lady of Perpetual Help (above), the Lamenting Mother of God (below), and a third that is now in Florida. While the flow of tears has long-since stopped (it first began in March of 1960), Father Nicholas J. Magoulias, the pastor, told *Spirit Daily* that other phenomena continue at this church that lost two parishioners to the tragedy of September 11.

One recent cure involved a Roman Catholic woman named Lilly Bertuccio, who was set for a major cancer operation. After praying before one of the icons she took oil from the shrine and applied it with a short prayer (*"I am applying this Holy Oil with the Blessed Mother's hand"*). Two days before the operation, she had a dream filled with remarkable light and the following Friday, when she went to New York Hospital of Queens for the surgery, a mammography indicated that the tumor was gone.

"We then went to another room for a different mammography," she noted. "The nurse, my doctor, and the technician returned to my room and the technician said to me, 'Do you believe in miracles?' I said, 'Yes, I do.' He said, 'For twenty years I have been doing this and this is the first time this happened to me. Whatever was there is not there anymore.'"

That was in 1997. According to the priests, the healings continue to the present day—with at least two remarkable ones a year. "For instance, there was one I know last March of a woman suffering from cervical cancer who was completely healed," said the associate pastor, Father Joakim Valsiad. "I heard this with my own ears. I know that every day three or four stop by, pray, and receive the assistance of the Virgin Mary."

"The icons are still miraculous," says Father Magoulias. "They still do healings. We had two this past year. It's a continuous thing.

When I first came we had an all-night service, and we had a lady here from Chicago who was deaf, and before I started the service she was moved to take a picture. Back in those days they used to have a bulb that they would place in the flash, and she went to take a picture and all of a sudden it exploded. I heard a big explosion and turned around and said, 'What happened? What happened?' and she was hysterical. She said, 'I can hear! I can hear!' Her doctor sent a letter documenting it."

The church is one of a growing list in the New York area involving alleged miracles. Reports of phenomena have also come from *Our Lady of the Island* Shrine in Eastport (47 miles to the east); from *a woman in Huntington* who claims apparitions of St. Therese the Little Flower; and even *a tree on the Upper West Side of Manhattan* that seemed to bear an image of the Virgin just weeks before the World Trade Center event. Meanwhile, the Pope has been vigorously seeking reconciliation between Roman Catholicism and the Orthodox Church, both of which have a profound devotion to Mary.

Is the Pope just mentioning *Revelation* in the course of things or as a message?

It's gotten hard, in the past month, to avoid signs of the times. From the quake in Seattle—on Ash Wednesday—to the Lenten outbreak of livestock epidemics (at a time when we are called to fast on meat), and now to the blackouts in California, God continues to tap us on the shoulders. His touch is becoming increasingly insistent. Is the Pope hinting also? We ask this for a simple reason: On February 15, Zenit News Service, which is based in Rome, commented that "never before, as in recent weeks, has the Pope quoted the Book of Apocalypse so much."

We don't know the Pope's process of teaching at midweek audiences. Maybe he was just stepping through the New Testament with midweek audiences. But it seemed odd. Just a week later, as he was installing a record 44 new cardinals, he exhorted them to read "signs of the times" (this time referring to *Matthew* 16:3), made references to martyrdom, and again took up the theme of persecution a few days later. Soon after a report came out saying that worldwide 200 million Christians are in political systems that in some way could or do persecute them. Persecution is a key component of *Revelation*.

Last week, at another general midweek audience, the Pope "again addressed a topic characterized by mystical overtones," reported Zenit. "The book he quoted most often was the Apocalypse. He described the struggle between good and evil, represented by the woman who gives birth to a son, and the raging dragon bent on destroying them. Both against the Church, and the Mother, of which she is a figure, is unleashed the monstrous devastating energy of violence, falsehood and injustice."

This came on the heels of a message in January from Medjugorje in which the Virgin referred to Satan as "without chains."

Through the years John Paul has often repeated messages from Medjugorje—knowingly or unknowingly. Either he is taking the messages to heart or receiving something himself.

Whatever the case, he is in a period of heavy teaching. We may never know if he is simply explicating Scripture, or subtly hinting of times to come to his billion sheep.

Angel appears in northern lights as world teeters on the brink of holy war

The other day, we ran a photograph of the northern lights from Finland, which on September 23 formed the extraordinary image of an angel (reminding us of the *third Fatima secret*). That the northern lights (or "aurora borealis") would form such a display is remarkable. It was the northern lights that constituted the "great sign" of Fatima in 1938—and presaged the Second World War.

Now we seem on the verge of another great battle. Will it be a long holy war? Have we seen the beginnings of World War III? Will it be Muslims versus Christians as it was during many of our darkest historical periods?

The words of terrorist Osama Bin Laden's group are chilling. "Wherever there are Muslims, they should prepare for jihad and by the grace of God, the victory will be Islam's," said one communique earlier this week. "Wherever there are Americans and Jews, they will be targeted."

Such evokes the tremendous oppressions from the eighth to 15th centuries—when Muslim hordes, often from Turkey, invaded Christendom, killing Catholics, taking over kingdoms, and destroying statues and crucifixes. It was during this oppression that a famous miraculous image of Mary was hidden in Spain at a spot called "Guadalupe" (centuries before apparitions occurred at a place in Mexico that was named after this earlier site), and it was during this takeover that a town in Portugal was named after Mohammed's daughter—Fatima. Indeed, the Muslims may well have eradicated Christianity but for a miraculous victory on October 7, 1571, at Lepanto when Spanish, Venetian, and Genoese fleets—bolstered by the special prayers of the Pope and a huge Rosary procession—defeated the Turks and prevented a takeover of Western Europe.

It was during the Muslim occupation that many in what is now Bosnia-Hercegovina were converted to the Muslim faith, setting the stage for recent conflicts. Throughout much of the 1990s Muslims, Orthodox, and Catholics viciously fought each other, with the Virgin appearing at Medjugorje to urge reconciliation.

Was all this a harbinger of a larger religious war? Is that what we approach now? A massive uprising of Islam against modern Christians?

According to statistics gathered in the newly-published "World Christian Encyclopedia," 31.2 percent of the world's six billion people are Christians but Muslims have increased their share to 19.6 percent (from 12 percent a century ago). There are now 1.2 billion followers of Islam, and in recent months they have been persecuting Christians from Africa to the Philippines and Indonesia—even beheading them. An alliance between Islam and Hindus (who have been viciously persecuting Christians in places like India) could cause a huge sway, as would an alliance between Muslims and China.

Are we headed for another "Lepanto"? Did the September 11 event already signal the start of a new centuries-long war?

All we know is that through prayer we can prevent it. But prayer is now urgent: we have an angel on the scene, as well as the aurora.

Atheist turns into minister after experience with hell

This is the account of a minister, Howard Storm, from Ohio, who "died" in 1985 from a perforation in his intestines and returned with an account of hell. While he's a minister now (at Zion United Church of Christ in Norwood), at the time he was an atheistic professor, chairman of the art department at North Kentucky University. Storm describes himself as a selfish man who not only didn't believe but detested those who did.

Then came the crisis on June 1, 1985, while he was leading students on a trip to museums in Paris.

"I needed surgery immediately but unfortunately when I got to the surgery hospital there wasn't a surgeon available," says Storm. "It was excruciating. I was in real agony for hours. I said to my wife that it was time to say good-bye. I couldn't hang on any longer. We said our good-byes and I closed my eyes, knowing full well that I was going to die and that when you die it's like an electric switch, the end of you. I knew that as certainly as anyone knows anything. I was waiting for the big zero, the big blackout, the one we never wake up from, the end of existence.

"I went unconscious and I don't know how long it lasted. I felt real strange, so I opened my eyes, and to my surprise I was standing up next to the bed looking down at my body in the bed. I tried to communicate with my wife but she was ignoring me. I tried to communicate with another man in the room, but he ignored me.

"Then I heard people outside the room calling my name in English. I went over to the doorway and I asked if they had come to take me for my surgery and they said, hurry up, we've been waiting for you a long time. I had bad feelings about them but I went with them. As I journeyed with this group of people beyond the room, down what would have been the hall, I began to be aware that the hall had no features and was just space, that I was traveling through a very hazy, ill-lit space and they were moving me along and we went for a very long journey—there was no time, it could have been days or weeks—and they became increasingly rude and abusive and hostile and I was becoming increasingly afraid.

"Now we were in darkness over this very long period of time. I said, 'I'm not going with you any further.' They said, 'We're almost there.' They started pushing and shoving me and I fought with them and there were many of them. A wild orgy of frenzied taunting, screaming, and hitting ensued. They had very sharp, hard fingernails. My impression was also that their teeth were longer than normal. I tried to defend myself but with this huge horde of people it was impossible. What they were doing was playing with me, initially scratching and biting, punching and slapping, pushing and taunting, very vulgar.

"Then it got much worse than that. That part's censored. They were playing with me as a cat plays with a mouse. Every new assault brought howls of cacophony. Then at some point, they began to tear off pieces of my flesh. To my horror I realized I was being taken apart and eaten alive, slowly, so that their entertainment would last as long as possible. I want to reiterate that what was happening was extremely real.

"After they had humiliated me to the best of their ability, I was lying on the floor of that place and I had been all kinds of ripped up and broken, outside and inside. I was devastated, having been stripped of any worth. I heard a voice that said, *'Pray to God.'* I thought, I don't believe in God, it's a stupid idea. I heard it a second and third time and I was thinking, what did I say when I was a kid? I was 38 and had probably said my last prayer when I was 15 years old. And in my attempt to remember I muttered a few phrases [of old prayers] and with that the people who were around me became very angry and they were saying to me in obscene language which is unimaginable—nobody has ever spoken like this in this world—in essence, 'There is no God. Nobody can hear you. And if you don't stop we're going to really hurt you.'

"But because the mention of God made them so angry, I tried to remember phrases about God—anything from my childhood. As I did that I was aware it was driving them away from me, as if the mention of God repelled them. It was as if I was throwing boiling oil on them. And eventually I was all alone in that place. My sense was that they were way, way off in the darkness somewhere.

I was left alone there for a time without measure and thought about my life. The bottom-line conclusion was that I had led a bad life. My god was my art career. That's what I worshipped.

"I thought of how cold-hearted and cruel and manipulative I was. I felt where I had ended up was where I belonged, and that the people who had come and picked me up and taken me to this place were people who had lived lives like mine. We were people who hadn't loved God and hadn't loved fellow human beings.

"Now in this place there was nothing left but to tear and gnaw on one another, which was essentially what we had done on earth. I was also aware that this was just the beginning, and that it was going to get worse. Much, much worse. I knew the only way to survive in this place was to be crueler than the people who were around you. There was no kindness, no compassion, no hope.

"I had no hope of seeing the world or getting back to life but I didn't want to be part of their world. I had gone down the sewer pipe of the universe to the cesspool and was still on the top of the cesspool. A memory from my childhood came very vividly of me as a small child sitting in a Sunday school classroom singing 'Jesus loves Me' and the memory was so simple and innocent and pure, believing in something good, and that Jesus cared about me and was good and powerful.

"I didn't believe in Him but I wanted to believe what I had believed as a child.

"So as an act of desperation I called out to the darkness, 'Jesus, please save me.'

"Off in the darkness I saw a pinpoint of light like the faintest star in the sky. I wondered why I hadn't seen it before. The star was getting brighter and brighter. At first I thought it might be some phenomenon like a meteor. Then it dawned on me that it was moving toward me at what apparently was an enormous rate of speed. As it closed in I realized that I was right in its path and I might be run over. But I couldn't take my eyes off it, because emanating from the light was more intensity and more beauty that I had ever seen before in my life. Almost immediately the light was very close. I realized then that while it was indescribably brilliant, it wasn't light at all. It was a living entity, a luminous being approximately eight feet in diameter and oval in shape. Its brilliance and intensity penetrated my body. In a very vivid and beautiful experience I slowly rose up with no effort into the light.

"As I was being picked up I saw all my gore blown away like dust and I was restored physically, and emotionally I was in ecstasy and I knew this person Who had come was Jesus and I knew instantly that He was very intelligent, very strong, and I knew that He was very good, and most importantly I knew that He had loved me more than any concept I had ever had of what love was. If I had taken all my experiences of love and compacted them into a moment, it would have exceeded that.

"And I knew that He knew absolutely everything about me. He knew my thoughts. He knew every moment of my life, even things I didn't remember. And He held me and I cried and cried and cried out of joy and He began to carry me directly straight up, like a helicopter. We started leaving that place.

"Fairly soon we were entering into a world full of light and off to the distance was a great center of brightness.

"The goodness and the love and the holiness were permeating through me, and I thought to myself, I'm a piece of garbage. They've made a terrible mistake, because I don't belong here. I was so ashamed.

"With that we stopped our movement and He spoke to me for the first time and He said, *'You do belong here, and we don't make mistakes.'*"

Part II:

Minister saved from hell claims he was granted a glimpse of angels and the future

When we left off Reverend Howard Storm, a Protestant minister from Ohio, was recounting how, during a brush with death in 1985, he found himself in what he describes as hell. At the time he was an atheist who taught art at North Kentucky University, a cold man who shunned believers and worshipped art as his god.

That changed on June 1, 1985, when his duodenum ruptured while in Paris and after hours of agonizing pain he found himself dead and out of his body [*see previous story*].

After demonic beings attacked him and tried to lead him to hell, Storm, who later entered a seminary, claims he was saved by a light that was Christ, a light that arrived at great speed. "He spoke in a male voice, and when I say He spoke, I could hear His words and voice in my head and it became apparent to me that He knew any thoughts that I had.

"He tried to comfort me and assure me, because a part of me wanted Him to throw me back down into the cesspool [of hell]. I was so ashamed. He was comforting me and said He had people He wanted me to meet. We were in space. There was no ground or features, somewhere between heaven and hell. Some spheres of brilliance came, people who knew me, and after some talk, they had the record of my life, so I've come to identify them as my guardian angels. They said they wanted to show me my life. At first I thought that would be great fun. We started out as a baby and things were pretty neat—seeing my mother and father love me and all that, everybody making a fuss over me."

However, says Reverend Storm, he went astray, losing his faith, entering the world of academia, and closing himself to love.

"As my life developed I saw how I had become more withdrawn and saw how God had done really wonderful things for me, like bring a woman in my life to love me and teach me how to love and how I had misused that love and how eventually God had brought children into my life so I could also learn to love by them and how I missed a lot of that and I saw how God had tried to reach out to me through people and things and how I had just blocked all those attempts by God to change or improve my life.

"I knew that what I was doing in my life had really hurt Jesus, had hurt the angels, and it hurt God, because that's not what I had been created for.

"They loved me but hated what I was doing—the atheism, the blasphemy. Basically I broke all Ten Commandments. I didn't murder anyone, but I certainly murdered people with my heart. And I don't think there's a whole lot of difference.

"From a societal point of view, I was just a regular, normal, healthy American guy leading the good life, which I think is a tremendous indictment on our society.

"When we completed that process the angels asked if I had any questions, and I asked everything I could think to ask. They were extremely good teachers. Historical questions, philosophical questions, religious questions, everything I could think of at the time. When I exhausted everything I could think to ask about, I said, 'I'm ready to go to heaven now.' They said, no, you have to go back to the world because you're not fit to go to heaven. We had a big argument and they tried to gently persuade me that I had to come back to the world and try again.

"When I said I was ready to go back, I was back and immediately when I was back the nurse said the doctor had arrived at the hospital for my surgery. [Previously no surgeon had been available.]"

Thus did Storm's encounter with death—the other side—end. We have to be cautious of all near-death experiences. As I have said many times, they must be discerned like apparitions. Too often, the people having such an experience (and there are millions) put their own spiritual spin on it, and sometimes this can stray into the New Age.

But often the insights remind us of II Corinthians 12:3 (where Paul mentions a man who was caught up into paradise), and contain profound lessons and images. Where does Reverend Storm see the United States heading?

"They made it very clear to me that God had given this country the greatest blessing of any people in the history of the world. We have more of God's blessing. Everything that we have comes from God. We didn't deserve it, we didn't earn it, but we happen to be the wealthiest, most powerful nation in the world. And God gave us all this so that we could be the instruments of God's light in this world, and we are not instruments of light. In other countries people see us as purveyors of exploitation, military might, and pornography. They see us as completely hedonistic and amoral—we have no morality. People can do whatever they want wherever they want with whatever they want. Our amorality is a cancer on the rest of the world, and God created us to be just the opposite.

"People get mad at me for saying it, but God's very unhappy with what we're doing. When I came back from the experience I was almost out of my mind trying to convert people. God wanted a worldwide conversion thousands of years ago. God pulled out all the stops 2,000 years ago with Jesus. From God's view, that was the definitive moment in human history. And the impact of the prophets and teachers and the Messiah has been a big disappointment to God because people have mostly by and large rejected it. And [I was told that] God wants this conversion. And if we don't get on the program fairly soon, God is going to have to intervene in some ways that from a human point of view are going to seem cataclysmic. God's really tired of what we're doing to one another and the planet and to God's Creation. We were put in this world to be stewards and live in harmony with His creation and one another and we don't realize the important spiritual consequences of what we do when we raise a child in a faithless society. And we're doing it all over the world, not just this country."

Was he shown anything specific?

"I asked how [purification] would come about, and they said it would be simple, that our society is very dependent on a lot of very fragile things—energy grid, transportation. In each geographical area of the United States people used to be relatively self-sufficient as far as agricultural products. Now, how long would any state survive without the transport of food and energy?

"What would happen is these very complex and delicate grids of our economic system would begin to break down. We've created a society of such cruel and self-centered people that the very nature of civilization would begin to break down. They (the angels) showed me that what would happen is that people would begin robbing the grocery stores, hording goods, and killing one another for gasoline and tires, and as a consequence everything would break down and would end up in chaos."

We've had scares every year—false alarms. We saw this with Y2K. We saw this recently. But Storm insists that we're not out of the woods, that there will be a purge as God ushers in a new Kingdom during the next 200 years.

How close is that? How close is purification?

"Too close," said Storm. "Way too close. And God doesn't want this to happen. God doesn't want to do it. What God wants is love, hope, faith, and goodness."

Texas woman describes alleged bilocation and glimpse of coming war

By coincidence, we happened to talk to a woman we know and respect, Pat Hull, who works for a Catholic organization, *La Promesa Foundation,* in Midland, Texas, the other day, and she told us of several remarkable experiences. Pat explained in her low-key, forthright way that four times in the last 16 years she has had what mystical theologians call "bilocation"—an alleged experience of being two "places" at once. Obviously, this is a spiritual manifestation (anything is possible in that realm) and two of the times, she said, involved famous mystic Maria Esperanza of Betania, Venezuela. Before Pat ever heard of Maria, she had an experience of suddenly being with and talking to Maria. That was 1985. Years later she met Maria in the flesh. "As soon as I sat down, through the interpreter, Maria threw her head back and said, 'I know you. I've met you before. I know you.' I said, 'Yes, we kind of passed in the night,'" recounts Pat, whose daughter operates a Catholic radio station, KJBC (1150 AM), in Midland.

Pat claims her most recent "bilocation" occurred a month ago. "This was July 12," she told *Spirit Daily*. "That was a Thursday. It started happening about 2 p.m. I was here at work. I didn't know if something physical was happening to me, like a stroke or a heart attack, but then I realized it wasn't that because I knew I was here yet going somewhere else. I don't know how else to explain it. Then [after a while] I recognized what was happening and sat down and got still, and even though I knew I was sitting here at my desk, I entered the room at Maria's at Betania, on her veranda, and we went into this small room—a very small room—and we sat down in chairs face to face and we talked. She doesn't speak English and I don't speak Spanish but we knew what we were saying. She was very tired and weak from all the heaviness and burden she's been carrying. She said that she was really concerned that we must get things together and get things right, and she meant in our hearts, get our souls right—not anything material. And then she said how sad she was because people were not listening and they were not changing. A great blackness of evil was being released. She said it that way. And God has held up His hand as long as He is going to, and He is going to take His hand down and there's nothing, nothing, that will stop this, this disaster, from happening. She didn't tell me what the disaster was. She didn't say any kind of a time. We got through with our visit and I wrote it all down. It was about 3:30 that afternoon. So our visit was between 3 and 3:30. I slowly sifted back. Even Friday [the next day] at noon, I still said to my daughter, I'm not all back yet, and I pointed up. I said, 'From here to over here I feel movement, I hear voices, there are angels, good spirits, they are getting ready for a mighty battle. I hear everything they are saying but I can't tell you what they said. They were rushing around going here and there like an army would getting ready to go in battle. That night, I didn't hear the voices anymore, but I sensed movement and feeling."

Incredibly, Pat told us this was before viewing an article we carried on this website that day about Maria in which her son-in-law related that she was telling her family precisely what Pat had "heard" in bilocation. Pat called us astonished when she read the *Spirit Daily* article.

"Humility drives the devil away"

That's what we hear from a mystic in the mountains of Austria (who we'll be featuring this week). It's one of the greatest weapons. It's something many have forgotten. It's no longer in fashion. But it's as powerful as ever.

Humility drives the devil away because he is the prince of pride and when we have humility he has no hold on our territory.

When we have humility, the devil *flees*.

When we have pride, the opposite happens. When we have pride, we are under the tutelage of Satan. Pride comes in many forms. There's pride over our brains. There's pride over our bodies (as if we created them). There's pride over money—especially over money. There's pride over possessions. There's religious pride. There's a haughtiness that even pervades our places of holiness. It was pride that caused Satan to ascend toward the Throne and pride that got him thrown out of heaven.

Pride is not apologizing. Pride is refusing to forgive. Pride is wanting recognition. Pride is trying to *control*. Pride is believing others are inferior. Pride is believing we deserve more from God than others. Pride is anger when things go wrong. Pride is jealousy. Pride is antagonism. Pride is criticality. Pride is besmirching another. Pride is believing we're above the rules. Pride is seeking after the latest fashion. Pride is materialism.

Humility, on the other hand, is the diminishing of "self" and the absorption into God.

It's recognizing that all we have we were given.

It's seeing others as equal.

It's showing charity.

It's having only good things to say.

It's wanting no more than others.

It's detachment from self, from the world.

And when it's fully accomplished—when it pervades us—it's what the Austrian calls a "golden key" to heaven.

Pope's take on Medjugorje: "I believe, I believe, I believe"

Those are the words John Paul II reportedly used in a hushed tone when an Italian cardinal mentioned the happenings at Medjugorje and if true join a pantheon of such statements attributed to the Holy Father on the monumental apparition site in Bosnia-Hercegovina.

"I spoke with the Holy Father on the 24th of February, 1990," said Bishop Murilo Krieger of Brazil. "I told him I had been to Medjugorje three times and that I was going to return the following week. He said simply: 'Medjugorje is a great center of spirituality!'"

That's according to a booklet, *Medjugorje: What Does the Church Say*. We have heard the same from other bishops. We have talked to men like Bishop Sylvester Treinen and Archbishop Philip Hannan about their own conversations with the Holy Father. And there is no doubt: while bishops and others wrangle over the apparitions, and while the authentication is currently in the hands of a national commission (as well as Vatican observers), the Pope has time and again expressed his strong support for a site that may one day rank with Lourdes—and that has indicated the world is approaching a critical spiritual period.

"Yes, it is good for pilgrims to go to Medjugorje," the Pope told Bishop Treinen on May 14, 1989. "It is good!"

According to a Cardinal Joseph Gray of Scotland, the Pope called for a Marian Year in the 1980s "because of the message of the Mother of God in Medjugorje. I know the Pope himself accepts the apparitions." Indeed, it is reported that the Pope regularly read the monthly messages from seer Marija Pavlovic-Lunetti in a publication called *Echo of Medjugorje*. Earlier this month Marija told us that when she met the Pope in 1982, he said, "If I were not Pope, I would be there hearing Confessions [our emphasis]." The seer noted that many times the Pope says things in a way that uncannily resembles messages from Mary. The same feeling was conveyed to seer Mirjana Dragicevic Soldo, who told us that at a brief private meeting with her the Pope likewise indicated to her his wish to be in Medjugorje.

As the booklet, by a Medjugorje proponent named Denis Nolan, points out, in 1988, Bishop Michael Pfeifer of Texas gathered the same impression from John Paul. "In a private conversation I had with our Holy Father, I asked his opinion about Medjugorje," related the bishop. "The Pope spoke very favorably about the happenings at Medjugorje."

One of the most dramatic quotes attributed to the Holy Father came from a papal advisor who said the Pope told a group of pilgrims heading to Bosnia from the U.S. that "Our Lady of Medjugorje will save America."

According to the *Korean Catholic*, in November 1990, when Archbishop Angelo Kim, president of the Korean Episcopal Conference, thanked the Pope for freeing Poland from Communism, the Holy Father replied, "No, not me, but by the works of the Blessed Virgin, according to her affirmations at Fatima and Medjugorje"!

And according to a Montreal newsletter, the *Message de Paix*, John Paul, when asked if pilgrimages should be permitted, told Archbishop Patrick Flores of San Antonio, "Let them go. . . Sometimes the people follow the bishops. *Sometimes the bishops follow the people.*"

To former Medjugorje Pastor Father Jozo Zovko the Pope said on June 17, 1992, "I give you my blessing. Take courage. I am with you. Tell Medjugorje I am with you. Protect Medjugorje!"

Still, there has been no final Church approval of Medjugorje, nor has there been a rejection. When such an attempt at a negative ruling was made in 1986 by the Bishop of Mostar, it was negated by the Vatican. That itself stood as an indication of the Pope's views.

Could this change? Yes. The Vatican could always decide negatively. There is a long way to go. But so far it has judged Medjugorje on its fruits and has seen it as a site that has created more converts and vocations than any other known situation since World War II.

"Authorize everything that concerns Medjugorje," the Pope told yet another prelate, Archbishop Felipe Santiago Benitez of Asuncion, Paraguay—and indicated his own desire to visit the site during conversations with both bishops and government delegations. "I want to go to Split, to Maria Bistrica, and to Medjugorje," the Pontiff told a delegation from Croatia in 1995. That same year, when asked by the Bishop of Mostar when he was going to visit Sarajevo, the Pope responded, "Oh, I thought you were going to ask me, 'When are you coming to Medjugorje?'" The same was expressed two years later to the president of Croatia—the country neighboring Bosnia-Hercegovina.

And indeed during his historic visit to war-torn Sarajevo the Pope mentioned the "*Kraljice Mira*" ("Queen of Peace," the title Mary uses at Medjugorje), and referred to the pilgrimages that continued there despite the war.

The "warning" or "illumination": will it really happen?

Is an "illumination of conscience" coming? Is a gigantic event that will affect the world—a "warning"—in the making? Are we approaching an event that will convert millions?

These are crucial questions at a time when so many are turning prophetic. Across denominations is the expectation of something tremendous. For Protestants it's a "rapture." For many Catholics it's "the Warning." As the world continues to descend into confusing times, the possibility grows that events will begin to happen—punctuated by an event, catastrophe, or miracle that many believe will cause an "illumination of conscience."

It has nothing to do with the year 2000 but it does have to do with an era like now when there is rampant evil. Some trace the idea of a global event back to a martyr, Saint Edmund Campion, who in the 16th century "pronounced a great day, not wherein any temporal potentate should minister, but wherein the Terrible Judge should reveal all men's consciences and try every man of each kind of religion."

The concept of a huge global event that would open the consciences of men—what some have called a "miniature judgment"—got further currency around the time of the French Revolution. From the end of the 1700s through much of the 1800s—in the wake of severe Christian persecution—seers began to repeat the prophecy of great coming events.

A seer named Elizabeth Canori-Mora had a vision in 1825 in which "a great light appeared upon the earth which was the 'sign of the reconciliation' of God with man." In 1836 Blessed Anna Maria Taigi had a similar vision in which she foresaw that "a great purification will come upon the world preceded by an 'illumination of conscience' in which everyone will see themselves as God sees them."

As pointed out by author Thomas Petrisko, the prophecy has been claimed by many. "I will give them a special light," seers in Heede, Germany, quoted the Lord as saying. "For some this light will be a blessing; for others, darkness. The light will come like the star that showed the way to wise men. Mankind will experience My love and My power."

These prophecies may tie in with signs seen by saints and popes. Saint Faustina envisioned a great luminous cross in the sky, and in the 19th century Pius IX saw something similar. "There will be a great prodigy which will fill the world with awe," he said.

In recent times the idea of something in the sky got a boost from claims at Garabandal, Spain, where alleged seers spoke about what they called "The Warning." When I was writing *The Final Hour* one of the visionaries, Mari-Loli Mazon, told me that she was given the prophecy of an event so powerful that it would seem like "the world is coming to a standstill." Others there spoke of an event that would sear the world. A seer named Conchita Gonzalez saw it as a cosmic event "like two stars. . . that crash and make a lot of noise, and a lot of light. . . but they don't fall. It's not going to hurt us but we're going to see it and, in that moment, we're going to see our consciences."

She said the Virgin announced the event "by a word beginning with 'a'."

It would be visible throughout the world—experienced by believers and non-believers alike—a sort of catastrophe but also miraculous. "The warning is something that is just seen in the air, everywhere in the world, and immediately is transmitted into the interior of our souls," another Garabandal seer, Jacinta Gonzalez, had said. "It will last for a very little time, but it will seem a very long time because of its effects within us. It will be good for our souls, in order to see in ourselves our conscience—the good that we have failed to do, and the bad we have done. Therefore, one should prepare for that day, but not await it with fear. God does not send things for the sake of fear but rather with justice and love."

I have to inform you that the Church has rejected the apparitions at Garabandal, and takes a dim view of several others that proclaim apocalyptic-like events, but the idea has grabbed the Catholic imagination and has been announced by major Catholic media outlets. "The most important thing about that day is that everyone in the whole world will see a sign, a grace, or a punishment within themselves," Conchita told an interviewer way back in 1973. "They will find themselves all alone in the world no matter where they are at the time, alone with their conscience before God. They will then see all their sins and what their sins have caused."

It will be "horrifying" but will not kill unless by sheer fright.

Conchita saw it as something that would be seen and felt but inexplicable to science. It would not physically burn but would sear the conscience. Everyone in the world would see "a sign, a grace, or a punishment within themselves," she said. "No one shall escape it and unbelievers will feel the fear of God."

It reminds us of the light people see during near-death experiences: a light that reveals one's entire life and the good and bad we have accomplished. Could it be that sometime in our lifetimes or in the lifetimes of our children the world will encounter something similar—but this time on a massive scale?

Will, as another alleged mystic, Father Stefano Gobbi, predicted, every person see himself or herself "in the burning fire of divine truth"?

As always, we have to be careful with prophecies. Already there have been dozens that have been wrong. Each year we hear of a seer or locutionist who sets a new time-frame for some kind of great event—only to discourage believers when it doesn't happen.

Moreover, our time is not the same as God's. He does things when He wills. Too many have overemphasized the year 2000.

But I do believe we approach a time in which many events will cause conversion.

At Medjugorje in former Yugoslavia seers have not spoken of any single global event, but they *have* mentioned a *series of events* that will occur on a regional level and serve as warnings (plural) to the world. According to seer Mirjana Dragicevic, three events will be given to the world, and after or as part of the third will come a "great sign" that will prove the supernatural nature of Medjugorje and convert those who do not believe—although they warn that by the time this happens, it will be too late for many who still don't believe.

Most indications from Medjugorje are that God will speak

through natural events. This is similar to Fatima, where a "great sign" ended up being an unprecedented display of the aurora borealis. I wouldn't be surprised if one day mankind gets a tremendous scare and it indeed has to do with something in the sky. But instead of anything overtly supernatural, it could be be a natural event.

In other words: I wonder if an illumination of conscience will come through fear of an asteroid or comet.

I was astonished to learn from the astronomers I interviewed for *Sent To Earth* of the many astronomical threats. There are between 700 and 2,000 potentially hazardous asteroids, objects that could hit the earth, and thousands of others that are a bit farther out and could jump out of their orbits—or that are as yet undiscovered. Just a couple months ago an asteroid passed 18 times the distance to the moon *and wasn't even known until several days before it made its pass.* I'll be writing more on this soon. In 1989 an asteroid missed earth by six hours. And then there was Hale-Bopp, a massive 40-mile-wide comet that was large enough to destroy all life on earth and wasn't known to science until amateur astronomers spotted it!

A high possibility exists, I was told by astrophysicist Dr. Brian Marsden of Harvard, "that in the next five to ten years, given the surveys going on, that we will discover a small object not too far away that in a matter of days is going to come into the atmosphere." Several asteroids are expected to make close passes by the midpoint of this century.

And we can imagine the tension of not knowing where such an object will hit—never mind the tension if it *isn't* so small an object.

We can only imagine what it would be like if a large comet like Hale-Bopp suddenly appeared, and scientists weren't sure it was going to hit or miss.

It would fulfill prophecies of a great light and at the same time of an event that may not physically harm but would be like fire and would cause tremendous soul-searching.

That would certainly cause us to search our consciences—and to return to God as has been so long prophesied.

Image of weeping virgin had been claimed – and ignored – on tree in Manhattan

Maybe Church officials need to take such things more seriously. Maybe they are signs of the times. We're speaking here of a tree: on August 27—just two weeks before the terrorist attack—*The New York Post* reported on a Siberian elm on Arden Street in Manhattan's Inwood section. According to witnesses, a stain on the tree resembled the Virgin Mary *weeping*. "Since last week, when one devout Catholic on the block spotted the Madonna on a common Siberian elm tree, thousands have visited the tree," reported the newspaper.

Candles surrounded it, along with what looked like small flowers and probably petitions. News had spread quickly—only to be dashed by city and Church officials who saw it as a product of overactive imaginations. Parks Commissioner Henry Stern asserted that the face was merely a scar from tree pruning. "And the tears are what's called 'slime flux,' which is seepage of sap from a wound in the bark," he claimed.

Perhaps they're right. But perhaps, in light of September 11, they may want to take a second look. Those who believe it and viewed it felt grace and cried themselves. Charles Nelson, who lives at 80 Arden, said the Madonna was weeping because there was so little love and had told the newspaper it was "a warning."

Laugh, grow strong, and chase away the devil

Laughter chases the devil away. He hates when we laugh because when we laugh we have joy. The devil is the antithesis of laughter. The only snicker he has is when we are in pain. This is the dark side of humor: when we laugh at the misfortunes of others. I'm not talking about that. We're talking about a good, clean, and honest laugh—a laugh that purges tension.

"Laugh and grow strong," said St. Ignatius Loyola.

It really does work. The other night I heard a preacher talk about how the devil tries to emotionally block us up like throwing stones in a well. He does this our whole lives, trying to halt the flow of positive emotions. Laughter is like a geyser that tosses the boulders aside. Laughter lets loose healing. Laughter releases hormones called endorphins that cause us to relax.

True, there's nowhere in Scripture where Christ told a joke. And, true, earth is serious business. We'd never deny that! We're cognizant indeed of the difficulties and dangers on earth, which is a place of trial. No one could accuse us of taking such things lightly.

But we need to have balance. We need to have joy. No matter the difficulty, the bottom line is that we live forever—eternity is a fact—and knowing this should expel all gloomy thoughts.

Want to say an effective prayer? Pray for a better sense of humor. Pray for a smile. Pray to make others laugh. You'll be amazed at how quickly the Holy Spirit will move in this direction, for God has a very cheerful side. His deepest essence is joy. Pray to lift your spirits. Pray to lift the spirits of others.

When we do, the devil flees because with good humor comes the light of heaven.

The Levels of Purgatory

When we die, we will learn that there are many levels to the afterlife. In fact, the levels are probably infinite. Through the ages we have heard from many mystics and seers, as well as those who had had near-death experiences, and they describe the in-between place of purgation or cleansing called purgatory (even those who are not Catholic).

From what we can tell, the lowest level is identical to hellfire, the same level of pain, but there is the knowledge that one will eventually reach heaven. As long as we are not in hell, we are saved. That's because once we die there is no more free will as there is on earth and thus no opportunity to sin. Upon death all souls are given a glimpse of God and after that would never consider offending Him. The soul only longs to see Him again. The greatest torture in purgatory, it is said, is a craving for heaven.

That's the chief suffering in purgatory—the longing to be back in God's presence—but there are others. And at the lowest levels they can be extremely severe. Through the ages revelations have informed us that there is loneliness, anguish, and pain in parts of purgatory that are worse than anything on earth, that a minute at the lowest levels is tougher to take than an entire lifetime of pain. In a word, it is a chamber of grief. Some say there are punishments comparable to extremes of heat or cold. Others are tortured by memories. They relive how they made others feel. They experience the hatred they once directed at others. If they enjoyed filthy things, they find themselves now in a place that is beyond filthy. If they enjoyed pornography, they may now find themselves with searing pain in their eyes. According to the revelations of a 19th-century nun, a soul here is as desperate for help—for a Mass, for a single prayer—as a thirsting man is for water on a desert. It is claimed that as part of their suffering some are not allowed to pray for themselves, and some cannot even benefit from the prayers of others until they are at a higher level.

As I have said, this is probably a place for the worst sinners but sinners who at the last moment, at the final mercy, accepted Christ and narrowly avoided hell. There are other, higher levels, and we will discuss them in a subsequent article. The vast majority of those who have near-death encounters do not see this far into the beyond and as a result often paint a rosier picture of the afterlife, making it seem like everyone goes to heaven. While death is in many ways a delight and heaven is beyond words, first one has to get there, and souls who are still tainted by sin, who have the residue of evil, willingly go to the cleansing of purgatory because having now seen heaven they may long for nothing else but wouldn't want to go there immediately any more than a person with muddy boots and ripped jeans would go to a wedding.

When we have taint, when we are dirty, we *want* to purify, and for reasons we will not understand until we're on the "other side," suffering, whether on earth or in purgatory, facilitates that purification. When we suffer well on earth, offering it up, we shorten our purgatory. Indulgences well said in a life well lived can also help, and Confession is crucial; once we have confessed our sins and asked for forgiveness, we are absolved; we are "saved." But we may still have to purify. There may still be expiation. We may have to remove the soil of the evil that we brushed against.

Purgatory is suffering. There's no getting around that, and I won't soften it. I am here to report the truth as best I can discern it. And that truth doesn't scare me, nor does it depress me. It excites me to action. It excites me knowing that while we are still on earth we have a chance at avoiding these sufferings. We have a chance at avoiding the worst of purgatory as long as we pray and as long as we love. We have a chance as long as we purify here and now.

Seer suggests intercession of deceased priest be studied

One of the most joyous times we've had recently was sitting around talking with Medjugorje seer Marija Pavlovic-Lunetti. She's the one who gets the monthly message to the world, and she is just filled with vigor and joy: a warm person who sets an example of both prayer and humility.

During a talk in Sacramento in September, Marija told the crowd that there should be a group studying all the claims of miracles being attributed to Father Slavko Barbaric—the holy priest who served at the parish since 1983 and died unexpectedly just over a year ago (November 24, 2000) on Mount Krizevac. The priest succumbed at 3:30 pm, after finishing the Way of the Cross. There is a memorial to him there, and now pilgrims also gather at his grave, where pilgrims feel grace when they invoke his help. Marija indicated that there are many cases of his intercession.

From time to time we also hear of such claims. Within two weeks of his death, there was the account of an American who was scheduled for knee surgery but suddenly was able to walk without a cane after Father Slavko was invoked to help. Others have been aided in emotional or spiritual struggles. A few weeks ago a woman from England claimed to have seen a priest fitting Father Slavko's description behind St. James Church (although we were unable to confirm this), and there are other reports of healings, both physical and spiritual. The day after his death, the Virgin, in her monthly message, told Marija, "*I rejoice with you and I desire to tell you that your brother Slavko has been born into Heaven and intercedes for you*"—lending credence to reports of his intervention. Already a statue of Father Slavko has been installed at a home for orphans founded by the priest.

According to a website called "Children of Medjugorje," last summer a pilgrim ran into a priest whom she later identified as Father Slavko on Apparition Hill. She claimed she told the priest her problems and received a blessing from him in Spanish. "He looked at me, and put his hand on my head," said the account. "He told me to go and seek Confession with a priest, a sacramental Confession." Later, the woman saw a small photo of Father Slavko and in that way identified him [*see this account*].

We talked to Marija about a number of things. Ironically, one subject was how we are supposed to view other religions, which led to a discussion of Muslims just a couple days before September 11. There is one God for all, emphasized Marija, citing the instance of a Muslim boy who was healed by the Virgin at Medjugorje. On other matters, she said that the seers are "forbidden" to discuss the secrets with each other; that during an apparition everything disappears except the Virgin; and that when an apparition is over—when Marija "returns"—it's hard to look even at people around her after seeing the beauty of heaven!

She deferred a question to another seer when asked if the chastisements can be lessened.

Marija also said she has visited historic shrines like Lourdes, Zaragoza, and Fatima where the Virgin has also appeared. At Zaragoza (a site in northern Spain where Mary appeared to the apostle James), the priest mentioned Medjugorje during his homily. "I felt like putting up my jacket and covering my face to partly conceal it," she said, laughing.

On the way to Zaragoza, after a visit to Avila, Marija said she had the car stop when it was time for her daily apparition. They found a spot and Marija noted that the Virgin did not stay long and that no one else was wasting much time either. Unknowingly they had wandered into the middle of a bull pen!

Interesting was Marija's impression that the Pope may have some form of mysterious communication with the Virgin. As she pointed out, John Paul II often seems to say the same thing that is said at Medjugorje by the Virgin—and often either the day after it's said, or the day before. She recalled meeting him in 1982, when he said, "If I were not Pope, I would be there (Medjugorje) *hearing Confession*."

National Catholic broadcaster relates miracle with Maria Esperanza

A former CBS radio broadcaster who now airs a national Catholic show was eyewitness to a miracle with famed mystic Maria Esperanza that is truly hard to fathom.

John Marion, once a newscaster in Boston and Philadelphia and now host of the spiritual show *Nightflight* with wife Barbaranne, says that on August 15, 1995, he was at the Church-approved apparition site of Betania, Venezuela, when what can only be described as an inconceivable event occurred.

As has happened with saints at rare times in history, an actual flower—a rose—came out of Maria's chest, says John and other witnesses contacted by *Spirit Daily*.

It's something said to have occurred with Maria on 15 occasions, as if to represent the Rosary. That they are roses may also be connected with her lifelong devotion to St. Therese the Little Flower. The phenomena first began on January 18, 1986, and while many believe they are at an end, that 1995 was the last, no one—including Maria—is sure. "We could never know for sure if it's the last one," Maria told us. "Only God knows. Maybe Our Lord is being more gentle with me. Whenever I remember the pain, it makes me feel very scared."

Those who have observed say it looks like she is having the palpitations of a heart attack or giving birth. The rose opens as in slow-motion photography with little sparkles of water, according to a son-in-law who was also there in 1995.

Among those who have also seen the phenomenon are Carolina Fuenmayor, a television newswoman for Venevision in Caracas at the time; many of Maria's relatives; and at least two Latin American medical doctors, Dr. Chebly and Dr. Alfonso Gutierrez Burgos. Fuenmayor shot a videotape of one of the events but at Maria's insistence will not release it until the seer's death.

The idea of a rose coming from someone's body stretches the most open of minds, but John Marion—who himself is now known for charismatic gifts—says there is no doubt about it, and both the current bishop of the diocese and his predecessor have lent formal approval to Betania and have expressed deep respect for Esperanza, who many believe is the greatest mystic since Padre Pio (whom she knew).

Her mysticism is especially pertinent at this time of the year because December 8 is the anniversary of another event that involved Betania—a miracle in which a Communion Host began to bleed in 1991 while handled by a priest, Father Otty Ossa Aristizabal, during Mass at the site of apparitions.

But let's focus here on the rose, which is perhaps the most remarkable single phenomenon claimed by a mystic in decades.

"My travel agent and I were down there on business, a hot summer night, and it was close to one o'clock in the morning," says Marion, one of the elder statesmen of both the charismatic and Marian movements. "We were seated in the compound area at the shrine site. We were wondering why Maria had kept us waiting so long. We had been waiting four to five hours. During that period a group of American pilgrims had also arrived wanting to see Maria. While we were waiting there we hear a cry from Maria's son-in-law. 'John, John, hurry! Come over here!' What they had done was set a chair in the compound area for Maria and helped by some family members, they placed her in the chair. They told me to keep looking. I couldn't imagine what would happen. She was experiencing some kind of pain. She was very uncomfortable in the chair.

"*All of a sudden Maria sort of parted the blouse she was wearing and a red spot began to appear.* I stared. It kept getting bigger and bigger and Maria was really in pain. Then this red spot began to take a shape and I recognized the shape as that of a rose—a deep red rose, first budlike as she continued to force it out right through her body, causing great pain—until finally it was through and fully in bloom. There was this big red beautiful rose.

"I couldn't believe it. I turned to my agent in amazement. He said, 'I know, I know. I see it!' After the rose cleared Maria's body, you could see this stem, about two inches of stem, and Maria broke it off, then she handed a petal first to a priest, three nuns, and then she called me over and gave me a piece.

"The next day I was told she passed the rest of the stem, with thorns on it. It was like she was giving birth—the same expression and same kind of pain and couldn't wait to get it out, then she held it lovingly in her hands. If you went into a florist shop for a single long-stemmed red rose in full bloom, that was what it looked like. It was absolutely beautiful and I couldn't believe my eyes—it was such a phenomenon."

What does Medjugorje say about the "antichrist"?

Back last summer, when we were visiting Medjugorje, I sat down with seer Mirjana Dragicevic Soldo and told her that once, years before, I had asked another seer, Vicka Ivankovic, if any of her secrets involved the Second Coming, the end of the world, or the anti-christ. I told her I knew that she couldn't tell me what was in her secrets, but that maybe she could tell me what was *not* in her secrets.

That was in 1997. Vicka had smiled that unforgettable smile and to my surprise deigned to answer. She told me she could categorically state that none of the above were in any of the nine secrets she has been given by the Virgin Mary.

I explained this to Mirjana, and asked her what *she* thought of Vicka's response. I wanted to know if Mirjana could answer the same question. Was the anti-christ, the Second Coming, or anything quite so apocalyptical in *her* secrets?

Mirjana is a wonderful and candid person but this she did not choose to answer. "I cannot give a comment," she said, speaking English with a Croatian syntax. "We don't know if we have the same secrets or different secrets. We feel we cannot talk about this. I don't know what Vicka told you, but I cannot say the same like her. I will be quiet."

The bottom line is that there has never been an indication that apocalyptic developments such as the anti-christ are in any Medjugorje seer's secrets, and this is important because Medjugorje may well be the most powerful apparition since Fatima. At the same time there has never been a dismissal of apocalyptical notions.

I bring this up because we've been quoting an alleged prophecy from 1990 from a source we have kept anonymous, a prophecy that allegedly came from the Lord in a dream on December 3, 1990, and has been startlingly accurate in certain aspects. For example, it seemed to uncannily foresee the development of cloning (referring to it as a great new evil), and it was right-on in describing how the first events, the first wave of chastisements (there will be others), would come as regional disasters. It forecast the breaking down of synthetic modern life. It said the world would not end but claimed that many of the inventions and constructs of man would be disassembled. The prophecy claimed that we are at the end of an era. What comes after will not be a barren world, it said, nor one depopulated, but the end of the technological era. There will be more a pleasant atmosphere.

That we can begin to digest, but then there was this:

"After this breakdown of false society will come persecution of Christians and also a new world order," said the 1990 prophecy. "Let me say that the anti-christ will start to rise only after the great evil. He will have tremendous influence—a man of influence, not actual raw political power. Hardly anyone will notice the extent of his influence until afterwards. He will not be of tremendous visibility until he is accomplished. That is to say, he will not rule, control, and be at all obvious to the world at the peak of his influence. He will not be unlike a figure such as Marx, except his ideas will be more immediate."

These are weighty words. They are to be mulled over. They are to be discerned. *Tremendous influence*—instead of raw power. Many are looking for a government leader to be the anti-christ, or *an* anti-christ—but perhaps, if indeed this is true, it will be more secretive. Perhaps it will be more subtle. Perhaps it will be more on a spiritual level.

We don't know. Your discernment is as good as ours. Will the anti-christ or at least a form of anti-christ come in our time—or is he something in the far-off future?

So far, no Church-approved apparition specifies the anti-christ, and so we have to be very careful. But some apparitions that have been sanctioned by the hierarchy (including occurrences at Kibeho, Africa), have had aspects that veered strongly in an apocalyptical direction. Also, we note that a mystic from Massachusetts who appears to have foreseen elements of the September 11 events had also mentioned the anti-christ—and had also used the verb "accomplished."

But that prophecy saw the anti-christ in the Middle East; the 1990 prophecy, on the other hand, said, "As for the anti-christ, remember Europe, and especially Central Europe."

Shock of recent events raises questions about first secrets of Medjugorje.

The questions are constant: Are the recent events—terrorism, war—part of the Medjugorje secrets? Are they what was foretold to those kids who claim to see the Virgin? And most importantly, do they foretell the coming of something larger?

These are logical questions. After all, one of the seers, Mirjana Dragicevic Soldo, has long indicated that the first secret she was given by the Virgin Mary is a regional event that will come as a warning to the world. She has hinted it's a disaster that will occur at a particular place but resonate everywhere—something that people will "hear about very far" away—and she once compared it to a dam collapsing in Italy. Since at least 1985 she has described the event in her first secret as some sort of a "suffering" or a "disaster."

These are words she used.

"It won't be good at all," Mirjana once told a priest. "It won't be pleasant."

If the people saw the first secret, said the seer, "all of them would most certainly be shaken enough to take a new and different look at themselves and everything around them."

She added that the event or events in her first secret will be "distinct" and "necessary in order to shake up the world a little. It will make the world pause and think."

In many ways, of course, that sounds like what happened in New York: The bombing of lower Manhattan was a regional event; it was decidedly "unpleasant"; there was great suffering; and it shook the world. It made everyone pause and think; it was on a scale similar to a dam collapsing.

But there is no indication that September 11 was part of any Medjugorje secret, and indeed, it can *not* be one of Mirjana's. She has made clear that she will give her first secret to a priest ten days before it happens, and that he will then publicly reveal it after prayer and fasting.

No such announcement came from Medjugorje prior to September 11, and indeed I was with another seer, Marija Pavlovic

Lunetti, less than 40 hours before the World Trade Center disaster. She gave no hint that anything related to her secrets was imminent.

This raises another question: Are the secrets of Medjugorje—even the initial warnings—of a *larger* magnitude than what we saw September 11?

That's impossible for us to know. There's certainly that chance, although there is also a chance that the initial ones are smaller. Let's remember that it's not just the size of the event that makes the event in Mirjana's first secret so special but also the fact that it will be announced beforehand. It will confirm the apparitions of Medjugorje because it will be predicted.

There is little doubt, however, that the events in the latter secrets, especially the ninth and tenth, are larger. Despite recent attempts at downplaying them, they have been described since 1983 as major chastisements "for the sins of the world." *These* events are almost certainly larger than anything we have seen thus far, and in all likelihood much larger. They will bring about a purification that in the end will be beautiful. They are nothing to fear. They are only to be prayed about, and their very existence should be a stimulus to our conversion.

Everything sent by God has a goodness that we may not understand except in retrospect.

"Something like a catastrophe?" Mirjana was asked in 1985 about her first secret.

"No," she claimed, "it will not be anything as huge as that. That will come later."

When asked if people would flock to where the first event occurs, the seer said, "Surely no one wishes to watch disasters, distress, and misfortune. I don't think that this kind of thing attracts people at all. Why would people go to see something of that sort? It is one thing to go and see a sign, quite another to go and see suffering or a disaster. Who would, for example, go to Italy to see a dam collapse? I don't think anyone does—and that is how it will be with this secret. Whatever is in the secret, it will, of course, be something that everyone, everywhere, will immediately hear about."

Intriguingly, when further asked about the first secret in 1985, Mirjana reportedly replied: "It is the upheaval of a region of the world."

How the Archangel Michael intervened in the case behind 'The Exorcist'

Although the famous movie and the popular media didn't describe it, the famous case behind *The Exorcist* was finally won when a statue of the Archangel Michael was placed next to the bed of the possessed boy (in real life it was a male named Rob) and pleas were made for the great angel to take the case before the throne of God.

While in the movie evil seems to win, terrorizing an exorcist, in real life the priests were plenty awed but stuck it out and with the intervention of Michael—the great nemesis of Satan (*Revelation* 12:7)—freed the boy from the horrid grip of full-blown satanic possession.

This was not a standard demonic infestation. It was the highest order of possession and was traced back to the boy's aunt, a spiritualist who had introduced him to the Ouija board, the "game" in which people try to communicate with the dead (but in actuality are often talking to demons.)

Whatever was at the root, it began during the winter of 1949 in a Washington, D.C. suburb called Cottage City when strange noises, including a scratching in the wall, joined a shaking of the wall behind a picture of Jesus. Soon the boy's bed was shaking and there were other strange furniture movements, eerie cold spots, and the inexplicable tossing about of objects.

At the first the boy's family took the matter to a minister at St. Stephen's Evangelical Lutheran Church in Washington, but when the minister sensed an actual diabolical presence he recommended that the parents seek help in the Catholic Church, which had formal procedures for exorcism.

After initial attempts at delivering the boy at Georgetown University Hospital (where, indeed, the case seemed too much for a young priest), the matter shifted to St. Louis, where a priest named William S. Bowdern from St. Francis Xavier Church headed a team that watched aghast as bloody red marks materialized on the boy—marks that spelled words like "hell"—and a vial of holy water flew and hit a dresser.

At one point a crucifix with relics moved from under the boy's pillow to the foot of the bed and a relic of Saint Margaret Mary, the mystic who saw the Sacred Heart of Jesus, vanished.

There was spitting. There was "fiendish" laughter. There was a guttural voice that spoke with great hate from the beleaguered 13-year-old boy.

After weeks attempting to free him, the priests decided to baptize the boy, and on the way Rob struggled madly to take control of the steering wheel and crash the car.

It was a clear indication of how the sacraments were hated by forces of evil. Finally Rob was baptized, but the next day, when the priests tried to give him holy Communion, the boy refused it, spitting it out for two hours—until a Rosary was said.

The exorcism took six weeks to accomplish, and the climax came at the Alexian Brothers Hospital in St. Louis. There on Holy Thursday a small statue of Michael was placed on a bed stand next to the boy, and the following Monday—Easter Monday—as the priest prayed for the angel's intervention—as prayer intensified, with near desperation—the boy's voice suddenly changed into a clear, commanding, and dignified voice from heaven. *"Satan, I am St. Michael,"* said the voice that now came from the boy, *"and I command you Satan to leave the body in the name of Dominus [the Lord]. Now. Now. Now!"*

At that precise moment what sounded like a loud gunshot was heard throughout the hospital. The boy sat up, had a vision of the archangel, and announced with near befuddlement but certainly terrific relief that the evil force was "gone."

At the same time, priests at St. Francis Xavier Church saw a light illuminate the sanctuary from the dome high over the altar and in the light a vision of Michael.

Removal of St. Michael prayer came as Church encountered "smoke" of satan

It has to be considered a mistake. It has left the Church without a vital safeguard. Someday, it may well be aligned with great smoke that rose in the sanctuary.

We speak here of the *Prayer to the Archangel Michael.* It's a prayer that was devised by Pope Leo XIII after some sort of mystical experience in which the pontiff was given to understand that Satan was in a special period of aggression. It was then that the prayer was devised, and in 1886 Leo XIII ordered it said at the conclusion of Mass, which was done until the fateful 1960s—when a torrent of evil suddenly poured into the world. In 1964, in the first wave of post-Vatican II changes—in what was known as the *Instructio Prima*—this magnificent and potent invocation to the archangel who threw Lucifer from heaven was removed from low Mass in the Catholic Church along with a reading of a last Gospel.

Since that time, what have we seen? Priests who have left the priesthood. Pews that emptied. And now, scandal. Across society, Christianity and particularly the Catholic segment has become the focus of disdain in a culture that opened itself to infernal legions. Removal of the prayer—along with the near-elimination of exorcism—allowed an influx of evil. In 1972, speaking in the aftermath of Vatican II, Pope Paul VI himself said "the smoke of Satan has entered by some crack into the temple of God."

It was in 1964 that the new standard was directed, and in 1968 that the new liturgy, minus the prayer, was authorized.

What happened in that specific period?

Our youth strayed. The choir was replaced by rock bands. Priests were made to feel outcasts. There were even songs dedicated to the devil. Television replaced the majesty of religion. Free sex. Drugs. Abortion. Instead of public prayer there was now public profanity. In the same chronological window that saw elimination of the Michael prayer, the first Church of Satan rose (1966) in the U.S. and the satanic Bible three years later.

It was against such things that the prayer was potent, as was the practice of deliverance, something Jesus had commanded. Most of the exorcisms were taken out of baptismal rites, and the Church eliminated the minor order of "exorcist" (which young men traveled on the way to priesthood). Exorcism became rare at the same time that the devil became pervasive.

Our current Pope is trying to stem this tide, and on at least two occasions, in 1982 and on September 7, 2000, personally conducted exorcisms. He was accompanied by Father Gabriel Amorth, the official exorcist of Rome, who says:

"I believe that it was a mistake to have eliminated, without a suitable replacement, the prayer to Saint Michael the Archangel that we used to recite after every Mass. I am convinced that allowing the ministry of exorcism to die is an unforgivable deficiency to be laid squarely at the door of bishops. Every diocese should have at least one exorcist at the cathedral, and every large parish and sanctuary should have one as well. Today the exorcist is seen as a rarity, almost impossible to find. His activity, on the other hand, has an indispensable pastoral value, as valuable as that of the preacher, the confessor, and those who administer the other sacraments. The Catholic hierarchy must say a forceful *mea culpa*. I am personally acquainted with many Italian bishops; I know of only a few who have ever practiced or who have assisted during an exorcism or who are adequately aware of this problem."

It's time to bring Michael back. Evil can not *stand* in his presence. The situation is growing severe—as we saw on September 11 when the very smoke from the World Trade Center formed demonic images.

Describing what it's like to see Mary, seer tells of transport to another dimension

When we visited with seer Mirjana Dragicevic Soldo at Medjugorje last month, she gave many insights into what it's like to see the Virgin Mary: how it is to be transported out of our time and space to a place where an indescribable woman stands in a splendor that's transcendental.

It is not our dimension. As it says in Scripture, the sanctuary of God in heaven opens. There are flashes of light. She is the great sign adorned with the sun. When she comes, says Mirjana, everything disappears. All that's left is a surrounding of blue. Although Mirjana has been seeing Mary since 1981, she says she could never treat it casually. "I could see her a hundred years, but I would always recognize that she is the Mother of God," says Mirjana, who spends a day of fasting and night of prayer before her apparitions and then takes several hours afterwards to recover.

Being transported from our reality to a place that's heavenly and then returned to earth after a few minutes of an apparition is excruciating. When Mary is there, says Mirjana, even her family disappears. If it were not for them, she would not want to return to physical existence.

It becomes obvious in talking to this astute, well-spoken seer that the power of an apparition is more than most realize. Mirjana, who now receives an apparition once a month (her daily ones stopped in 1983), says that when she is about to see Mary a tremendous feeling wells up inside. "I think, if she doesn't come in a second," says Mirjana, indicating a feeling of bursting, "I'll die!"

There are a lot of misconceptions about seers. People tend to think the Virgin directs their every move when in fact the seers ask few if any questions during the apparitions. They are too in awe. They are in the presence of a woman who has been given an extremely high place in heaven. They are left alone to decide many things. Mirjana says she has to pray like anyone to understand many of the messages.

"A visionary is not special," the seer emphasizes. "We can make mistakes like all of you."

Back in the early days of the apparitions the Communists would often follow, detain, and threaten the seers (Mirjana was once shown a mental hospital, as well as a morgue), and yet on one such especially tense occasion, when Mary next appeared, she said nothing about what had happened that day. "At the beginning it was very different. I never knew if I would be alive tomorrow. They were coming every day in my home and taking me and returning me at about one or two in the morning. When they sent me home I would have an apparition but Blessed Mother didn't say anything about this. She would give me a message and then leave. I would think, 'She doesn't know what's happening with me? How is it that she isn't saying anything?'"

There are thus limits to the communication. Seers face trials like everyone.

How do the rest of us communicate with Mary? How does she respond to prayer?

According to Mirjana, it's fine to write petitions, but before we even ask, the Virgin, who is an emissary for her Son, realizes our needs. "Blessed Mary reads our hearts and knows all these things that we want," says Mirjana. "If you pray, she is reading your hearts and knows all these things."

Mirjana says that an image of Mary hanging in her basement [see below] has the closest feeling of the Virgin, although it is not a replica by any means. "This was made by an Italian, and Father Slavko [Barbaric, a deceased priest in the local parish] gave it to me," says Mirjana. "I like it because Blessed Mary is not like this, but this painting has something, maybe in the face, or how she is taking her hands, or how she is looking. In this painting I have something from Blessed Mary."

Mirjana also likes the Shroud of Turin.

And she says she has been told parts of the Virgin's life story.

"She gave it to Vicka [Ivankovic] and myself," says Mirjana. "I have small things. I need to receive more."

Were there things that surprised her? she was asked.

"There were so many surprises, so many things. But when she will tell me, I will give it to everybody—not like a book, because it is not a book, but like a script of her life. It will be revealed generally."

In unreleased interview:

Medjugorje seer hints that first secret is not spectacular global event but will be "severe" regional event

by Michael H. Brown

Visionary Mirjana Dragicevic Soldo from the famous Medjugorje site of apparitions in Bosnia-Hercegovina indicated in a previously undisclosed interview that the first of ten secret prophecies she was given by the Virgin Mary involves not a global miracle but a "severe" regional event.

In an interview conducted by a priest a day after a vision in which she was shown the first secret, Mirjana, the first seer to obtain all ten secrets, said the first occurrence "will be something that [people] hear [about] very far" and added that people would not race to the place where the first one occurs because "surely no one wishes to watch disasters, distress, and misfortune. I don't think that this sort of thing attracts people at all. Why would people go to see something of that sort? It is one thing to go and see a sign, quite another to go and see suffering or a disaster. Who would, for example, go to Italy to see a dam collapse?" She said the first secret needs nothing to precede it and will "abundantly speak for itself." She said that people in Medjugorje "will know immediately that it is in connection with the secrets." It will be something, she said, "that everyone, everywhere, will immediately hear about."

Although the Virgin has instructed the seers not to become obsessed with the secrets (and in recent years they have assiduously declined further comment, turning away discussions of the secrets and instead emphasizing the joy with which the Blessed Mother often appears), at the same time she has expressed the need to warn the world and during certain apparitions the seers have shown great anguish. "[Our Blessed Mother] told me that it is necessary to pray a great deal until the first secret is revealed," Mirjana said. "But in addition to that it is necessary to make sacrifices as much as possible, to help others as much as it is within our abilities, to fast—especially now before the first secret. She stated that we are obliged to prepare ourselves. She not only asks but pleads with everyone to convert, to pray, to fast. They have no idea what awaits them, and that is why, as their Mother, she is in deep anguish for them. It is not enough to just simply pray. It is not enough to just quickly say some prayers so that one can say that they prayed and did their duty. What she wants from us is to pray from the depths of our souls, to converse with God. That is her message."

Although her first secret does not appear to involve a global event (nor a single massive warning), there is little doubt that what she has been told is serious. During a vision on October 25, 1985, Mirjana, whose daily apparitions ceased in 1982 (but proceed now on certain occasions), said she was shown the first secret like pictures projected on slides and that it "shook me the most. That was, of course, due to seeing the first secret. If the people saw the first secret, as it was shown to me yesterday, all of them would most certainly be shaken enough to take a new and different look at themselves and everything around them. I now know things that are not particularly pleasant. I believe that if everyone knew about these same things, each one of these people would be shocked to their senses and would view our world in a completely different light."

"The manifestation of that secret, will it only be a momentary thing or will it be something that will last for an extended period?" she was asked by the priest.

"It will last for a little while," replied Mirjana in the interview.

"Will its effects be lasting and permanent or will its effect be momentary and passing?"

"How can I explain that without encroaching on the secret?" said Mirjana. "Let me just say that it won't be good at all. It won't be pleasant."

"Will the interval between the first and second secret be lengthy?" she was asked.

"That varies according to the secrets," answered Mirjana. "What I mean is that, for example, the time between the first and second secret is of a certain period, between the second and third is of different length. For example, and I stress, the first secret may take place today and the second one already tomorrow."

"Are they perhaps of a notable character or more of a spiritual nature?"

"Distinct, distinct. It will be visible; it is necessary in order to shake up the world a little. It will make the world pause and think."

"Something like a catastrophe?"

"No, it will not be anything as huge as that. That will come later. It will be something that will give the world something to think about seriously, allow it to see that she was, indeed, here, to see and realize that there is a God, that He exists."

"And after that, will there be anyone who will say, 'This is some sort of a natural phenomenon' or something along those lines?" asked the priest.

"Perhaps some staunch unbelievers might say something like that after the first and second," replied Mirjana in the biggest hints to date about her secrets.

She said her prophecies involve what the Blessed Mother herself described as *"many horrors"* and that some of the later secrets are "*really* unpleasant" [Mirjana's emphasis]. The seer said the apparitions have been a preparation. "Just as any mother, she cares for her children," said Mirjana of the Blessed Virgin. "She wants us to come and meet God the Father well prepared. She doesn't want us to weep and wail when it's too late. God said that He forgives at any time—providing the soul repents sincerely. All she asks for, the one thing she waits for, is for all of us to repent so that we may be forgiven. What follows are the secrets which are really unpleasant. I would be happy if everyone would finally understand that. I cannot tell them (much more), but once they begin to be fulfilled, then it will be too late."

No times or dates have been indicated from the seers. Mirjana said she will reveal the first secret to a priest she chose, Father Petar Ljubicic, who appeared to be the one conducting the 1985 interview, ten days before it occurs, and he may then reveal it to the public, which would prove it is part of the secrets.

Although at points it's not always clear from a translation of the interview, conducted in Croatian, which of the first three secrets the visionary is referring to, Mirjana has indicated that there will be three warnings given to mankind along with a great sign. Mirjana declined to say if the event or events in the first secret will occur at Medjugorje itself but said it would be convincing or witnessed by "all those who will be here [Medjugorje] or in the place(s) where the secret will unfold."

It is thus unclear whether the first event will involve just one locality or a number, although, again, it does not appear to be global.

The only certainty, said Mirjana, is that the world has taken a turn to evil and the first secret is needed wake it up. "It will make the world pause and think," said Mirjana in this interview, which I obtained during the writing of The Final Hour but which has not been previously released in this detail. "There never was an age such as this one, never before was God honored and respected less than now, never before have so few prayed to Him. Everything seems to be more important than God. This is the reason she cries so much. The number of unbelievers is becoming greater and greater. As they endeavor for a better life, to such people, God Himself is superfluous and dispensable. This is why I feel deeply sorry for them and for the world. They have no idea what awaits them. If they could only take a tiny peek at these secrets, if they could see—they would convert in time. Still, Gospa [Our Lady] gave us God's ten secrets. They may still convert. Certainly God always forgives all those who genuinely convert."

"Something like a catastrophe?" asked Ljubicic another time.

"No," replied Mirjana, "it will not be anything as huge as that. That will come later. These first two secrets are not all that severe and harsh. What I mean is, yes, they are severe, but not as much as the remaining ones."

Mirjana, who has been discreet about the secrets and has even downplayed them in public appearances (criticizing those who have put forth spectacular prophecies), nonetheless said the secrets are such that she was sometimes "distressed" to the point of "weeping."

"First and foremost, it is necessary to pray much," she emphasized. "Many people ask me to pray for them. That's fine, but some think that my prayers are better than their own. But to God all sincere prayers are good. Still, when I promise that I will pray, then I must. Most of all I now pray that people will convert, particularly in view of the secrets."

Mirjana said she must be in Medjugorje when the first secrets begin to unfold. She said she does not know if large numbers will come to the village as the secrets begin to unfold, but that there will be conversions.

"I was never really acquainted with such serious matters," said Mirjana, referring again to the secrets. "I couldn't even believe that Mary could come to this world in such a way, never mind being able to grasp the first thing about such great secrets and especially not that these would be entrusted to me. She explained everything to us and gave us perfect instructions. She gave us some sort of power, I mean special strength which actually restrains us from telling [anyone what the secrets are]. I was in a situation many times where I came close to disclosing a secret, but then, suddenly, something flashes through my head. It is then that I sober up and ask myself, 'What am I doing, what is the matter with me?' The fact is, we are incapable of divulging the secrets."

Leading up to the first secret, mankind must work at eliminating greed and disrespect for God, warned Mirjana. The seer singled out Sarajevo, where a vicious war was focused shortly after her comments. She mentioned the sin of cursing by using God's name. She said she does not know if her secrets are the same as those to the other five visionaries, except for the third secret of a great sign that will appear. A miracle is necessary, said Mirjana, for the godlessness to stop. It is now especially urgent, she said, to convert the young.

"She especially mentioned the need to pray for one's own soul," said the seer. "There are many people who think: 'I am good. I don't need to pray for myself.' No one knows how good or bad he or she is. God will judge that."

Mirjana and other seers from Medjugorje (which has not been officially sanctioned by the Church) have said they would at least live to see the first several secrets. (They are currently in their thirties and the priest to whom Mirjana will confide her secret is believed to be in his fifties.) She said her secrets are on a substance like paper that was given to her by the Virgin. "Actually this is not paper but some sort of unusual material," said Mirjana. "She gave me instructions how to handle it and what to do with it. She also told me to choose a priest [who will receive the paper], because the day is approaching when I will have to give this paper to the priest, on time. I will have to give it to him ten days in advance, so that he too will have enough time to prepare himself for this. She will give him the grace to be able to see the first secret. You see, if anyone else were to look at this paper they would see something entirely different on it. But he will receive her grace which will enable him to read the first secret. Once he reads the first secret, he will have to make its contents public [if he so discerns after prayer and fasting] and afterwards he may do with it whatever he thinks is necessary."

Seer recounts meeting with Pope and says secrets can't be changed

by Michael H. Brown

She was one of the first to see the Virgin. She is an intelligent, humorous, and sophisticated seer—perhaps the most urbane of the Medjugorje visionaries—and has also been one of the most hidden. But as Mirjana Dragicevic Soldo rises to the forefront—as she meets more and more pilgrims, as her mission to the public has grown in recent times—it is also apparent that this talented and gracious woman has a mission of tremendous gravity. She has been given among the weightiest "secrets." Indeed, indications are that all of her secrets pertain to the world or the Church (as opposed to some seers whose secrets may include many matters that are personal), and she told me last week that none of her secrets have changed or been lessened. Where in the 1980s it was announced that part of the seventh (at some point it was said the eighth) had been mitigated due to fasting and prayer, she told me that since that time neither the dates of the secrets nor the extent of her secrets have been altered, including the last two, which she has always described as serious.

"Once Blessed Mary spoke to me and said, 'Yes, this part of the secret is changed, but I can not ask any time more for the secrets,'" said Mirjana. "[The Virgin said] 'the secrets are secrets and they must happen as they are.' She only said it is not possible to change the secrets more."

Mirjana, who knows the dates of each secret, says those deadlines have not been altered in any way.

But it is Mirjana's view that the world has somewhat improved since 1981. Emphasizing that this is her own opinion (not anything the Virgin told her), she said she believes such is true because there are more prayer groups. But she leaves no doubt that it is a "time of decision."

In coming days we'll have more on what Mirjana said—especially her spiritual advice. She has important words of encouragement. And she always emphasizes that there should not be a focus on the secrets—but on the message of prayer, fasting, conversion, peace, and love.

We watched her during a monthly apparition on July 2. (Where three of the six seers at Medjugorje in Bosnia-Hercegovina still receive daily visits from Mary, Mirjana's daily experiences stopped in 1983 and now she receives them on a monthly basis.) The apparition began at about 9:39 a.m. Croatian time and lasted five minutes. It started during a song between the second and third decades of a Rosary. Just before the Virgin came Mirjana began to take occasional deep breaths, sighed several times, and rubbed her eyes as she prayed with simple wood beads. Then suddenly her eyes teared as she looked up, first very serious, but within a minute or two smiling, although still very intent. She nodded and at times squinted as if trying to understand Mary, who she said appears with a great background of blue, with all else disappearing. The visionary said the visit pertained to the secrets and thus there was no public message. After the apparition she looked fatigued and emotionally spent; it took her two hours to recover.

Mirjana also recounted to me a 1987 private visit with the Pope at his vacation residence. She is the only seer who has had a private meeting and it lasted just ten minutes. "We talked normal, but he didn't ask anything about secrets. He asked only about Blessed Mary. He was funny because he thought that Polish and Croatian are similar and he was talking Polish and I didn't understand. I was so enraptured being in front of the Holy Father that I was looking at him and crying and he was talking in Polish and I didn't have the force to tell him I don't understand. Then I asked him to speak Italian, and then we tried Italian. He didn't ask very much, really. He kept looking and asking some questions and then he said, 'If I wasn't the Holy Father, I would already be in Medjugorje.'"

More later...

"Monkey-man": prank, hysteria, or spiritual?

The panic over a 'monkey-man' in India has grown more mysterious as police say there are no physical clues from a "creature" that has supposedly been stalking people in New Delhi.

"After an intensive search in which some 3,000 extra officers were put on the case, police said they had come up empty-handed in their quest for the so-called monkey man," according to Reuters. "'If there are no physical clues, then it has to be the product of a fertile mind,' assistant police commissioner Rajiv Ranjan said. 'It's nothing but fear psychosis.'"

That may be. It may be hysteria. It may also be a prank, or even a criminal. But we note the worship of a monkey "god" in India (Lord Hanuman), and we also note that last year similar "creatures" caused a panic.

And indeed there has been an outbreak of demonism in the midst of earthquakes and Christian persecution and other upheaval across India—steeped as it is in occultism.

Last summer in Mochi Para, Loot Para, Jaruadih, and Rasikpur were similar tales of an "invisible" assailant called the *Murkatwa* that was haunting the night and causing such fear that people in remote areas like Godda and Sahebganj were fleeing to West Bengal.

For years we have heard of spiritual problems in India—which may trace its origins to ancient Egypt and Babylon. We have heard of possession. People thrashed on the ground. They went into convulsions. It's said that powders (or *prasaads*) dedicated to Kali—a violent, snarling goddess—were slipped into food of the unsuspecting. "The devas who are worshipped as gods and goddesses by pagans are actually devils because, in hundreds of cases of exorcisms, I have come across these devas or devils under various names confessing against their wills that they are coming from the depths of hell," a priest named Robert Lewis, who is stationed near Ajmer, wrote us some time ago.

Could this tie into the "monkey-man"?

Could it link to the *Murkatwa*?

Or is it all just a prank?

All we know for now is that reports of the creature attacking people at random have triggered panic in the city of 13 million and led to at least three deaths. Dozens of other residents complained they were injured by the "monkey man." Descriptions of the nocturnal entity have varied wildly—with some saying it was a monkey-like creature with metallic claws while others said it was like a cat with tawny, glowing eyes, according to Reuters, which reported one witness who said it had "flaming eyes and green lights on its chest."

Stay tuned. . .

Mysterious mountain at Medjugorje: are its secrets hidden in biblical mounts?

One of the enduring mysteries of Medjugorje is the mount known as Krizevac. Located just south of the village, it towers 1,760 feet above sea level and has a cross at its summit that dominates the landscape for miles around.

In the twenty years since Medjugorje first erupted on the world scene, pilgrims flocking to this holy place have seen the cross spin or fade or disappear. They have seen phantom smoke and fires—flames that upon inspection did not actually occur. They have seen the Virgin in large images descending from the summit; indeed, it is here, the seers were told, that Mary prays to her Son at the foot of the cross every morning. They have seen auras of color around the mountain.

According to legend (and here we emphasize the word *legend*, for we have never been able to confirm it), a priest from the area, Father Bernardin ("Brno") Smoljan, was called to Rome in 1933 by Pope Pius XI, who supposedly had a dream in which he felt inspired to raise a cross "on the highest Golgotha in Hercegovina" and related this dream to Father Brno. We don't know if there is truth to it, but the fact remains that around this time the parishioners set about building a cross ten meters high atop the mountain known back then as Sipovac ("Pomegrante Hill").

Most likely the cross was erected as a holy talisman against the violent hailstorms that used to destroy crops in the fields. It is also possible, say some, that it was constructed in reparation for the bitter and bloody clashes between Croatians and Serbians.

Whatever the precise motive—and whether or not the Pope had any such vision—the point is that a highly visible cross made of concrete was erected in 1933 by peasants lugging achingly heavy buckets of material up a rocky and often treacherous goat path. At the very least, it was an act of great community penance that commemorated the 1,900th anniversary of Christ's Crucifixion—and the mount soon became known as "Krizevac," which means "Cross Mountain."

A cross now predominated over a mountain that had been known for its poisonous snakes (*poskoci*) and wild boars.

And the mountain set the stage for the famous apparitions that began on a connected hillside in 1981—with Mary often manifesting on the mountain.

"I am often at Krizevac, at the foot of the cross, to pray there," the Virgin told the seers. *"The cross was in God's plan when you built it. These days especially, go up on the mountain and pray at the foot of the cross. Pray before the cross. Special graces come from the cross. Consecrate yourselves to the cross."*

"You are at a Tabor," the Virgin said in 1986.

And so we ask: is there a relation between Medjugorje and Israel? Is there a connection between Krizevac and biblical mounts?

It indeed brings to mind Tabor. That's where Jesus Himself had an apparition of Elijah and Moses—and where He dispensed His own secret, asking His disciples not to discuss what they had seen at this site of apparition. It also brings to mind Mount Sinai. There are those who have seen a column of light come from the cross, a light recalling the one that led the Israelites out of Egypt—an unworldly pink or white light which has later given way to the outline of a luminous woman. "The turning of the cross and the white light and the figure of Our Lady were often seen by hundreds, sometimes thousands of people," said one priest who published a report about Krizevac.

There have been funnel-shaped lights. There have been "meteorites." Stars above seem to turn colors. One evening in 1981 an inscription of the word *MIR* ("peace") appeared above Mount Krizevac in fiery letters. Others have been luminous doves.

Are there hidden indications of Krizevac's role in the role of biblical mountains? Can we glean anything from Scripture?

It was Mount Sinai where the Lord promised to come down in the sight of all the people [*Exodus* 19:11]. It was also that mount where signs were shown in *smoke and lightning and thunder*. It was Mount Hor where the Lord spoke to Moses. And Mount Carmel where Eijah battled the evil Baal prophets. It was yet to another mount, of Olives, that Jesus often went, and where He was asked many questions, including about the end-times.

Are there hints in all this? Is there a connection? Is Krizevac an extension of Sinai and Hor and Carmel, of Perazim, of Olives? Will there be battles fought between good and evil as at Carmel and new dictates as at Sinai and a great apparition as at Tabor?

We all know that the Virgin has dispensed secrets at Medjugorje and now we wonder if the mountain will somehow figure into those secrets. Will Jesus one day appear in apparition as has His mother?

Only time will tell but we think the mount may figure into future events and the realization of something that whatever it may entail will be of biblical proportion.

In nation's capital, a sense of peace as warning graduate

By Michael H. Brown

I paid a visit to Washington Monday and the mood was somber but calm. Snipers patrolled the roof of the White House and there were cops on the street leading to the home of our president. Around the Capitol and other landmarks are cement barricades—some there for a while now, some since September 11. At the Pentagon sightseers cross a knoll to glimpse the blackened side that was hit by an airliner, the missing walls a gaping reminder that the country is in the midst of a war.

Everywhere are reminders of how fragile our infrastructure is. Things we take for granted can crumble around us. For years we have been hearing people prophesy that a day would come when our constructs would begin to disintegrate, and it's no longer hard to envision.

To travel this week was to stand in a line so long at airport security in Albany, New York, that they had to herd us into the *parking lot*. Later in the day, at Baltimore-Washington Airport, the line for security was more than half-a-mile long. It took two hours to reach the x-ray machines.

In the meantime, news was coming of events: a supposedly deranged person who tried to break into a cockpit while in route from Los Angeles and a report that in Florida there was a second case of anthrax. Once at the gate at Baltimore-Washington, I encountered the deplaning of another flight that was emptied for security reasons. There were two rumors: that several Afghans had been asked to leave as passengers, or that a suspicious package had been found.

Yet in the midst of all this I felt a great tranquility. When we pray, there is nothing to fear. Prayer means God is with us. I felt peace driving around the nation's capital and peace as I said a prayer and watched what seemed like a pulsing sun near the White House and when there is any tension in the days ahead I will simply pray until the tension vanishes. I urge everyone to recite at least 15 decades of the Rosary and I especially urge use of the Scriptural Rosary. I can't tell you the graces I have experienced from that!

In the days ahead, there will be reports that unnerve us, and we need to know the truth. Here, we will not shirk from reporting those threats to you. There is a tremendous threat. It is greater than we thought. But none of this is through the prism of fear. No: in the midst of it all, in the upheaval of our times—in this stage where warnings are beginning to graduate into purification—there is only the peace of prayer and the joy of knowing that we're in the hands of God.

Did my nephews encounter an angel?

by Michael H. Brown

On our recent pilgrimage to Medjugorje two of my nephews had a unique experience. It happened June 29, a Friday, on what's known as "apparition hill." They were sitting enjoying the evening when a stranger approached wearing white shorts and a white shirt. They didn't look to see if he had anything on his feet.

But his behavior was strange. The man said nothing, just approached and sat inches away from one of them, Richard Jenkins, nearly in his lap—and then just quietly stayed as Rich finished praying the Rosary.

Every once in a while the man opened his palms to the sky or pointed upward. Rich didn't understand what he was trying to say.

Most unusual was the man's face. He looked young from the sides but like an old man from the front, perhaps a local Croatian. His mouth puckered as if he had no teeth.

For some reason, the proximity didn't bother them. There was an inexplicably peaceful feeling emanating from the man, who greeted my second nephew, Joseph, when he approached and kissed him on the cheek, offering peace. "Peace and love," they said as they left. Joe also felt the flow of tranquility.

Later that night they saw an unusual light fall on the village. They were still up on the hill. It was like a meteorite, but was too big and thick to be a meteorite, and it split into four or so lights before vanishing from view.

Perhaps that's what the "man" had been indicating.

Or maybe he was just praising God.

When we got back we were interested to learn that when angels appear as mysterious strangers they are often dressed all in white. . .

The astonishing apparitions in Nicaragua: an untold story

Somehow, in the rush of modern life, in the avalanche of alleged Catholic phenomena in the past two decades, we lost site of a gem at our doorstep. It involves apparitions that allegedly occurred during 1980 in Cuapa, Nicaragua, and it's no small story.

First is the fact that the apparitions, to a humble sacristan named Bernardo Martinez (above), received the endorsement of Monsignor Pablo Antonio of Juigalpa, the local bishop—a rare event in an era when the majority of such claims are rejected or ignored. It joins two other Latin American apparitions (Betania, Venezuela and San Nicolas, Argentina) in at least partial ecclesiastical acceptance, and indicates a willingness to embrace the supernatural in Spanish-speaking areas that is missing from the modern scientific terrain of North America. Although there are messages that have received imprimaturs, no apparition has been officially approved in the United States since the nation's foundation.

The second significant fact is in what the Nicaraguan apparition allegedly said. Like the messages in Argentina (which we reported on *two weeks ago*), the Nicaraguan revelations contained a warning that if people did not come back to loving each other and God, mankind would experience a terrific war and natural disasters.

Cuapa is a small valley in the Chontales Mountains where most people work on small cattle ranches. Here, on the night of April 15, 1980, Martinez first saw a statue of the Blessed Virgin Mary illuminate and at first thought it was light coming from a hole in the roof. "The light was not coming out of anything," said Martinez. "The light came from her. That was a great mystery for me: with the light that came from her, one could walk without tripping."

Soon Martinez saw Mary in several dreams and apparitions. The visions took on the aspect of both Our Lady of Fatima (with one event occurring on the Fatima feast day of October 13), and Our Lady of the Miraculous Medal (grace streaming from the Virgin's hands). As at Fatima and Medjugorje, her feet were on a cloud.

"Covering her was a veil of a pale cream color with gold embroidery along the edge," said Martinez. "The rays that came from her hands touched my breast."

The Virgin gave Martinez—who later entered the priesthood—a number of profound spiritual lessons. For instance she advised that the Lord did not like prayers made in a rush or ones that were recited mechanically. She recommended the Rosary *with the reading of biblical citations* (the Scriptural Rosary) and First Saturday devotions (Confession and Communion on the first Saturday of each month). She also urged the faithful to read the Word of God—and put it into practice.

"Love each other," Martinez quoted Mary as saying. *"Fulfill your obligations. Make peace. Don't ask Our Lord for peace because if you do not make it there will be no peace.*

"Nicaragua has suffered much since the earthquake [in the 1970s]. She is threatened with even more suffering. She will continue to suffer if you don't change.

"Pray, pray the Rosary for all the world, my son," the Virgin said. *"Tell believers and nonbelievers that the world is threatened by grave dangers. I ask the Lord to appease His justice, but if you don't change you will hasten the arrival of a third world war."*

It's unclear if the war mentioned at Cuapa was the same alluded to at other apparitions. At Fatima Sister Lucia dos Santos reportedly said a consecration of the world to the Immaculate Heart of Mary by the Pope in 1984 prevented a nuclear war from occurring in 1985. The threat of war was also mentioned in the 1980s at Medjugorje while at San Nicolas in Argentina—more than 3,000 miles south of Nicaragua—an alleged seer named Gladys Quiroga said she was warned (*precisely in 1985*) that the world was "*hanging by a thread*" and "*in great danger*."

It's unclear whether the threat has now passed or was simply postponed but we should note that a *fourth* Latin American apparition—this time to a young woman named Pachi Talbot Borrero in the remote city of Cuencha, Ecuador—warned of a similar threat, with Pachi shown a vision of what looked like great nuclear destruction if mankind did not convert.

Impressive is the fact that these seers were unknown to each other at the time that their visions occurred. In Nicaragua the Virgin came with lightning-like flashes similar to what has been described at both Fatima and Medjugorje. She materialized over a little morisco tree, reminding us of the way she appeared over a small holm oak at Fatima. She came both as a young woman and a child. Her hair fell to her shoulders, brown in color. She faced the east. Significant was that one major apparition took place at 3 p.m.—which Catholics honor as the hour of mercy. In one vision, played like a movie, the Virgin showed Martinez a large group of people dressed in white and bathed in a luminosity. "They sang," said Martinez. "But I could not understand the words. It was a celestial festival. It was such happiness, such joy. . ."

"These are the very first communities when Christianity began," the Virgin reportedly explained. *"They are the first catechumens; many of them were martyrs."*

Martinez said he was also shown a group who had been given the first Rosary. One man carried a large book, would read from it, and then the others would meditate. "After this period of prayer in silence, they then prayed the *Our Father* and ten *Hail Marys*," explained Martinez, who said the Virgin told him that many people pray for things that are *"unimportant"* when they should *"ask for faith in order to have the strength so that each can carry his own cross."* She said certain requests were granted but not those designated by God as sufferings to be endured while in the world. *"Pray for faith in order that you will have patience,"* Mary told the sacristan—now Father Martinez. *"Pray, pray, my son, for all the world. Grave dangers threaten the world. Pray the Rosary. Meditate on the mysteries. Listen to the Word of God spoken in them. Forgive each other. Make peace. Don't ask for peace without making peace."*

Bernardo said there were also visits by an angel who prophesied events that came true—including the murder (September 9, 1980) of a cousin who had scoffed at the heavenly warning. "Everything that the angel told me was fulfilled exactly," said Martinez.

Told by the Virgin to disseminate the messages, Martinez was granted permission to let others know of the happenings on June 24, which was the patron feast of Cuapa (and a year to the day before the beginning of apparitions in Medjugorje). Mary told Bernardo to invoke her by saying, *"Holy Virgin, you are my mother, the mother to all of us, sinners."* And after having said this three times she was elevated as if the clouds were pushing her and disappeared.

Was last week's display of the northern lights a sign of "anguish among the nations"?

It says in *Luke* that there would be signs in the sun, moon, and stars (21:25), and for the past decade we've been seeing exceptional solar activity, mainly in the way of increased dark areas called sunspots and now in the way of mass ejections that have caused tremendous displays of the aurora borealis, better known as the "northern lights." They have been seen as shimmering curtains of yellow, green, and blood-red during the last week. Although initially visible only in places like Alaska, by last weekend they were seen in a spectacular way from California to Kansas, Georgia, and Texas.

It was the result of a geomagnetic storm on the sun that hit the "severe" category on March 31—the most intense emission in a decade and by some standards in half a century. So large was a solar flare on Monday that space weather forecasters had to estimate its intensity at X-22—on a scale that goes only to X-20.

According to scientists, current changes in the sun may account for much of global warming—the current swerves in climate. Prophetically, they may also be omens. It was precisely a display of the northern lights on the night of January 25-26, 1938, that Lucia dos Santos, the sole surviving seer from Fatima, said was the "great sign" prophesied by the Blessed Mother in 1917—a sign that mankind was about to be chastised by war. So pronounced were the lights that Portuguese peasants went screaming through villages fearing the end of the world. In London residents thought Windsor Castle was afire. According to *The New York Times,* they watched as two magnificent arcs of light rose in the east and west, "from which radiated pulsating beams like searchlights in dark red, greenish blue, and purple."

The "aurora" was swiftly followed by Japanese aggression and the rise in Germany of Hitler to war minister. A year later the Germans invaded Poland; France and England declared war.

It was the beginning of World War II, and the lights that foresaw it—that appeared in the night skies just a month before Hitler annexed Austria—were also described as "a shimmering curtain of fire" and huge "blood-red" beams—terms eerily similar to what was described this week, when the Associated Press wrote of "shimmering colors" rippling across the heavens and an observer in Albuquerque described the color he saw as "blood red."

Moreover, while the lights themselves were not as intense as in 1938, and while it thus seemed only a pre-sign (part of a more gradual build-up), the geomagnetic event that generated the lights may have been a once-in-fifty-year event—just as the "great sign" of 1938 was likewise described as the most brilliant display of the aurora in at least half a century.

That display had affected areas like LaSalette (where there had been prophecies of war and great natural disasters), and was seen as far west as New York, Ohio, and Canada. But here we come to a key difference: Where the 1938 display was focused around the Atlantic—and specifically in Europe, where war would soon break out—the recent display was seen by looking to the west—toward the Pacific and Russia and China.

Is there meaning in this?

If we take it from *Luke*, signs in the sun and the moon and the stars (there was also a brief eclipse last month) are followed by "anguish" among the nations.

You can interpret that anyway you want.

Why are angels appearing in the northern lights?

Photographs of the northern lights have been showing some strange things. One we ran of the lights over an area about 37 miles north of Jyvaskyla, Finland, on September 23, was especially curious. If you look at it, you'll see a number of images. One face, smack in the middle of the photograph, looks like an angel facing directly frontward with flowing hair. But looked at another way, it is part of a *larger face* that is also at the middle but looking downward to your left, his hair also flowing but upward, with the purple streak of light right through the middle of his head.

This larger image is strikingly similar to a *painting* by an artist named Mario Macari of the Archangel Michael looking upon the Crucifixion. The faces are much the same, and so is the purplish hue (although Macari's is a painting, not a photo of the aurora borealis!).

We're interested in the northern lights because they constituted the "great sign" of Fatima in 1938 (when their appearance signaled the onset of World War Two)—and also because the Third Secret of Fatima had a luminous angel in it.

It seems that angelic helpers—the big angels—are on the scene. Below is another photograph of the northern lights by the same photographer—who presented them to the secular and scientific press without noting any of these images. We watch many such images as they are presented on goverment sites or in secular media such as BBC.

And we have wondered if they signify a war, this time a "holy war." Many have noted that one of the last great battles between Muslems and Christians, the Battle of Lepanto, occurred on October 7—the same day the war in Afghanistan started.

But let's look at the bright side: Bishop Fulton Sheen once predicted that the Muslims would be converted through Our Lady of Fatima. Indeed, many Muslims visit the Catholic shrine because Fatima is named after a queen who was named after Mohammed's daughter!

Priests express fear as cults grip "paradise" island

An American priest who has just returned from the Caribbean island of St. Lucia says fear is rampant after the demonic attack last New Year's Eve at the Basilica of the Immaculate Conception.

It was on December 31 that Rastafarians—a cult that uses marijuana in its rituals—burst into the church and began dousing churchgoers with a flammable liquid that was then set afire. They arrived in eerie robes bearing torches and wildly attacking just after Communion. An elderly Irish nun was killed and Father Charles Gaillard, who was celebrating Mass, was critically injured when he was set afire. A dozen others were also injured.

The good news is that Father Gaillard has made what has been described as a "miraculous" recovery. This occurred shortly after a statue of the Virgin of Fatima arrived, according to Father Clement Machado, an America priest who often appears on the Catholic network, EWTN, and who has just returned from the island. "Thanks be to God that the Virgin has come and brought some healing to the area," he says.

But Father Machado, who specializes in spiritual warfare, says he received "a lot of dirty looks" when he wore his collar on the once-idyllic island. "There are a lot of people there I wouldn't be in a dark alley with, who if they could get me they would," he told us Tuesday.

"The people around me were trying to protect me and told me my life was in danger. A lot of groups, including evangelical groups from the United States and elsewhere, have spewed out a great deal of anti-Catholic propaganda, saying the Pope is the Anti-Christ and the Church is the whore of Babylon. There has been a lot of violence and a lot of threats. Last year they had vandalism at churches. Just after my visit they've taken seriously some new threats they've received. They're right now in a state of shock and outrage. The bishop is trying to call for calm. There is a lot of occult activity in St. Lucia, a whole underworld. There's a tremendous amount of voodoo and Santeria, black magic, sorcery, and witchcraft. In Trinidad there are now now full-time exorcists involved but not in St. Lucia and from the capital of Castries to the outlying areas, cult activity is strong, especially among young people. It was particularly evil. I could sense it. I had to watch my back constantly. There was a dark oppressive spirit over the island, a tremendous danger. Spells and curses are rampant."

An evangelical deliverance expert has told us the same thing: that voodoo is prevalent and that there are death threats against Christians of all denominations. Voodooists are sometimes brought in from neighboring islands.

Police have arrested two men, although one or two more may have been involved in the attack. Other Rastafarians claim the men acted alone. Adherents are recognizable by their reggae music and dreadlocks. They believe that former Ethiopian king Haile Selassie was a manifestation of God. Although they are not directly associated with black magic, it is an undercurrent in all cult religions on the island and an Egyptian ankh—the cross with a loop—was etched onto the church just before the attack.

Machado says it was not an isolated incident and that cult activity in other countries, including the United States, is creating a growing danger. He recalled an incident in which a chalice was stolen by a satanic cult from a church where he ministered in Canada and when it was found—after prayers to the Archangel Michael—had to be reconsecrated. "We're not exempt," he warns, "anywhere."

When you have to make a tough decision, go with what gives you peace

When you have to make major decisions, the simple rule is to decide on what gives you the greatest peace. Make the decision that offers tranquility. Look for calm waters.

Often, that's not what you want. It's not what your *brain* tells you. It's not what you might prefer. We're all creatures and we often desire things that seem great on the surface but in the end bring tension and cause us to stray from the Lord.

On the other hand, when we flow with peace—when what we are about to do brings us calm, when we go with what brings about the greatest feeling of peacefulness—we're operating in accordance with God. This is a great hidden truth: peace—a feeling of serenity—means we're operating in accordance with the plan of God. That's because peace is what it's like in heaven, where all are perfectly doing what God wants.

Don't get me wrong: there are times we have to make tough decisions; there are times we have to suffer; there are times we have to go against the grain. There are trials of tension.

But that's different. That's standing up to the world. That's doing what Jesus had to do. There are times when the right decision is what everyone else thinks is wrong!

But if it gives you peace, it's correct. It's the right one. And it comes only through prayer. To pray adequately is to pray until all the mental noise is shoved to the side and we have a clarity and calmness of spirit.

Don't make decisions *unless* you feel peace. If you feel jangled or uneasy or rushed while you're praying, pray until that disquiet has been dispelled. If you're under duress, pray until the duress is lifted. If you feel aggravation, cast it to the foot of the Cross.

Then pray long. Pray for the right direction. Pray until you've pierced the clouds.

It's incredible how insights fly into our heads or we suddenly remember something we need to remember or how we gain that sudden clarity—that clear vision—when we take the time to pray.

On occasion, this can mean praying a half an hour straight or longer.

To some people that's a lot but it's crucial because a lack of prayer brings the wrong decisions. Oh, it may be what we want right away, it may bring us immediate gratification, it may be what gives us the immediate "rush"—but in the long run it will be counterproductive. Whatever brings too much electricity and overexcitement is in all likelihood out of heavenly accordance.

Remember that. Remember that Christ was peaceful. He taught us that whatever gives us peace—peace in our innermost depths—is good and is the correct choice.

He was the Prince of Peace, and when we find peace we also find Him.

Seers at Medjugorje still describe "permanent sign" as future

Last month, when we were at Medjugorje, our priest, Father John McFadden, asked seer Mirjana Dragicevic Soldo about the "permanent sign" long prophesied to occur at the apparition site of Medjugorje. Could it be something related to the statue of Christ that has been exuding a watery substance? Could it be a miracle along that order?

"The sign will be indestructible and permanent," was Mirjana's only answer.

Like the other visionaries, when asked anything about secrets, she replies only in the briefest way. For years they have been asked about the secrets. For years they have patiently answered without infringing in any way on what they have been told. For years their answers have been adroit. But for years they have confirmed that after several warnings are issued to mankind, a supernatural sign of some sort will appear on Apparition Hill, where the Virgin first appeared.

For Mirjana, the sign is involved with the third secret she was given, and others have indicated the same. It's the only secret we know that they share. And the purpose, they say, will be to show once and for all that the Virgin has indeed appeared at this place in Bosnia-Hercegovina.

Will the sign be in the heavens or on earth? another seer, Vicka Ivankovic, was once asked.

"On earth," Vicka responded.

Will it come gradually—or spontaneously?

"Spontaneously."

Will everyone be able to see it?

"Whoever comes here will," said Vicka.

Will it be temporary or permanent?

"Permanent," Vicka responded.

The seer once added that she had at least three visions of it and that she'll see the Virgin less than an hour before the sign appears. She's says it's "very beautiful."

This has led to all sorts of speculation. Will it be a light? Will it be something physical (like the miraculous spring at Lourdes)? Will it be at the exact spot where Mary first appeared, or just generally on the hill?

A third seer, Jakov Colo, once said that even the mayor—even people of the highest social standing—will run to the hill. Even they will understand it as what Mirjana described as "a place or occasion to convert."

Back on November 30, 1983, the parish at Medjugorje sent a formal letter to the Pope informing him that the Virgin "has promised to leave a visible sign for all humanity at the site of the apparitions" and that "before the visible sign is given to humanity, there will be three warnings to the world. The warnings will be in the form of events on earth."

There has always been a mystery around this. At times it has seemed as if three warnings will precede, but at other times it has almost been expressed as if the sign itself is part of the third warning. We know from an interview Mirjana granted to a lawyer named Jan Connell years ago that the secrets will occur in Mirjana's lifetime (she was born in 1965).

Vicka says that when the permanent sign appears, healings will occur.

But we also know that we're not to become obsessed with either the past or the future. We're to live in the here and now. Today is a period of grace. It's a time for conversion. It's crucial to enlighten unbelievers. These are the ones in the greatest danger. These are the ones who grieve the Blessed Mother the most.

If only each of us could draw one person to Christ, we would rejoice for eternity.

But that still does not answer our question: what could the sign *be*?

When will the permanent sign at Medjugorje occur?

By Michael H. Brown

"Everybody will be able to see that it's coming from God, that human hands could not make it," says seer Mirjana Dragicevic Soldo of the permanent sign prophesied to occur at Medjugorje.

It will be "beautiful," says a second seer, Vicka Ivankovic.

There will be healings, says a third, Marija Pavlovic Lunetti.

But when will it occur?

That's the question of the hour: when will the secrets unfold?

And of course no one but those who have been told could provide an answer.

While there has been disappointment among many that so far—after twenty years—"nothing" has happened and while many became skeptical because little happened in the year 2000 (as if God operates on the human calendar), I have no doubt that the secrets are real and no doubt that they are still pending.

Mirjana told us that the dates have not altered and can't be.

They will happen and when the first occurs, it will break the power of Satan.

On Monday we'll see an old prophecy from a nun in South America that ties into this.

Nothing said in the formal messages from Medjugorje has proven to be false, and while there has been confusion in certain things, we can say that Mirjana will live to see the secrets materialize and will inform a priest, Father Petar Ljubicic, ten days before the first is to occur. He is then to pray and fast before releasing the information publicly. Since Father Petar is about sixty, and the life expectancy of Croatian males in 69.3 years, one might speculate that the first secret will occur in the next ten years.

But then again Father Petar (and we certainly hope so!) could live to be 100. He will know the incident in advance and will announce it.

That's Mirjana's first secret. She told me the priest will be privy only to that first one. He may not be privy to the third—which involves the permanent sign—and so all we can say is that this will occur in Mirjana's lifetime. She has said and so has Vicka that they would live to see the secrets.

Mirjana was born in 1965. She's 36. The average life expectancy for a female Croatian is 77.

Rumors swirl around Medjugorje, and one is that a seer will die before the secrets. We've never heard any confirmation of this, and thus caution that at this point it should not be believed. We also caution about other dates. Recently we carried an item about how a seer attached to the Church-approved site of Betania in Venezuela foresaw a special enlightenment from heaven around the year 2004, but this does not necessarily mean an event on earth; she was referring to heavenly light; and we should always bear in mind that heaven follows no earthly timetable.

Personally, I did not expect the secrets to have occurred by now. In my book *The Final Hour*, I concluded that they would begin between now and 2040 (see page 338). But I must say that signs in the world are quickening. And as we head into a new world of cloning and stem cells, it will quicken yet more. Soon, an event—an event attached to a secret—will be precipitated.

What does "soon" mean?

Soon is in our era. Soon is in many of our lifetimes. At Fatima it took 21 years for the prophesied sign in the first two secrets to occur and 64 years for part of the third secret (which apparently involved the shooting of the Pope in 1981) to materialize. But all occurred in the lifetime of seer Lucia dos Santos. One visionary at Medjugorje has said that if we pray we will in some way understand the secrets for ourselves and most importantly if we pray the Virgin's plan for mankind will be fulfilled. She needs our prayers. She needs them now.

So do unbelievers. It has been said at Medjugorje that when the secrets unfold, those who don't believe will despise themselves for not doing so. For many, it will be too late. Now is the time for decision. Now is the time for conversion. "Our Lady always says, don't talk about secrets but pray," says Mirjana. "'Those who see me as mother and God as Father have no fear of anything.' Our Lady says only those who don't believe have fear."

As darkness grows, so does need for personal

Right now the devil is all over the place. We need personal protection. We need to protect our families. Since Pope Leo XIII in 1884 we've been warned that a period of evil was on the way and now we find ourselves in the throes of it. It's a battle that's been raging for a hundred years and will one day soon reach a crescendo. This too was said at Fatima, and most recently at Medjugorje. It is the hour when Satan is allowed to exercise his greatest force, and we see it all around us. We see it in lust. We see it in demonism. We see it in the eyes of terrorists.

So how do we avoid it? How do we protect ourselves? We start out with prayer. We're running one of the *most powerful prayers* we've ever seen against evil on today's site, and we urge everyone to use it. When we pray we're connected to God and the more we have God the less room there is for evil, the less is the devil able to gain a foothold. If we're filled with the light of God there's no room for the prince of darkness. While he may seek to attack from the outside, in the end he must flee; in the end we can trample on him. We know he's around when we're consumed by anxiety or fear or depression, when we're obsessed, when we're consumed by jealousy, when there is *confusion.*

So we start out with prayer. We go directly to Jesus. With that Name satan must flee, as he also must in the presence of Scripture. Read the Bible. Keep one open in your foyer or living room or bedroom. Keep it open to *Ephesians* 6 or *Psalm* 23. The devil hates this book and can do little in its presence.

Use holy water. Sprinkle some each day, especially in your bedrooms. It's at night that the devil likes to attack, or when we first rise. That's why morning prayer—prayer right away, at the start of each day, and then the last thing at night—is essential. Salt blessed by a priest is equally powerful. Sprinkle this in every corner of the house, and use holy oil on you and your children if your diocese permits it. Last year we carried a story on Father Gabriele Amorth, the official Rome exorcist. Listen to what he says: "Exorcising salt too is beneficial for expelling demons and for healing soul and body. The specific function of this salt is to protect places from an evil presence or influence. When there is suspicion of evil infestation, I usually advise people to place exorcised salt across the threshold and in the four corners of the room that are affected."

Blessed candles can also be efficacious. So is the Scapular. While we don't have to become obsessive about religious objects, placing anointed ones in every room is an important way of keeping an evil spirit from taking root. At the same time, we have to cast out. We are told by the Bible that in Jesus' Name we can command away evil spirits and when we feel such spirits coming around we should immediately cast them away. You'll be amazed at how quickly an oppression or prickly situation can be dispelled when in the Name of Christ you command it away. "I command you evil spirits away and to the foot of the Cross to be disposed of according to the Will of God in the Name of Christ! In the Name of Jesus!"

Command evil out of your house and bless the doors that no evil may enter.

Also, fast. If you are haunted, if a problem persists, denying yourself food for a day can make a world of difference. It's potent. You'll be amazed at its power. It lets you transcend the prince of this world, the prince of the flesh.

These are crucial tools and then there are the sacraments. "Confession and Communion," Father Amorth noted in a book, *An Exorcist Tells His Story,* "are worth as much as a strong exorcism." These practices are a form of *immunization* from evil. They are also tools of deliverance. If you are oppressed, if there is evil in you, or around you, if a spirit haunts you, this can be cleansed by the Eucharist and especially by receiving the Blood of Jesus. It's that Blood that defeated satan. It's that Blood that has won us our victory. Few prayers are as powerful as those implored the moment of consecration.

Then there's the Rosary. This is our lifeline, a ring of protection. When we pray it with our hearts and with our families, they too are protected. In these times the Virgin has been granted special powers and it's a tragedy that many don't seek it!

From all corners come reports of illness and division and quarreling and anxiety and stress and unhappiness and depression and this we can transcend. This we have the power to defeat. Prayer. *Fasting*. No matter what you see on the news in the days to come, no matter how many times they replay footage of the World Trade Center, no matter how things seem to be crumbling around us, remember that nothing crumbles with Christ and that when it is darkest the Light of Heaven can be made to shine brightest.

The vanishing oil in the case of an allegedly miraculous statue *of St. Philomena*

A statue of St. Philomena that's exuding oil in Michigan has a new twist: the oil seems to vanish when the statue is touched by anyone but a priest.

That's the testimony of Kevin Khidhir, proprietor of All Saints Gift Shop in Sterling Heights and owner of the statue, which has been making news in Detroit.

When we called him Tuesday, Khidhir explained that he had purchased the statue from a Florida church on August 9. "We were giving it to another church in Saginaw, Michigan," says Khidhir. "The church rejected her—said she was too small, even though it's three feet—and two weeks later, on August 26, the oil first started. Four customers and I saw the oil, but we didn't think anything of it. We thought it was just accidentally put on there. It was just like three drops. But we wiped her down and more came out the next day and then more came out the day after that. It kept increasing in volume."

The statue, which is currently at a secret location in Troy, exudes the oil from its body for up to seven days at a time, "then stops for a day or two or three," according to Khidhir. "We never know when it's going to start or when it's going to stop. It continues for hours as long as no one touches it. As soon as someone touches the oil, it just automatically disappears. You can't put it on any type of cloth. If you touch the oil, it will wipe it away, but there's nothing on the cloth itself."

More like a supernatural substance than actual oil, Khidhir said it does remain intact when there's anyone sick. In that case they're able to take a small amount of the oil on a finger and anoint the person with it. Or a picture of the statue is placed next to the ill person. He claims the result has been at least nine cures—four cancers (including a "stage four" lung malignity), one massive heart case, a thyroid problem, a person with broken ribs, a paralyzed arm, and a non-cancerous throat tumor.

Let's make it clear that at this point these cases are only hearsay. As yet nothing has been documented. We'll await medical records. In any case like this we have to be cautious of exaggeration, delusion, trickery, or even demonic deception.

But according to Hawke Fracassa, an otherwise skeptical news reporter I spoke with, Khidhir and those around him seemed sincere. The store owner—who has long had a *devotion to Philomena*—said that when a priest touches the statue, the supernatural oil increases.

The statue has also wept on two occasions. "The first time she cried was in front of a priest who had taken all his statues out of his church," said Khidhir. "He stood in front of her and all of a sudden the tear came down. Does that mean it was because of that? I don't know. It was October 31. The second time she cried was the day she left here to go to her investigation (by the Church). She let drop one tear and then everybody started crying with her. That was November 1."

Khidhir believes the message is for everyone to come back to the "saints of God, which so many people have lost." It comes at a time, ironically, when Catholics are debating *a return to more traditional architecture.* It also comes at a juncture when Church authorities have been rejecting many alleged miracles—some for good reason, some because it fears "sensationalism," some out of over-skepticism.

Khidhir believes the statue of Philomena, a young martyr executed at the order of a Roman emperor, is also a warning about the sins of our times, including abortion. He has been having dreams connected with the statue but declined to discuss them.

Terrorist plot against Pope was foiled by miraculous explosion

A published report says that a terrorist plot by Osama Bin Laden against Pope John Paul II during a visit in 1995 to the Philippines was foiled when a miraculous accident caused an explosion in the Manila apartment where a bomb was being readied just a week before the pontiff's visit. The plot involved use of a fragmentary bomb and timer inside a digital watch. When officers investigated they found the apartment laden with a crucifix, Bibles, and cassocks—indicating that the terrorists were going to disguise themselves as priests. Italian police are now on high alert at all papal functions.

In recent years, John Paul II has been the object of at least three failed plots on his life by fundamentalist terrorist groups, according to political and press sources. The CIA says the mastermind behind the Philippines plot was terrorist Ramzy Youssef, who has worked under the direction of Bin Laden and who two years earlier organized the first attack on the World Trade Center.

One of the terrorists set in place in the Philippines was Abdulhakim Alihashim Murad—who was arrested at Doña Josefa apartment on Quirino Ave., Manila, which is only 150 meters away from the Papal Nunciature House. Murad had training as a pilot. "Authorities also recovered a map covering the areas of Manila, indicating [a plot] to disrupt the visit of the Pope at the Federation of Asian Bishops' Conference at the San Carlos Seminary along Edsa, Guadalupe, Makati City on Jan. 15, 1995," according to the *Cebu Sun-Star.* Recovered from Murad were also a laptop computer, a map of the Pope's itinerary, and photographs of John Paul II.

U.S. officials said the plot against the Pope was discovered in January of 1995 when Filipino firemen were summoned to the apartment in response to reports of smoke billowing from the windows. The firefighters called in police when they found smoldering chemicals in the empty apartment, according to the *Charlotte Observer.* Later, authorities confiscated a computer disk that described plans to blow up a dozen 747 jumbo jets over the Pacific Ocean and to assassinate John Paul II.

Potter arrives in occult tidal wave

It looks innocent enough, even cute. There is the bespectacled boy, Harry Potter, and he stands up against the forces of evil. He does this by using magic. He's a wizard. He trains under witches. He *is* a witch—more technically, a warlock. But it's all in fun. Harmless. Those who complain are on the fringe.

And so it is that at the most spiritually vulnerable time in recent world history comes an occult tidal wave, packaged irresistibly. This is the Beaver Cleaver of witchery. Never has the occult come in such a desirable form, and never has it come in such a massive fashion. We don't pretend to be experts on Potter, but we know all we need to know. We know that Potter casts spells, that he employs witchcraft (there is no such thing as "good" witchcraft), and that the books about him contain the names of actual demons. One former witch—now a pastor—described the Potter series as "witchcraft manuals" written at a surprising level of sophistication.

There is the Hogwart's School of Witchcraft. There is a witch's actual incantation.

Such is anything but harmless and the residue will be with us for years. For to orient our youth in the direction of the occult and to expose them to such forces in the name of fun is very dangerous and comes at a time (remember September 11?) when we're supposed to be in the mode of repentance. Societies in Egyptian and Roman times were chastised for involvement in precisely such paganism.

It has nothing to do with fanaticism. It has everything to do with the Bible. Again, the bottom line is simple. As it explicitly states in *Deuteronomy* 18:10: "Let there not be found among you anyone who immolates his son or daughter in the fire, nor a fortuneteller, soothsayer, charmer, diviner, or caster of spells, nor one who consults ghosts or spirits or seeks oracles from the dead. Anyone who does such things is an abomination to the Lord." In another version (the King James) it explicitly uses the term "wizard" as a condemned practice and in *1 Samuel* 15:23 we see mentioned "the sin of witchcraft." In *II Chronicles* is the account of a man who "wrought much evil in the sight of the Lord" because he "used enchantments, and used witchcraft, and dealt with a familiar spirit, and with wizards."

It doesn't get much more direct then that. You believe the Bible or you believe J.K. Rowling. As we recall, Rowling told an interviewer she was given the idea by an entity that popped into her head. We wonder what that could have been, but we do not wonder about her books. However cute, to embrace Potter is to expose our kids to the energy of darkness. We realize that many of you have done so unknowingly, and so that's excused; we know you meant no harm. But you know now, or will if you open up Scripture. Whenever we have books or see movies involving the occult, there is the potential for infestation. Often unrecognized, spirits are allowed to attach themselves to people who willingly expose themselves; let's not forget that the child behind the case in *The Exorcist* became possessed after playing with a "harmless" Ouija Board.

Hopefully, Potter will quickly fade. But it doesn't look like he will. It looks like it could be one of the biggest movies ever. And it couldn't come at a more spiritually vulnerable time. During a moment when the Lord is calling us back— *and specifically calling us to guard our youth*—here we are sending what can only be described as the occult's version of a tidal wave.

The next time something hurts, it may be God "pruning" you

Did you ever wonder if God is disciplining you, or just trying to tell you something? Do you wonder why you get rapped on the head?

It isn't always a test or a punishment. Often, it's what might be called "pruning": the Lord simply taking away some things or situations that are inhibiting you, that are preventing you from being more fruitful spiritually. This is what we do to a tree or vine: When the branches and leaves are too thick, they're pared back in order to get more fruit, and the more mature a plant, the more shearing it often necessitates.

We're borrowing this metaphor from author Bruce Wilkinson, who has written an inspiring little book called *Secrets of the Vine*. It's based strictly on Scripture, and it underscores the importance of detaching ourselves from the world as we head in the direction of Christ.

Sometimes this means weaning ourselves of unproductive friendships.

And sometimes it can hurt.

How many of us can cite relationships we dearly wanted to succeed but that God took away—and that we now thank Him for ending?

Left alone, a vine will always favor new growth—growth for the sake of growth—over grape production. You'll see a full, leafy, beautiful plant, but few grapes. This is because all of the water and light and juice are going to the production of leaves instead of the fruit!

As we grow in our Christianity, Christ prunes that. "If necessary, He will risk your misunderstanding of His methods and motives," writes Wilkinson. "His purpose is for you to cut away immature commitments and lesser priorities to make room for even greater abundance for His glory." In pruning, how we respond makes all the difference. When we suffer, notes this author, we should offer it up to Jesus and respond with joy, comfort, and gratitude—

not complaint or rebellion or resentment.

Think about it: once you came to Jesus, did you notice how certain of your relationships changed, and how hanging out with certain friends began making you feel empty or out of place? Indeed, we start to gravitate to people who are on the devout side. They're the ones that now fulfill us.

This isn't to exclude people, and this isn't to encourage folks to ditch long friendships (and certainly not spouses!). It's to advise us that we must go with the flow of the Lord—and recognize when God is weaning us.

He weans us from money, physical attachments, and bad habits. His first command is to seek first the Kingdom of God, and as Wilkinson points out, "this is why God will always prune those things that we slavishly seek first, love most, and begrudge giving up. Again, His goal isn't to plunder or harm, but to liberate us so that we can pursue our true desire—His Kingdom."

If disciplining is about sinfulness, weaning is about ego. The Lord wants us to let go of things that inhibit us; He wants us to ditch what is unnecessary; He wants what's best for our ultimate good. It's how the Lord changes us from an empty basket to one full of fruit!

[And if you really want to bear fruit, try this little prayer each day: "*Lord, let me make a difference for You that is utterly disproportionate to who I am.*"]

Quakes of last week may presage great earthquake "storm"

Last week, as we all know, a large quake hit western India, killing thousands. It was a magnitude-7.9—not anywhere near as large as a quake can get, but larger than what we have recently seen in California and an indication of what's to come. The Indian quake was accompanied by reports *that same day* of quakes in Greece, Mexico City, and northeastern Ohio.

Was that a coincidence? Or was it something we can expect to see more frequently: earthquake "storms"?

It was minor this time (the quakes in Ohio and Greece were magnitude-4 or less) but the next one—the next *ones*—may not be so minor. There is a momentum building. In 1998 the number of deaths from earthquakes tripled from the previous year and then more than doubled from that in 1999. There's an excellent chance, with 10,000 to 20,000 dead in India alone (more than for all quakes in 1998 together), that the figures will soar even higher for 2001.

More importantly, there's the growing prospect of seismic clusters.

In other words we may see one quake set off one that is larger.

While seismologists and geophysicists still debate the point, there's a growing feeling that quakes in widely dispersed parts of the world can be connected, that they "conversate" with each other, that one can provoke another.

Is there thus a chance that a quake in Asia could set off the "big one" in California—or vice versa?

Might there be a flurry like we have never seen, including one of a magnitude we have not yet recorded?

The answer is yes.

Consider that in 1906, year of the famous San Francisco earthquake, there were even more powerful quakes in Japan and Ecuador. Indeed, shortly after the great Frisco quake there was a huge tremor in the Aleutian islands, and just *thirty minutes* after that was a yet greater one in Chile. There were major quakes that year in New Guinea, Australia, the Antilles, China, and again in Chile.

They were all more powerful than what just struck India.

"Normally you have one magnitude-8 earthquake every one and a half to two years," we are told by Lowell S. Whiteside of the National Geophysical Data Center. "That year there were about ten of them."

For decades seismologists believed that earthquakes were unrelated and that it was just a coincidence when they came in a cluster. It is no longer looking like a "coincidence." Instead it's looking like when one tremor resonates through the earth, others—sometimes others that are substantially larger—follow. As another example an earthquake in Landers, California, on June 28, 1992, was followed within hours by increased quake activity across the western United States, from Mammoth Lakes in California to Washington State and even the Yellowstone area! According to Dr. Whiteside, the 1989 Loma-Prieta earthquake in San Francisco may have triggered seismic activity as far away as Hawaii!

As we head into a time of natural turmoil, we can expect some of God's warnings to come in the form of major and perhaps unprecedented seismic activity, activity that will rumble for days or weeks, that will be without modern precedent, that may even form major chastisements. It is just such regional events that have been indicated by some of the recent seers. Visionaries in Ireland have forewarned of sounds coming from the ground like claps of thunder and the sensation of an immense wind and a split in the earth. *In Venezuela Maria Esperanza has warned that the earth's core "is not in balance."*

Such is also predicted by scientists who say we're overdue.

"It's like putting a bullet in a gun," says Dr. Whiteside. "If the stresses are there and they're just waiting for a trigger, it's like putting a bullet in a gun. All you have to do is pull the trigger."

For your discernment: an alleged description of Christ's manifestation

[full 1990 prophecy]

We submit the prophecy below for your discernment. We have mulled it over for more than ten years. It came in a dream. We think it may bear credibility. However, we are keeping certain details, including its source, anonymous for the time being. It quotes Jesus and occurred as a two-fold locution after a most unusual vision of an angel or young Jesus early in the morning of December 3, 1990:

"In four years there will arise a new evil the likes of which mankind has never before encountered. It will arrive almost imperceptibly, with few people noticing the depth of its evil, for it will appear to have beneficial and convenient aspects. It is an evil comparable to abortion—that is to say, that even if evils as great and widespread as abortion were to be eliminated, this is enough of an evil that it would present mankind with an enormous challenge. This evil is being allowed as a test because of the prayers inspired by Mary to put off chastisements. How mankind responds to this new evil will determine the extent, length, and severity of the first chastisements. These chastisements will differ according to regions, and like the great evil, will not always or usually be immediately noticeable for what they are. In the period also will be a warning that involves not fire from the sky but *fear* of fire from the sky, and strange loud rumblings. This, according to mankind's response, will then be followed by another chastisement, or the inevitable onset of the change of era. Your era is ending. Soon the world will not be the world you know. I am not speaking of a barren world, or one depopulated, but of the end of your technological era. Many inventions of mankind will be broken down and there will be more of a peasant attitude and way of life everywhere. After this breakdown of false society will come persecution of Christians and also a new world order. The anti-christ will be on earth trying to affect the new world order. Hardly anyone will notice the extent of his influence until afterwards. He will not be of tremendous visibility until he is accomplished. That is to say, he will not rule, control, and be at all obvious to the world at the peak of his influence. He will not be unlike a figure such as Marx, except his ideas will be more immediate.

"I will come not as a man of flesh, but like My mother, who already nurses Me and holds Me in her arms, as a light and power. I will manifest Myself in a series of supernatural events similar to the apparitions but much more powerful. In other words, My second coming will be different than My first, and like My first, it will be spectacular to many but also unknown initially to many, or disbelieved. Yet truly I tell you, the arrogance of the world will have been broken, and so many more than normal will believe.

"I will come in towering light.

"My mother held me in her arms at Medjugorje, as an infant.

"I will come as she has come, in light.

"Know this about the world: I would not appear on television, nor ride a car, nor travel in an airplane.

"Would I come in such a manner?

"Would I live in such a world?

"You think of the changes in very simple ways, without realizing the fundamental mistakes of mankind.

"The very artifice of your societies is false and against the accordance of God's Will.

"This artifice shall not last.

"Your very conceptions of happiness and comforts are a great evil and falsity.

"They will not stand.

"My greatest nemesis is science, even more so than the media. The science that alters life, the science which creates a counterfeit heaven, the science that toils with the womb and genes, the science that has filled the air with the power of the enemy, the science which creates chemical witchcraft and fouls the earth, the science which seeks to create life but cannot in actuality even sustain it, the science which has denied God.

"This will fall, and all of its creations with it.

"The seat of Satan in America is north of San Francisco.

"New York City is under an evil cloud and will be for 12 years. Do not go there. The pride there will be broken.

"As for the anti-christ, remember Europe, and especially Central Europe.

"Yet know too that God's Hand will be evident in South America.

"The world will not end but change."

Data support link between stem cells, cloning, and prophecy that warned of "new evil" and dire

The mail keeps rolling in: late last June, after more than ten years of discernment, we printed an anonymous prophecy that resulted from a dream the night of December 3, 1990. We can document the prediction's existence at that time. It began with a warning that *"in four years there will arise a new evil the likes of which mankind has never before encountered. It will arrive almost imperceptibly, with few people noticing the depth of its evil, for it will appear to have beneficial and convenient aspects. It is an evil comparable to abortion—that is to say, that even if evils as great and widespread as abortion were to be eliminated, this is enough of an evil that it would present mankind with an enormous challenge. This evil is being allowed as a test because of the prayers inspired by Mary to put off chastisements. How mankind responds to this new evil will determine the extent, length, and severity of the first chastisements."*

What could this revelation—said to have been by a man who looked like an angel or young Jesus—have been? Did anything happen four years or so after that alleged forewarning—around 1994?

Our readers resoundingly say yes. They tell us that around that exact time there were major moves in the scientific world that had to do both with cloning and stem cells. If so that means we are now in the very throes of that new "test." Did President Bush meet the mark in his response? Or have we opened the door to an expansion of embryo meddling—and greater chastisements?

One microbiologist who asked to be kept anonymous wrote us that "in 1994, the director of National Institutes of Health (NIH) created a Human Embryo Testing Research Panel to recommend guidelines for reviewing applications for federal research funds. The panel endorsed human embryo research, finding that the 'promise of human benefit from research is significant, carrying great potential benefit to infertile couples, and to families with genetic conditions, and to individuals and families in need of effective therapies for a variety of diseases.' The NIH Advisory Committee to the Director accepted the panel's recommendations." In December 1994 President Clinton announced that human embryo research would be permitted, but the use of federal funds to create embryos solely for research purposes would be prohibited.

There it is in cold print: by 1994 a new evil was on the rise, something that indeed would seem beneficial and be comparable in moral controversy to abortion.

"In November 1998 the first report of a method for isolating stem cells from frozen human IVF embryos was reported in the journal *Science.* The principal author is J.A. Thomson of the University of Wisconsin. The article was submitted on August 5, 1998. Assuming that it took several years to conduct this work (a reasonable assumption), that would have put it starting in 1995-1996. The same author reported similar results with Rhesus monkey embryos in 1995. Perhaps the work turned from monkeys to humans about that time?"

A science *website* notes 1994 in a timeline as the "first cloning of more advanced embryo cells. Neal First cloned calves from embryos that have grown to at least 120 cells. Nucleus taken from a multi-cell cow embryo. Nucleus implanted into egg. Cell division. Fetus. Calf...In Wisconsin, Dr. First had actually beaten the Scottish group to cloning a mammal from cells from an early embryo; that occurred when a staff member in the laboratory forgot to provide the nourishing serum, inadvertently starving the cells. The result, in 1994, was four calves."

If that isn't enough to further consider this prophecy seriously (and we'll be investigating the rest of it in future articles), in an encyclical letter called *Evangelium Vitae* written around this same period on March 25, 1995, the Supreme Pontiff noted, "The various *techniques of artificial reproduction,* which would seem to be at the service of life and which are frequently used with this intention, actually open the door to new threats against life. Apart from the fact that they are morally unacceptable, since they separate procreation from the fully human context of the conjugal act, these techniques have a high rate of failure: not just failure in relation to fertilization but with regard to the subsequent development of the embryo, which is exposed to the risk of death, generally within a very short space of time. Furthermore, the number of embryos produced is often greater than that needed for implantation in the woman's womb, and these so-called 'spare embryos' are then destroyed or used for research which, under the pretext of scientific or medical progress, in fact reduces human life to the level of simple 'biological material' to be freely disposed of."

According to the 1990 prophecy the new development predicted to occur in the mid-1990s would affect God's judgment. It also warned of coming events to the regions of the world, a worldwide breaking down of technology, and a major supernatural manifestation.

We'll be investigating other dramatic aspects of the prediction shortly. . .

Event in New York part of prophetic trend that will now heighten in every region

Within 12 years, the pride in New York would be broken, said the 1990 prophecy. There would be the rise of a great new evil, an evil comparable to abortion. How mankind responded to this new evil would determine "the extent, length, and severity of the first chastisements. These chastisements will differ according to regions, and like the great evil, will not always or usually be immediately noticeable for what they are." In the period, said the anonymous Catholic prophecy, would also be "a warning that involves not fire from the sky but *fear* of fire from the sky, and strange loud rumblings. This, according to mankind's response, will then be followed by another chastisement."

There has been fire. There has been the fear of fire. There have been strange loud rumblings. There has been a tremendous move toward cloning and stem cells and genetic manipulation—the "great evil," which the prophecy predicted would come in four years and which in fact reached the critical juncture in 1994. That has come to be. The prophecy was strikingly correct in predicting stem cells, and startlingly accurate with regard to the nation's largest metropolis, which has indeed seen its pride broken.

But now comes the question: *what next?*

It's a question that can be answered only with the intuition. It's a question that we ask the Holy Spirit. It's a scenario we pray to avert. By all odds, we are only entering the beginning of a steeper curve. We are still in a period of smaller chastisements and warnings. This period will peak with the first secrets of Medjugorje. For years now, since 1989—when a quake hit San Francisco—there has been an unrelenting build up, and now the curve, the trend of warnings, is taking another sharp upward curve.

Is this the "warning"? Is this a chastisement? Is it one of the secrets of Medjugorje?

So far nothing that has occurred appears to be among the secrets of Medjugorje but it is doubtless related to the general tenor of prophecy and so we look at this: what has happened appears to be part of a first wave of general chastisements, chastisements that vary according to region—that have materialized in the New York region in the way of terrorism and that will be followed by heightened events in all parts of the world.

Expect a host of situations to now arise. Expect events caused by man (such as terrorism and war) to be joined by natural events. Expect unusual societal occurrences.

The world is in upheaval and will be in upheaval for some time to come. We have reviewed that besides the fall of two enormous skyscrapers the fear of fire and "strange loud rumblings" may pertain to other and possibly greater events—perhaps an astronomical fright, or a series of earthquakes. We have reviewed the fact [see previous stories] that the quake may go beyond magnitude-9.5. We have constantly warned that we will be visited by a wide array of natural events.

These are what the 1990 prophecy called the regional chastisements, and how we respond to them—whether we go back to God, or go back to human pride—will determine the severity of what is to follow. The array of regional events and the strange loud rumbling are to be followed—if we believe this prophecy, allegedly given in a dream by Christ—by another trend of chastisement. It is this second wave of chastisement which may be related to the chastisements predicted at Medjugorje.

In the coming days and weeks we'll be taking a closer look at the most likely scenarios. We know that, except for those with secrets, no one can pinpoint exact times and places. We are also aware that we have to be careful: our goal is not to frighten. Our goal is not to alarm. But our goal is to communicate to a society whose collective head has been in the sand. We warn that it is not only America that will suffer—although it is headed for a distinct purification, which will involve a lessening and breakdown in its infrastructure. Latin America has already seen enormous events such as the hurricane in Honduras and Venezuelan floods and while this region will see more, and while already-huge events in places like China and India will increase, Western Europe—now moving so rapidly to becoming a super-state—should beware of a series of major events. Keep your eyes on Europe.

The events in this first wave of warnings and chastisements will be surprising. They will often occur where they are not expected. They will occur in *ways* they are not expected. And at some point—as we'll explore—they will involve the ocean. . .

For now, the cities at greatest risk of natural events in the United States, in our belief, are: Miami, Los Angeles, San Francisco, Seattle, New York, New Orleans, and Hilo as well as the rest of Hawaii, in that order. Internationally, Tokyo is at greatest danger.

But this level of specificity is difficult and nature always has surprises in store for us (as do terrorists).

A seer we are keeping anonymous due to security concerns says that several countries are involved with the recent terror attacks on the United States and that in the middle is "a fatal enemy who is still roaring. And it hasn't passed yet. The enemy is getting ready. It was an order they received. Not now, but they are getting ready, they are preparing. They want to scare the country even more. They are capable of doing anything. They don't have limits. There are two countries trying to provoke us. In all three or four countries are involved." The seer added that an escalation of current tensions will come although prayer can stop a "big event" that will otherwise occur.

Lost in the commotion: the link between prophecy, cloning, and September 11

Lost in all the commotion over recent events is the fact that on the very morning of September 11—as office workers settled in for coffee and glanced at the newspaper—there on the front page of *The New York Times* was the headline:

"Scientists Urge Bigger Supply Of Stem Cells," it said. *"Report Backs Cloning to Create New Lines."*

It was what many had feared: with the door to embryo stem cells cracked open by a decision in August to allow limited research, scientists were now going to try to barge right through—in fact, to break down that door—demanding that human cloning and the manufacture of more embryos be allowed in the name of "medical breakthroughs."

The trend toward cloning appeared unstoppable. Scientists in the U.S., Italy, and other countries were working feverishly to create the first cloned human, or at least embryos that could be used as a source of stem cells.

Now, they had all the more momentum.

That was the headline in *The Times*, which is located about seven miles from ground zero; meanwhile, in the Washington area, the same headline was splashed on the front page of America's largest daily newspaper, *USA Today,* which is four miles from the Pentagon.

While it was good that such research was limited by President Bush (who we have no doubt is a sincere Christian), we were concerned back then that scientists would be clamoring for wider use of stem cells if they were given even an inch, and we warned, in our own front-page headline, that as a result and for other reasons as well America would soon see a chastisement. The Pope himself warned that the wrong decisions on this issue would be "tragic."

It was just 33 days later that September 11 occurred, and it seemed tied to what we have called the *1990 prophecy*—an anonymous prediction seemingly from the Lord on December 2, 1990, which had foreseen *"a new evil"* in four years that mankind had never before encountered and that would *"arrive almost imperceptibly"*—appearing to have *"beneficial and convenient aspects."*

That certainly sounded like cloning and stem cells. According to the prophecy, *"it is an evil comparable to abortion—that is to say, that even if evils as great and widespread as abortion were to be eliminated, this is enough of an evil that it would present mankind with an enormous challenge. . . How mankind responds to this new evil will determine the extent, length, and severity of the first chastisements."*

We don't carry every prophecy. In fact, we try to limit things rather strictly. But this stands out. This *cries* out. It was exactly four years after the prophecy that landmark decisions were made pertinent to both stem cells and cloning. In 1994, the director of National Institutes of Health created a Human Embryo Testing Research Panel that endorsed human embryo research, finding that the "promise of human benefit from research is significant, carrying great potential benefit."

The prophecy went on to say that "regional chastisements" would occur according to our response to the "new evil."

Few can deny that since 1990 the U.S. and other nations have seen a baffling array of local disasters. It's not just over genetics. It's over our greed. It's over our general morality. But cloning is clearly a key part. *"My greatest nemesis is science, even more so than the media,"* said the alleged prophecy. *"The science that alters life, the science which creates a counterfeit heaven, the science that toils with the womb and genes, the science that has filled the air with the power of the enemy. . . the science which seeks to create life but cannot in actuality even sustain it, the science which has denied God.*

"This will fall, and all of its creations with it."

Prophecy that mentioned San Francisco may have warned of one world religion

In 1990, during a message granted in a highly unusual dream [*see previous stories*], an angel allegedly spoke on behalf of Christ about coming trials. In the message was the warning of disasters that would occur on a regional scale (which soon took the form of events like Hurricane Andrew); a "great new evil" within four years (which fit the description of cloning breakthroughs four years after the prophecy); and a "cloud" over New York (which the prophecy correctly implied would undergo a major event).

We are usually careful with such drama, but there is little doubt that elements have come to pass (for example, the event in New York was predicted to occur within 12 years of the prophecy, which indeed did happen), and, if true, the message had elements that may serve as a major warning. We submit it for your consideration. It's up to your own discernment. As we said, elements have come to pass, but tucked away in this prophecy, which we have only begun to flesh out, was also a stark and perplexing sentence we would like to explore now. It came in a package of less than a dozen words. "The seat of Satan in America," said the prophecy, after warning of the other events, "is north of San Francisco."

The seat of Satan. North of San Francisco.

What could this mean? Was there any one spot in America that represented a special form of threat? Was this all overheated apocalypticism—or might it be true?

What could it be about a spot *north* of San Francisco?

Again, we present this all for your discernment. What is north of San Francisco? There are the ritzy suburbs like Sausalito, and they certainly are drenched with materialism. There is Novato, where there was a town resolution to install microchips in pets, something that serves as a bad harbinger. But none of these seems to fit the bill. Farther north is Santa Rosa and then Ukiah, where drugs have been rampant, and the New Age mecca of Mount Shasta.

Those are the places directly north. To the northeast, just across the Bay Bridge, is a better candidate. That's the city of Berkeley.

We look at this place, and especially the university, and it has led the way into darkness—the place where a rebellious spirit turned into the Haight-Asbury hippies who along with Greenwich Village turned the country on to what we saw explode in the 1960s (which was the most dramatic infusion of evil in the country's history). It is where free love, drug use, radical feminism, and all sorts of liberal extremism took root, not to mention also the center for proponents of evolution and witchcraft (which is practiced openly).

That certainly seemed to argue in its favor as a candidate for the seat of evil, but even more poignant as the most likely explanation for the alleged prophecy is what is known as the "Presidio"—a plot of land at the extreme northern tip of San Francisco just before the Golden Gate Bridge. On a map it may look like it's *part* of San Francisco, but technically, as part of the national parks system (an old military reserve), it was federal land at the time of the prophecy—which separates it as its own entity and technically makes it the place most immediately and directly north of the city proper.

This is very interesting because it was at the Presidio that there was a major initiative to unite the world's spirituality and here where a foundation was started to conceptualize a new world order and the "U.N. of religion." This idea has circulated in other parts of the Bay Area and has been the focus of meetings in nearby Stanford. "Nearly 200 delegates wrapped up a week-long interfaith meeting at Stanford on Friday, predicting they had given birth to a movement as well as a spiritual institution: the United Religions," reported the *San Jose Mercury News* in 1997. Such may all seem well and good (it is good for religions to get along with each other), but such assemblies have been attended by prominent New Agers as well as a major United Nations official and a former leader in the Soviet Union (who indeed instituted a new foundation dedicated to this purpose at the Presidio). The united spiritual purpose tended to one based on environmentalism and "Mother Earth" (as opposed to God).

Such is dangerous, not because environmentalism is evil (it certainly is not), but because we have to be careful not to go to an extreme with it—in which case we might begin to worship the cre-

Eruption of volcano comes in wake of warnings issued in approved apparition

As major mystics like Maria Esperanza have warned, there are currently signs in nature, and one has come in dramatic fashion in deepest Africa. A volcano in the Congo has chased more than half a million people from their homes, and most important is its location. The volcano, named Nyiragongo, is near Goma, and this is fascinating because it was Nyiragongo that glowed ominously in 1994 as refugees were fleeing to Goma from a prophesied holocaust just across the border in neighboring Rwanda.

It was Rwanda where seven seers had seen the Virgin Mary starting in 1981 (the same year as Medjugorje) and during those apparitions, which were given the *official approval of the Catholic Church* last summer, messages were granted by the Virgin Mary, who showed them a "river of blood" in that area, headless corpses, and villages abandoned due to sinfulness, especially promiscuity. This materialized in the form of a brutal war in which thousands were decapitated with machetes (there was even a headline in the *New York Times* that said "Blood in the River") and the decimated villages came to be when AIDS swept through (and may have originated from) this very part of Africa. The seers also had seen "trees on fire."

Has this now come by way of the volcano? "The lava river that has poured from Nyiragongo since it erupted Thursday has killed dozens of people, razed buildings and forced hundreds of thousands to flee the city of Goma," reported MSNBC. "Fires and new fissures threatened to increase the damage, while continued lava flow was closing in on a Rwandan border town." It sounds like something out of ancient Pompeii. And like Pompeii it is a sign to us. The bishop, Augustine Misago, solemnly proclaimed that the Virgin appeared to three of the alleged seers, Alphonsine Mumureke, Nathalie Mukamazimpaka, and Marie Claire Mukangango. At the time, the three were 17, 20 and 21 years old. This is significant because while the ruling left out four of the seers (and some dramatic messages), Alphonsine, who gained an approval published by the Vatican, told inquirers that the Virgin came to Kibeho "in order to prepare us for the coming of her Son," according to Father Gabriel Maindron, a priest who has studied the situation. The seers said Mary came like an eagle that swoops down in the valley but without flapping wings. She often came with what were described as "flowers of incomparable beauty."

There were tremendous messages granted at Kibeho. We will be looking at them in coming days. They are poignant. They are prescient. Their time has come. For the moment, let's leave it at this:

"Nothing is more beautiful than a heart which offers its sufferings to God," said Mary. *"Pray, pray, pray. Follow the Gospel of my Son. Do not forget that God is more powerful than all the evil in the world."* There had to be cleansing, said Mary. There had to be *"reconciliation."* The world, Mary told Marie-Clare, *"is on the edge of catastrophe."* The only way is God, they emphasized. *"If you don't take refuge in God,"* said the Virgin, *"where will you go to hide when fire will spread everywhere?"*

Businessman in fight of his life details life-saving vision of the Virgin Mary

He was on the ropes. He was millions in debt. A huge corporation was trying to take his patent, ruin his company, and break him legally. His marriage was full of tension. He wore a pattern on his kitchen floor, pacing. So desperate was Louis P. Saia III that he thought of stalking the executives trying to break him. There was nothing left for him and his wife (even his lawyers were dropping him) and he was so beside himself with anxiety—an upheaval he describes as nearly worse than if a loved one died—that he could think of nothing to do but put on his running shoes and try to run it off.

The legal battle—a true struggle against Goliath—is detailed in *article* that we linked to yesterday. But there was also an incredible spiritual element. Indeed, Saia's life and marriage and business were saved, as it turns out, by an apparition of the Virgin Mary. It was March 17, 1996, that Saia, of Houma, Louisiana, who operates Pallet Reefer Company, came to the end of his rope, and began running down a gravel road. He was not a religious man—Catholic, yes, but the kind who thought nothing of missing Mass. That was about to dramatically change.

After dispelling the violent thoughts—getting rid of what he now perceives as having come from the devil—he jogged near his home.

"I began to run, and I get about 600 feet down this road and the road turns," he says of that fateful day. "When you make the turn, about 300 feet, is a little office building where we conducted the business that we were all fighting over [an invention for a new shipping container]. And I see someone on the porch. I was thinking, that's my secretary. I wondered why she'd be there on a Sunday. When I got about thirty feet at an angle, I look up to wave to my 'secretary,' but it's not her. On the porch, hands in prayer, is a woman with a white linen veil and a white gown. My thought was, gee, now I'm hallucinating. I rub my eyes and I'm still jogging and getting closer and I shake my head and now I'm 15 feet away—

and this time when I look, not only do I see her, with her hands in prayer, but I see a little bit of hair coming out from her veil and it's blowing in the breeze.

"I see her eyebrows, I see the wrinkles on her gown, and her eyes—which were very blue. *Blue, blue, blue.* A blue like I've never seen. Her hair was a light brown, like a chestnut brown. She was dressed in clothes like women wore in Jerusalem 2,000 years ago. She was rather short, about 5'3", and I got scared—too close and I was seeing too much. I decide that I'm going to run past the porch as fast as I can, and that's what I did. I was scared. When I got directly across from the porch—she was looking straight out—I looked as I ran past and her eyes hit me and I was stopped cold in my tracks."

Now he was looking at her from only 12 feet away, and her eyes, her incredible eyes, were touching his. From them came a wave of love unlike any he had ever felt. "I mean, my mother loves me and my wife loves me but it wasn't even comparable, it wasn't an iota as compared to the kind of love I felt from her," says Louis, who spoke to *Spirit Daily* yesterday and has also presented his testimony at church meetings. "Her love, the compassion in her eyes: if you took all the mothers in the whole city of New Orleans and you bottled up their love for their children, maybe that doesn't even come close.

"I didn't get on my knees. I wasn't very religious. She looked like a holy person, and I just stood there and she read my mind. Her face was not smiling and wasn't frowning. It was serious. We were eye to eye and she says, *'I am praying to protect you.'* The thing she says was not only the answer to my problem at that point in time, but an answer to my life. She says, *'Just have faith in my Son Jesus.'*"

That simple. That direct. "All these Harvard lawyers and Yale lawyers made my problem so complex, with the business situation, and she solves the business situation but more importantly the situation of losing my life from dying from stress and also my eternal life with one sentence: Just have faith in my Son Jesus."

Now Saia knew who she was—the Mother of God—and felt drawn like a magnet. The aroma of roses was so pervasive he could taste it in his saliva. "I walked up to her, not even thinking, and when I got close, she looked as human as anyone," says Louis. "After looking at her, I decided I want to touch her. I moved to do that and when I went to touch the bottom part of her arm, I realized that my hand would go through and I backed off. I had leaned forward and my eyes were four or five inches from her and that's when I could see through her, like translucent, you could still see the linen, but it was like liquid, and I backed off one arm's length, and when I did, she looked again like she was as much flesh as we are—as human as anyone—and that's when I decided I needed to get on my knees and pray, so I got on my knees and prayed the *Hail Mary*. And when I opened my eyes, she was *gone*."

But in the meantime, like a light switch, Saia had gone from the worst despair in his life—a despair so bad he says that "death would have been welcome"—to the best moment in his life. "It happened in a matter of a second," says the businessman. "The *peace* that I felt—not only was there no panic, but I had never felt the joy and peace in my entire life like I felt then. And it wasn't leaving."

Indeed, soon after, when his wife saw him, she couldn't believe the transformation. He looked 15 years younger. Incredibly enough, from total misfortune, from abandonment by his lawyers, from what appeared to be sure defeat—with a huge corporation taking away his invention, and leaving him bankrupt—he went on to a miraculous victory, a victory so dramatic that it was featured in a national business magazine.

We'll get to that next: the incredible intercession right there in a courtroom and a remarkable ray of light that changed everything and against all odds allowed him to defeat Goliath.

N.Y. woman claims apparitions of St. Therese in week before WTC

A Long Island woman says that St. Therese of Lisieux—long a famous saint, but one rarely reported in mystical events—began appearing to her just before the nearby World Trade Center bombing.

Sandy Mazzitelli, 45, of Green Lawn, New York, claims Therese, also known as "the Little Flower," came as a clear, distinct, and full-bodied apparition on the night of September 4—the beginning of five consecutive nights of apparitions in which the saint allegedly urged recitation of the Rosary and warned that "bad and terrible things" were about to happen.

Mrs. Mazzitelli claims the saint appeared in her classic garb of a brown habit with roses and on one occasion, the second night, September 5, was accompanied by a long appearance of the Blessed Virgin Mary. She also says the appearances greatly relieved and may even have healed an untreatable cancer she had been suffering. She said lumps in her body began to disappear during or soon after the events.

As always, we urge great caution with all this. We urge no involvement before prayer and fasting. We submit this for your discernment. And we do so because it unfolded under the close watch of a respected parish priest, Father Gregory Yacyshyn of nearby St. Francis of Assisi Church, who was praying with Mrs. Mazzitelli before the experiences were initiated.

If true it marks a new aspect in current mystical claims. While Therese the Little Flower, who lived in the late 1800s, once vowed to spend her heaven helping on earth and is famous for intervening with miracles—often in the way of roses—her appearance with messages allegedly pertaining to the world may mark a new phase in her intercession. Most of her previous appearances have been fleeting. In the 1990s it was claimed that she was seen at grottos in Ireland and she has also appeared to famed Venezuelan mystic Maria Esperanza—who likewise foresaw elements of September 11.

"I was sick and I wasn't getting better and I was in a lot of pain and Father Greg was helping me a lot, and one day he was telling me about this saint who was a man, that maybe I should pray to him, because the pain got really bad, and after he left I couldn't remember the saint's name," Sandy told *Spirit Daily*. "I was so desperate that day that I prayed for any saint to come and help me. It was like my last resort of a prayer. And then that night St. Therese came."

Significant is the fact that Mrs. Mazzitelli saw the saint not as a vision in her mind but with her eyes open, as what mystical theologians know as a "corporeal apparition." At first Sandy, a weekly Mass attendee, but not overly devout, didn't know it was Therese.

"It was late at night and everybody was in bed and I was getting ready to doze off," recounts Mrs. Mazzitelli. "I was just sitting on the couch and all of a sudden I smelled this pretty-like rose smell, and then I looked up a little bit and I could see her, and she was kind of glimmering, but then when I looked at her more, the more I looked at her, the more solid she became. At the beginning I was actually a bit frightened and amazed at the same time. I didn't ask her anything. She said she was here and she came to heal me."

The next night at around the same time Therese allegedly came again. This time Sandy knew who it was. She had looked at Mass cards and Therese had been one of the pictures. That night—September 5, a Wednesday—she told St. Therese she knew who she was. "And she told me that Jesus had a special purpose for me, that was the reason she was healing me, that I had special work," says Sandy. "She was like full-sized, but I could only see down to her ankles. She was telling me that bad things were going to happen. She stayed a while and was talking to me, that bad and terrible things were going to happen, and that for people to get through them they had to pray the Rosary more, that no matter what people tried to do, nothing was going to work unless everyone went back to the Rosary."

That such a warning would occur in a suburb of New York in the week leading up to September 11 is galvanizing. It was this very area that lost an especially high number of people who worked at the World Trade Center or surrounding buildings. Indeed, after September 11 this part of Long Island took on the bearing of a town in the midst of a war—with some families knowing not one but several victims and attending more than one funeral in a single week.

Mrs. Mazzitelli, the wife of an engineer and the mother of a 13-year-old, said the visitations greatly relieved her cancer but said that is not supposed to be focused upon—that it was only a sign to accompany a serious message and further warning of events that are still to happen. She said it was on the second visit that the Virgin also appeared. "And Mary was really sad. She had these tears coming out of her eyes, and she was sad because people weren't praying the Rosary, and she was telling me that so much more could be done if people prayed the Rosary, and that no matter what happens, there will never be peace until people start praying the Rosary."

The first apparition was short—perhaps five minutes, says Mrs. Mazzitelli—but the second one, which felt like just a few minutes, spanned more than two hours. "It was like the Virgin on the statue where she's the Virgin of grace. She had the blue robe and white and a blue sash, and then she had something over her head and over her were these stars, and as she was talking to me the stars moved. There were ten or 12 of them. The veil was light blue."

Mrs. Mazzitelli says Mary did most of the talking the second night, as St. Therese looked on. The woman was told she had to pray the 15-decade every day and help at the local church. It was then that Father Greg started a special Mass for Sunday afternoons, with an exposition of the Blessed sacrament and the Rosary. Every week more and more are coming, says Mrs. Mazzitelli, who believes many will be experiencing the Virgin as well as St. Therese in the days ahead—bringing to mind a message from Medjugorje that the Virgin would appear in every home if necessary. She says it's the obligation of everyone to pray the Rosary and start a prayer group immediately. "I basically had to change my whole lifestyle," says Sandy. "The Virgin told me the friends I had weren't good friends for me, and after she came all these new friends came."

Mary also allegedly told the woman—who was unfamiliar with other claims of apparition—that she was "picking people and starting an army or something, that the future was going to be worse and she wanted me to pray the Rosary. She said if everyone prayed the Rosary—they wouldn't realize all the power they had, that things could change."

According to Mrs. Mazzitelli, the Virgin especially indicated the Scriptural Rosary. "I didn't know what this was," says Sandy. "I had never done it."

This was all days before the events that would change America. Key among the warnings, says Sandy, is that things will get worse before they get better. "She wasn't talking like it being done in a month or a year, but over a period of time," claims Mrs. Mazzitelli. "I think it's going to go on for quite a while. And then she told me things for just me myself."

On one occasion she says that hundreds of rose petals materialized in the room and that after they were distributed, some claimed they had a healing effect. Mrs. Mazzitelli says she was told that St. Therese will be appearing to other people as will the Virgin, "and that I'm not the only one, and they have to do the same thing I'm doing. The point is, if you teach one person to say the Rosary, that person teaches another person and it will keep on going and that's what she wants."

The Long Island housewife adds that St. Therese appeared taller than she expected and with a wider face. "She wears the brown nun outfit, and the pictures I see of her have the Cross with roses, but she doesn't always bring the Cross. Sometimes she brings the Cross. In pictures her face is oval, but when you see her its wider. And her eyes were an unusual color. Some of the pictures showed them to be brown, but they were more like greenish blue or grayish blue, like a color you don't see often.

"The only thing I had seen before she came was a Mass card, but now since she came a lot of people have shown me photographs, and not all the photographs look like her. Every now and then one does. There's a photograph at a shrine nearby in Happauge and there was a picture of her there in the middle of the altar that looked just like her."

"Every time I saw her, I felt better and better," adds Sandy. "When I went to talk to some people, they were shocked that I was healed and they were dwelling on that, but they're supposed to dwell on what can happen if they don't pray the Rosary. The Rosary is more important than my healing."

Mrs. Mazzitelli said she has not returned to a doctor for an official evaluation and that she is now just doing things on her own. She says when she was told there was nothing else they could do for her, the insurance no longer covered treatments. "I had these lumps on my arms and everything, and they went away. And I had this tumor on my hip, and it went away, and now I'm walking without pain. And I was on all these medicines, including morphine, and I'm not taking anything now. I went from using everything to not using anything except steroids, because you can't stop them suddenly. I'm weaning off of them."

The Long Island resident says that the night before the World Trade Center attack she woke up and "was crying for no reason at all. I was just so upset." She says she knew it was part of what she had been warned about.

The last apparition was October 2, the day after St. Therese's feast day. It was the next day that Sandy says she regained her vision, which had been badly blurred. Mrs. Mazzitelli says she was told she would receive one more apparition. In her last appearance, claims Mrs. Mazzitelli, the Little Flower was not as solid as she normally was. "I knew myself that I wasn't going to be seeing her much longer, and she finally said it," says Sandy, choking back tears. "She said she is leaving me for a long while but that I will see her one more time. I don't know if it's going to be weeks or years. It was such a beautiful feeling. Everything was perfect. I didn't think of anything else."

Maryland priest says angel visited in full view of congregants

A devout priest in Maryland reports that on the feast day of Guadalupe an angel appeared during Mass in front of him and about 200 congregants.

The priest, Father Richard Scott, 41, of St. John the Evangelist Church in Clinton, Maryland, in the archdiocese of Washington, tells *Spirit Daily* that on December 12 he had started the day asking Our Lady of Guadalupe for confirmation pertaining to a special request he had made. Originally from Peru, Father Scott, who says he has a special devotion to the angels ("in the Catholic sense, nothing at all New Age") and recites the litany of angels every day, and conducts healing Masses at a church dedicated to the Archangel Raphael, recounts that at about 6:45 a.m. he was praying to the Virgin. "Blessed Mother, I know you are Our Lady of Guadalupe," he had said. "You know that I love you very much. You are also Queen of Angels. I know I am not worthy, but because of the merits of your Son Jesus and His Divine Mercy, I humbly beseech you to send me St. Raphael to give me a sign that what I have heard in my heart is from your Son."

That night Father Scott celebrated a Mass in honor of the Guadalupe Virgin at 7:30 p.m. He says that he had gone through the day without much further thought as to his request. "I forgot about it," he says, "but God didn't.

"I was saying the prayer of the faithful and I had closed my eyes and I opened them and looked up to see the people that I was praying for and I was indirectly praying for my special intentions and also praying for a man with cancer—and for our bishops that they always be filled with the Holy Spirit and faithful to the Holy Father—and just as I was saying that all together, I looked up and in the back of the church, I saw this Hispanic woman who works in the parish preparing the little kids at the time of the offertory, bringing the gifts—they were going to present roses and carnations to the Blessed Mother—*and right next to her I see this young man in his twenties with light brown hair with a big picture, a big painting in a frame, with a radiant face and around his body like an aura.* He looked different—but completely human, nicely dressed, with corduroy pants, a shirt, a sweater, and like a suede jacket.

"He was *radiant*—the most penetrating loving eyes. They exuded love, and he had a huge smile, as if he was my best of friends, surprising me. He walked like he was on a mission to fulfill what God wanted him to do. He walked up the aisle reverently but quickly. He was in control. Nothing would stop him. He just came down, but he didn't do it in a way that was pompous. He didn't float. He walked like a normal person, but quickly with this big painting on his right side and it was like there was a light, a spotlight on him, like an aura around his body, even though his body was normal, and throughout the whole thing his eyes were in contact with me. He gave reverence to the Eucharist and to me as a priest. He genuflected near the tabernacle and presented this painting. He laid it against a lectern on the left-hand side. He was not far away from me. He went up two steps and laid it against the lectern and he said to me, 'You have to bless it.' I did say as he was approaching, is there anything I can do to help you. I was *shocked*. Even as he said, 'You must bless this,' his facial expressions never changed.

"There was complete love and tenderness but he was there on a mission. I couldn't walk up to him. I couldn't move. Something kept me from moving. I couldn't speak. All I could do was observe and receive. Afterwards he turned around, once again genuflected to the Blessed Sacrament, and then he went again somewhat fast down the aisle, turned around, once again looked at me, raised up his arms to heaven, and said with a smile, as if he was exuberantly happy, 'Amen, alleluia!'"

It is an angel story as there have been many angel stories but with this twist: Father Scott actually saw the mysterious stranger disappear. Most who have angel encounters describe a stranger who then was nowhere to be seen, but the Maryland priest actually saw him vanish.

"After saying, 'Amen, alleluia,' he put his arms down and I don't know how the wooden doors opened, but as he was going down the steps, before he got outside—there is another set of glass doors—I saw him disappear. He went down five or six steps and disappeared. I saw him disappear. He disappeared just before he got to the glass doors. I did not see the glass doors open, and from the altar I can tell when people leave Mass early."

Of course, we leave this all for your discernment. So far we have no reason to doubt it and if true we find it tremendous—a Christmas gift. It confirmed something major for the priest, who says that painting was a replica of the famous Michelangelo masterpiece, "The Creation," in which God is touching the finger of Adam. He said there was a man in a car who had been out front through Mass waiting to drive a relative, and the man later testified that he saw no one enter or leave. Those attending Mass were equally shocked at the mysterious visitor's actions and way of walking.

Father Scott believes the mysterious stranger was the Archangel Raphael. He says the painting was expensively framed in wood with cardboard protectors on the corners. The priest left the painting in the church for four days, waiting to see if anyone would claim it, which no one did.

Scriptural Rosary: a powerhouse of grace and a source of the miraculous

By Michael H. Brown

We're finally able to make available what I believe is the most powerful prayer outside the actual Eucharist. It's called the Scriptural Rosary, and through the last 15 years I've seen it cause tremendous results. I've prayed it around the world, and have worn out several of them. They're so valuable I keep them as relics. I have personally found it to be more powerful than saying the Rosary with standard beads and perhaps this is because it's a more extensive Rosary. It has a meditation not just for every mystery but for every single prayer—and the results are potent.

Whenever there's a problem, and especially if it's a severe problem, an immediate recitation of this powerful prayer brings clarity. It takes about 45 minutes and is worth every second. I like to start the day with it, and on the rare occasions when I can't, things don't go as smoothly. The Rosary dispels anxiety and brings you immediately to what's important. It puts things in perspective. It has always amazed me how things that concern me suddenly vanish during recitation or how answers dawn on me. It grants us an exit when we're boxed into a corner.

I have prayed it in deepest Africa; I've prayed it in zones of war. I've prayed it over people who were dying or extremely ill. I've prayed it in New Zealand and Tokyo and Israel. I have prayed it at the site of the Annunciation, at the site of Crucifixion. I've prayed it at dozens of sites of apparition.

And it has enhanced every one of those experiences. It's packed with power because it has 150 little passages from the Bible and involves 15 recitations of the *Lord's Prayer*, along with 150 *Hail Marys*. This is a potent combination because both Scripture reading and the Rosary are each special tools against evil.

It's a book of solutions. It's a book of miraculous intervention. Nothing brings me closer to Mary. Nothing puts me closer to Jesus and heaven (except, like I said, the liturgy). I've prayed it at Knock and Fatima and Lourdes and Guadalupe and Betania and Medjugorje and Zaragoza and Montserrat and at the graves of saints like Francis of Assisi and Therese the Little Flower and Padre Pio and Catherine Laboure. I've prayed it at the Vatican in the presence of the Blessed Sacrament—and what power that unleashed!

Once when I was in Rome walking near the Coloseum a couple of teenage girls rushed up to me speaking hurried Italian and showing me something in a newspaper as if to divert my attention. Immediately I suspected them as pickpockets and placed my hand over my wallet. Finally I was able to shoo them away, but a minute later I heard a commotion and they were running back to me—*holding my Scriptural Rosary.* Apparently, while I was guarding my back pocket, they had taken it from my shirt or jacket pocket—and now they were returning what they had stolen, as if impelled by an unseen force.

[Further note: The Scriptural Rosary is based on the original Rosary, an outgrowth of the 150 Psalms of David. Most historians trace the origin of the Rosary as we know it to the Dark Ages of ninth-century Ireland when monks recited or chanted the psalms and devised ropes with 150 or 50 knots for laymen so they could keep count when they recited an abbreviated version. Soon after clergy and lay people in other parts of Europe began to recite the Angelic Salutation as a repetitive prayer (it's the first part of the *Hail Mary*) and integrated it with the old technique of chanting the *Psalms*. Then, during the 13th century, another prayer form, which would soon give the Rosary its Mysteries, began to develop.]

Medjugorje had warned that now as never Satan wants to show his shameful face

It could not have been more blunt. In 1991, in the monthly message for September, the Virgin Mary had told Medjugorje seer Marija Pavlovic Lunetti that great vigilance was in order. "For now, as never before," she said, "Satan wants to show the world his shameful face."

And so it was, on September 11, that he did. We have carried links to those photos you have seen: of smoke forming demonic features. We don't show them on our front page. We won't grant him that glory. Suffice it to say that when the World Trade Center blew, the face of Satan came forth for all to see. He was bearded. He was sneering. He was happy, at least satisfied. There are dozens of images. They're in many photos of the fire. One was so awful I didn't even want to keep it in my files. They were various demonic forms. They are even seen in video. Most famous was a photo taken by Mark Philips and splashed across Associated Press.

It was a blatant fulfillment of the Virgin's warning as the countenance of evil formed in licks of fire; even President George Bush has noticed. He has been using the term "evil" on an all but constant basis, and there's every reason to think he means what he says, that he takes the Bible seriously.

And anyone who takes the New Testament seriously knows and is not afraid to mention the role of the devil.

"I know that many Americans at this time have real fears," said the President. "We've learned that America is not immune from attack. We've seen that evil is real."

And so we have. It is the devil's hour. There are manifestations all around. We are seeing people take ill and friends in crises and the disintegration of friendships as Satan nudges us into competitions and jealousies and selfishness.

This is one of Satan's defining traits: selfishness. And there is nothing more selfish than exalting one's own image—an image formed in the agony of a fire that took 5,000 lives and caused real terror across America.

This is the devil's great suit: fear. He is the master of it. He drinks it like fine brandy. He wants us to fear him because when we fear him that means we have faith in him—it means he has more power.

So it is with terrorists. Knowingly or unknowingly, they serve his purpose and it's there in their eyes if you want to see it in the flesh. Under the guise of religion—and blinded by their fanaticism—they serve him. He is a master of extremes and he is now seen as a dark glazed look that emanates from the eyes of those he has infested.

We're not supposed to go around pointing to the speck in others' eyes until we look at the lumber in our own and so at the same time that we realize our own evil (and America is *filled* with it), we can also note the presence of the demonic in the glazed robotic looks of poor young Muslims who believed they were serving Allah but whose crashed planes sent up the fire that formed the devil's image.

The devil is "unchained." He is roaming like a lion. Back many weeks ago when a seer from South America warned of coming events she mentioned a "roaring lion" who would cause the United States trouble and now we see with stunning accuracy that Bin Laden's first name—*"Osama"*—translates as "roaring lion."

This is doubly interesting because we know Scripture (*1 Peter* 5:8) warns that "your adversary the devil, as a roaring lion, walketh about, seeking whom he may devour."

It was at Medjugorje at the beginning of this year that Marija had come out with another message mentioning that Satan was on the loose and now he is mentioned once again in the *latest monthly message.* In fact what the Virgin is saying is nearly exactly what she had said *back in 1991.* That was just before the height of the Yugoslavian turmoil and now we see Christians and Muslims rising against each other again—this time at a potentially vastly greater scale. We have warned that we could be approaching a "holy war" and let us issue this warning again.

We approach extremely interesting times. The key word is "intensification." What many who follow prophecy have been expecting (but what others discounted because it didn't happen precisely at the turn of the millennium) is now upon us. At times it will unfold slowly or even seem like it has stopped and at other times with the speed of lightning.

That's how Satan fell: as a bolt of lightning.

We're in a curve of purification and that means that the face of the devil must be purged. That means that he must be tossed from our lives. That means that we must not allow that shameful face.

For if he is not purged, if he is not defeated now—as we will discuss soon—his evil will precipitate an actual evil personage.

Why the Shroud of Turin is real

by Michael H. Brown

As we near the height of Holy Week, we are reminded of the controversies surrounding the Turin Shroud. Let's put them to rest: the shroud is real.

I'm not going to get into a long argument here with so many dates and places that your eyes will glaze. Let's get right to the heart of the matter. The shroud is a length of linen with an image of a strong tall bearded man who looks very much like older paintings of Jesus (before artists began to modify them). It's in negative. Only when the camera was invented in the 19th century did the details of its features become clear.

While scientists debate a bunch of technicalities, an overwhelming fact stands out: No one can explain how the image got on a piece of cloth in the first place. Even with modern technology, it would be impossible to inflect such an image on imperfect fabric in a way that displayed no use of pigments or any type of artistic substance and left no distortion. You could not do the image with a laser without scientists detecting the technique. You couldn't do it any known way. The image is just *there.*

Only a single layer of fibers is affected in a way no one can discern.

That overwhelming fact—that no one in the world can explain the technique used to form the image—is enough for most people. But let's take it a step further. Even if there *was* a way of inflecting the image in the way it was inflected, how could anyone have done it in negative, especially back in the Middle Ages?

Those who dispute the Shroud would have us believe that back in medieval times someone forged this image and magically was able to do so in a way that anticipated the later invention (six *hundred* years later) of the camera. It is not a very convincing argument. They base such views on so-called radiocarbon dating that they say places the shroud's age in the Middle Ages, making it only 600 years or so old and not 2,000 and thus "proving" it could not have been what many claim, the burial cloth of Jesus.

The problem with the carbon dating, however, is that the shroud had been through two fires up to that point in its history, one of which scorched the linen itself. When something is in a fire it picks up carbon residues that skew radiocarbon dating. And radiocarbon dating is suspect to begin with. Scientists throw out a lot of dates for everything, but I've seen cases where such dating, at least with ancient fossils, has been off by thousands of years.

Incredible are other tests that confirm authenticity by revealing that there are spores and pollen in the shroud, as well as images, that come from flowers and plants *that are only found in Israel* (despite skeptical claims that it was forged in Europe) and that furthermore *only come from the vicinity of Jerusalem*! The pollen of one plant, *Zygophyllum dumosum*, was especially significant because its northernmost extent is in the area of Jerusalem. In all more than two dozen of the species whose imprints were found on the shroud have been correlated with plants listed in Israel. "We discovered that there is one square of ten kilometers to a side that contains 70 percent of the species were were seeking—and is located midway between Jerusalem and Jericho," says Israeli botanist Avinoam Danin of Hebrew University. "Another check determined that five of the five-kilometer-sided squares containing 27 of the 28 species are in the Jerusalem area."

Scientists scrutinizing the shroud are amazed at the precision of its detail, the way the wounds correspond exactly with the wounds of Christ, the indications of actual blood, the precision of how the bones were structured and the blood flowed, the exact portrayal of how a body would be after crucifixion, the spots indicating where the crown of thorns were, the marks on the back that precisely resemble what would happen with the type of implement used back then to scourge, and even the fact the computer-enhanced images of the eyes show they had been covered (as was the custom) with coins—coins found to have the image of a ruler who reigned at that time.

More scientific details can be found by clicking onto some of our shroud links on the front page of *Spirit Daily,* or by clicking on the image of the *shroud* itself. You can also find pilgrimages there; it will displayed until October 22. We could go on forever with details supporting authenticity. To me the bottom line is how I felt when I visited the Turin Cathedral in 1990. Although the shroud was not on display, it was in a chamber above the altar and as I approached the vault in which it was kept, I felt a tremendous force come upon me, one that pressed me to my knees on that hard marble and led me through the most perfect prayer of my life. I then spent 45 minutes reciting the Scriptural Rosary as a fantastic grace came upon me. No scientist could ever diminish that and I will never forget it. It was as powerful as visiting Lourdes or Medjugorje.

A few years ago, there was another fire (Satan is always trying to destroy this greatest of relics), but a fireman heroically saved the shroud by breaking into the vault as flames roared around him. The fireman had been a nonbeliever but said he felt an incredible force as he was trying to save it. Something came upon him too. He is an atheist no longer.

Tips for healthy living from Sirach:

1) Be joyful - "Do not give in to sadness, torment not yourself with brooding; gladness of heart is the very life of man, cheerfulness prolongs his days.

"Distract yourself, renew your courage, drive resentment far away from you; for worry has brought death to many, nor is there aught to be gained from resentment.

"Envy and anger shorten one's life, worry brings on premature old age." (Sirach 30:21-24)

2) Be moderate - "Distress and anguish and loss of sleep, and restless tossing for the glutton! Moderate eating ensures sound slumber and a clear mind next day on rising."

"In whatever you do, be moderate, and no sickness will befall you." (Sirach 31:20, 22)

3) Be temperate - "Let not wine-drinking be the proof of your strength, for wine has been the ruin of many."

"Wine is very life to man if taken in moderation."

"Headache, bitterness and disgrace is wine drunk amid anger and strife." (Sirach 31:25, 27, 29)

4) Trust God - "He who fears the Lord is never alarmed, never afraid; for the Lord is his hope. Happy the soul that fears the Lord!"

"The eyes of the Lord are upon those who love
Him. . . He buoys up the spirits, brings a sparkle to
the eyes, gives health and life and blessing."
(Sirach 34:14-17)

5) Praise God - "Send up the sweet odor of your hymn of praise;
bless the Lord for all He has done! Proclaim the
greatness of His name, loudly sing His praises. . ."
(Sirach 39:14-15)

++++++

Our soul waits for the Lord,
who is our help and our shield.
May Your kindness, O Lord, be upon
us who have put our hope in You.

Psalm 33:20-22

JOHN

Father Slavko, famed Medjugorje priest, dies suddenly while leading group in prayer on Mount Kricevac

Father Slavko Barbaric, 54, a Croatian priest who has been stationed at Medjugorje in former Yugoslavia since the early days of apparitions there, died suddenly Friday while leading parishioners and pilgrims up Mount Krizevac, where they were praying Stations of the Cross.

Known around the world by millions who have ventured to the apparition site—and who have heard him at countless conferences and church gatherings—Father Slavko was a brilliant Franciscan who fully believed in the phenomena reported at Medjugorje and served as a spiritual counselor to the seers.

Initial reports are that he suffered a heart attack. According to Sister Margaret Sims of the Marian Messengers in Framingham, Massachusetts, Father Slavko sat on a rock and was unresponsive when those accompanying him went to summon him.

It's not yet clear exactly where his death occurred. A source in Medjugorje, tour guide Zeljka Rozic, said the priest was carried down the 1,760-foot mountain and was dead by the time they got to the church of St. James in the village itself. Fr. Slavko was born March 11, 1946 in Dragicini, Bosnia-Hercegovina. A member of the Hercegovina Franciscan Province, he had joined St. James Parish in Medjugorje in 1982. Often in the early mornings he could be found in prayer on Mt. Krizevac.

Details remain sketchy [this was very initial report]. But the grief has been immediate. "He was really like the adviser to the visionaries," said Sister Sims, who started the first Medjugorje peace center in the U.S. "Ivan (one of the seers) is very upset."

The same was said of other seers such as Mirjana Soldo, described Friday as "devastated."

The priest often stressed the tranquility that the Blessed Mother brings and while advising pilgrims not to focus too much on chastisements, warned that abortion is an "all-out war."

"Her message—calling us to faith, peace, prayer, penance, reconciliation, fasting, and conversion—is meant to bring all her children in the world back to her Son Jesus," he once told a writer.

The irony of dying on Mount Krizevac (which means "Cross Mountain") is significant. The mountain, just south of Medjugorje, has a large cross on top and has been the focus of phenomena, including reports that the cross spins and at times disappears. Legend has it that the cross was built after Pope Pius XI had an inspired dream and told another Croatian priest, Father Bernardin ("Brno") Smoljan, to build a cross "on the highest Golgotha in Hercegovina."

While we can't confirm that particular legend, a cross was erected in 1933 as peasant villagers hauled up buckets of sand and water. It was set on a rostrum overlooking the village as a protection against severe hailstorms.

The Virgin has been reported in the area since 1981 and even Protestant and Jewish visitors have offered testimony to the presence of the Holy Spirit. While it is not yet approved by the Church, the Vatican allows unofficial pilgrimages and Father Slavko coordinated many of them. He will be missed by all.

Priests said to bear the wounds of Christ

In recent years a new phenomenon has developed: the claim that certain priests have stigmata, the mystical wounds of Christ. This is interesting because while many have reported the phenomenon of stigmata through the centuries (and dozens in just the past several years), it's unusual for a *priest* to bear this phenomenon. Indeed, we have seen an estimate of at least 321 major stigmatists since the time of St. Francis, but until the 20th century, when Blessed Padre Pio of Italy (who hopefully will be canonized next September), burst upon the scene, there were no known stigmatic priests—or at least such is the common wisdom.

We believe there have been more than that through history, and they're certainly around today. One of them is James Bruse of St. Francis de Sales parish in Kilmarnock, Virginia, about 60 miles northeast of Richmond.

The phenomena around him began ten years ago this week, when, on November 28, 1991, droplets of water welled in the eyes of a statue in the home of his parents. It was a statue of Our Lady of Grace. Soon, dozens of other statues began to weep anytime the priest was around, and thousands saw it. Interestingly, this was in a diocese that includes the FBI academy, a Marine base, and the Pentagon. It had started at a point in his life when Father Bruse, a young priest, began to question whether he should be a priest at all.

The day after Christmas that year, Father Bruse complained of sharp pains in his wrists, and before long blood appeared to seep from unbroken skin on his wrists, feet, and right side. Meanwhile the phenomena included statues that not only wept but changed color—followed by healing and the fruit the Church looks for: conversions.

"There were spiritual and physical healings," said Father Bruse. "Then there were people coming back to the Church. If that's what the Lord wanted, He got it."

Father Bruse strictly obeyed his superiors, and at the height of the phenomena was under the strict control of the bishop. At one point, a statue wept in the bishop's very office. There was at least one claim of a bilocation in connection with Father Bruse (something that was frequently claimed for Padre Pio), and other unusual phenomena. He approaches these matters in a low-key, humble, and circumspect fashion.

He is a pastor now, and takes care of two churches, and so his energy, to a large extent, has been diverted but the feeling—the sensation of speaking with a holy man—is still there. He is near the Chesapeake Bay, and says the more recent phenomena have involved rosaries turning color, which is also reported at Medjugorje.

As we said, there are many laymen and women who claim stigmata. There are dozens in North America alone. We've seen it ourselves. We've been in the presence of one alleged mystic when blood began to appear on the forehead. But why are priests now experiencing it? Is it just that it now receives attention, and that in the past it was kept quiet by bishops?

Indeed, Father Bruse's bishop attempted to keep it low-key, but so many people experienced phenomena that it even made the cover of *U.S. News and World Report*. The healings have included a girl who recovered from partial blindness and a tumor.

What does it mean?

"Something is getting ready to happen," believes Father Bruse. "The Lord is just making us aware that He is there and He is real." As for our times and especially what has happened recently, in New York as well as the Pentagon: "I see that as something getting ready to happen. I think it's a major wake-up call that's going on, and I think that all that I see—the weird temperature, the polar caps, the earthquakes—there's a lot going on and I think we should all be prepared. I really do. I've had a lot more come back to church and Confession. I think it's all different than a few years back. I think we're in a different era now."

Whatever doubts about God he may have had, or at least about the priesthood, are gone. "We don't have to worry about what's beyond death," he was reportedly to have said. "We know. It's total love. Christ is the real power behind all these phenomena. Christ is preparing us for the Kingdom of God, saying 'be prepared,' but shouting it out now. It's as if Christ is saying 'wake up! Let's get moving on our spirituality.' I believe it's building up to something big."

We come in close contact with God with tears and cries from the heart

By Michael H. Brown

A short while ago we had an article about laughter—and how, even in times like these, we need to have a sense of humor. Laughter clears out our emotions; it removes bad feelings like removing boulders from a well.

The same is true of tears. Every once in a while, it does us good to sit down and have a good *cry*. You heard me right. Crying is a gift from God and it has a cleansing effect, it empties us, it releases emotions that can eat away at us like acid. They're important because when we cry the heart is engaged (whereas a dry eye can indicate a parched heart).

Christ wept. And so did those whose prayers He answered. There was the blind man in *Mark* 10:47-51. He cried for healing and Jesus heard those cries. He responded to the man's cries because Jesus responds to all prayers *from the heart.*

The Spirit Himself bears witness when we cry out. It is the strongest form of prayer. It can be a wail. It is the strongest request. We're told that this is how the Pope has prayed: directly, with a wailing that has been heard outside of his chambers. There is even a charism know as the "gift of tears." My wife has this. Whenever she comes across something that's anointed—something that's especially powerful—tears fill her eyes and she can't stop them.

That's the Holy Spirit at work—touching us, cleansing. We are healed by the tears of miraculous statues. One man we know who has this gift says he knows regular crying from spiritual crying because when the gift of tears comes, his nose doesn't run!

For the longest time, I had trouble crying. I couldn't do it even when I tried to force myself to. Then, in 1995, during a trip to France, I visited the tomb of St. Therese the Little Flower, and as I approached it I suddenly found myself in a flood of my own tears. In an instant emotions were released that had been pent up for years. I have cried since then and am happy about that. As one preacher noted, if you look at the Son of God without tears to protect your spiritual eyes you'll go blind. The greatest reapers, he said, are the greatest weepers!

In our tears, heaven touches us. God saves them up. Did you know that? The tears we weep with a good heart are gathered in heaven like precious jewels that are kept in a spiritual bank. "My wanderings you have counted," says *Psalms* 56:9, "my tears are stored in your flask."

I have actually spoken with people who had the near-death experience and testified that all their tears had been kept by the angels like jewels.

With God, nothing is wasted, no emotion is unnoticed, and no cry—when righteous—is passed. Jesus said that to get to heaven we must be like children and children cry. As they depend on adults so we must depend on God. Did not Jeremiah cry out for his eyes to be a "fountain" of tears?

"I have heard thy prayer," says II Kings 20. "I have seen thy tears." We suffer because we are joint heirs with Christ. Did He not cry out to the Father?

So must we. In weeping, our souls, our needs, our anxieties are poured forth. "They that sow in tears shall reap in joy," the Bible (*Psalms* 126:5) promises us. What a promise that is! The Lord wants our emotions engaged. He doesn't want crybabies, but He wants us to put our hearts into *everything*, especially at times like this. Our hearts are more important than our minds. Let us remember how valuable—how precious—it was when the woman who had sinned wept tears on the Lord's feet!

Weeping is a source of revelation. When we weep we are in touch with God and new things come into our heads. There is clarity. The boulders are moved. In our tears is our humanness. "I have seen thy tears: behold, I will heal thee," says *2 Kings* 20:5.

So now and then, go ahead and wail. Let your eyes gush forth with waters. Cry up to God. Let Him know what you need. Let Him know where you're at. Show Him your tears—and watch how powerfully He responds.

Mother Teresa's love knew no bounds

As many reflect on the saintliness of Mother Teresa—who died four years ago this week, and whose canonization process is actively underway—aspects of her miraculous life keep coming to the surface. Most of them involve examples of her fantastic love. Perhaps none is more surprising and even amazing—certainly not more telling—than a request she made during a tour of Africa. "In Yemen," recounted Mother Teresa, "which is entirely a Muslim country, I asked one of the rich people to build a Masjid [a mosque] there. People needed a place to pray, I said to him. They are all Muslim brothers and sisters. They need to have a place where they can meet God."

A nun asking for construction of a Muslim mosque!

It was charity that Mother Teresa emphasized as the hallmark of her faith, and it was a charity that knew no religious bounds. She was careful, yes, to adhere to the Catholic way; no one was more orthodox; no one had greater appreciation for the sacraments; but she was most careful to *love*. Her heart was a fountain of mercy and her openness was a manifestation of selflessness.

The root was in her humbleness.

"Humility always radiates the greatness and glory of God," she said. "Humility is the beginning of sanctity. Through humility we grow in love. "

These are important words at a time when pride runs rampant. It is the small things in life, said Mother Teresa—the things many think of as inconsequential—that mean the most to God. The food we give the poor. The help we grant the elderly. "I do not agree with the big way of doing things," said Mother Teresa. "To us, what matters is an individual. To get to love a person, we must come in close contact with him. If we wait till we get numbers, then we will be lost in numbers, and we will never be able to show that love and respect for the person."

It is one-to-one contact, emphasized Mother Teresa, that counts the most in our final spiritual evaluation. It's that upon which we will be judged. It's how we treat members of our families. It's how we look on strangers. It's our charity—and not just to the poor, but to all we know, all we have met. "The very fact that God has placed a certain soul in our way is a sign that God wants us to do something for him or her," Mother Teresa said. "It is not chance; it has been planned by God."

If we want discernment, if we want guidance in life, the key is in humbleness. The key is in seeing Christ in every person. The key is making proper use of religion and not letting it cause us to judge harshly. This means focusing on others. "Dear God," said the nun, "when it comes to helping those in need, help me to see more than myself"!

Nothing brings us closer to God than thanking Him

"We gather together, to ask the Lord's blessing."

Remember that old Thanksgiving song? The sincerity? The way it came from the heart of a good nation?

America was once a country that acknowledged God in everything: its major river, now known as the Mississippi, was the "River of the Immaculate Conception"; its first city, St. Augustine, was dedicated on the feast of the Virgin's Nativity; and its early bishops consecrated the nation to Mary's Immaculate Heart in its earliest days. In New York, Lake George was originally known as the "Lake of the Blessed Sacrament."

It's time to get back to that. It's time once more to acknowledge our great Creator. It's time to thank Him. As in our nation's early days, it's time to bring His Name back (with gratitude) to every public place.

When we do, when we give proper thanks, we feel His blessing. God likes our thankfulness. He likes to be acknowledged. He likes us to appreciate what He has given us—*which is everything.*

Think about it a moment: your very existence—the fact that you are conscious, that you ever had a thought, that you ever inhaled a breath—is solely out of God's goodness. It's solely His direction. And the Lord wants us to know this so we will be holy and grow close to Him. Without purity we can't approach His throne, and the Lord is lonely when even one of His children is missing.

"Thank you, Jesus," we should say every day—not just at Thanksgiving. "Thank you Christ." Repeat it. Keep saying it. It lifts our hearts. It transcends all else. Thank God and love God and you'll feel closer to Him than ever. "Oh give thanks to the LORD, call upon His name," says *1 Chronicles*. "Save us, O God of our salvation, And gather us and deliver us from the nations, To give thanks to Your holy name."

"I will give thanks to the LORD with all my heart; I will tell of all Your wonders," says *Psalms*—and may we highly recommend reading the entire Book of Psalms at crucial times in your life when first and foremost you should thank God. We have seen this cause wonders! "I will praise the name of God with song," it says in that wondrous book. "And magnify Him with thanksgiving."

"Always giving thanks," says *Ephesians*, "for all things in the name of our Lord Jesus Christ to God, even the Father"!

Thank Him for everything: for your life, for your friends, for your children, for your spouse, for your parents, homes, food, for your work—for your trials. Thank Him for allowing you the opportunity of heaven!

That's what heaven is: thanksgiving. We'll be spending an eternity at His throne praising and adoring and thanking. He is worthy of all worship and is *the* only one worthy of worship and in these times when so many forget Him—when they forget how much He has restrained His anger, how long His mercy has endured—we must thank him all the more intensely. We should do this hundreds of times a day: in the shower, while we're dressing—while we're stuffing the turkey. We should do so full-heartedly!

"Praise You, Lord Christ. Thank You God. Thank You Lord. You are great beyond great! You created all. You gave us all. Thank You Lord. Thank You Christ. Thank You Holy Spirit!"

Was the third secret of Fatima altered?

For months now, the rumors have been rampant. In the secret corridors of the Vatican, in corners the public never sees, powerful forces worked to conceal the true Fatima secret. The stories have flowed since last June 26, when Rome finally revealed the full contents of the message given to Lucia dos Santos more than eighty years before.

There have been mutterings of a Vatican conspiracy. Dark influences, say some, have taken the power out of the message.

Is this possible? Could—*would*—authorities really have altered the famous secret?

It seems unlikely.

Sources close to the situation—and to Lucia—say that the version given to the public is indeed the authentic one, that it naturally progresses from the previous messages, and that there has not been the slightest indication that anyone manipulated Sister Lucia or altered what she had written. They point out that the seer was videotaped reviewing what the Vatican was to release and has never indicated even the slightest hesitation with what has been publicly represented in her own handwriting.

For the secret to have been altered (at least recently) would have taken the complicity of Pope John Paul II, which makes a conspiracy theory all the more improbable. The Pope is intimately familiar with the secret, which he studied while recovering from his gun wounds in 1981, and, simply put, would not allow a fraud to be perpetrated.

Could it have been done without his knowledge?

Could someone have slipped it by him?

The answer to that too appears to be no. The Pope is still on top of his job and well aware of what is being said and done out in the world. Despite a body addled with Parkinson's, visitors describe him as in command of his faculties.

Moreover, the secret flows organically—with great symmetry—from the two previous Fatima secrets. Consider:

In those previous parts Mary had prophesied that "the good will be martyred," and, indeed, in the third secret, the vision includes martyrs.

The previous secrets said the Pope would "have much to suffer," and in the third secret, as revealed by the Vatican, an image was given of the Pope being shot.

The previous two secrets emphasized the dangers of Russia—and, indeed, the third secret has the image of an angel about to set the world on fire with a flaming (nuclear?) sword.

The symmetry is not only present but a work of beauty.

"Based on Sister Lucia's interviews in conjunction with the Fatima message and the secret, you get a perfect image of what all of this really entails," claims Carlos Evaristo, a Fatima historian who has also served as a translator for Sister Lucia. "Anybody will see that the third secret could not be anything else. It fits perfectly."

The question, then, is not whether the secret is legitimate, but what it refers to.

Some believe the flaming sword relates to a nuclear war that almost occurred in 1985.

Has the secret all played out, or does it have implications for the future?

Has Fatima been totally fulfilled? Or do we now move on to the secrets of Medjugorje?

Those whose focus is Fatima believe the secret may still have future pertinence.

"It's an image that refers to the past, the present, and the future," claims Evaristo. "In Sister Lucia's opinion and my opinion it doesn't hold itself to that particular event but can be used to interpret both that [nuclear] event, other past events, and other future events."

John Haffert, co-founder of the Blue Army, which is centered on Fatima devotion (and has millions of members worldwide), agrees that the Vatican released the actual secret but that it may pertain to more than just the tensions of the past. "I think this is finally saying, 'deadline,' the sword is there, Our Lady is holding it back," he says. "She said at Akita (Japan), so far, I've been able to hold it back by offering the passion of my Son to the Father, in union with victim souls, who joined their offering of passion. And now what do we see? The angel with a sword of fire about to strike the earth and Our Lady holding it back. It requires a lot more study, but the bottom-line is that it's very serious."

The third secret of Fatima and the flaming sword

As we mark the year anniversary since the entire text of the third secret was released, let's take a close look at what the most dramatic element, the flaming sword, meant.

The first two parts were revealed in 1941, but it was only last summer, on June 26, that we learned the third secret, and what we saw was stark: a vision of an angel holding a flaming sword.

"After the two parts which I have already explained, at the left of Our Lady and a little above, we saw an Angel with a flaming sword in his left hand," wrote Lucia. *"Flashing, it gave out flames that looked as though they would set the world on fire; but they died out in contact with the splendor that Our Lady radiated towards him from her right hand: pointing to the earth with his right hand, the Angel cried out in a loud voice: 'Penance, Penance, Penance!'"*

Why the flames? What does the image mean? What does it imply for the world?

It was a prophecy, I believe, of nuclear war. I believe that it relates to the other two secrets, which warned of Russia and Communism. I believe that it fits precisely with the rest of the Fatima message. While many think that there had to be something else—that the real third secret must have said something about the end of the world, or the collapse of the Church—I believe that the secret as presented last June is the full one and dramatic enough.

Why do I say it pertains to nuclear war?

First of all, the obvious: the vision implies falling fire, which is exactly what would occur during a nuclear holocaust. Lucia mentioned more than one flame—she used the plural—which in my mind conjures the image of a multi-tipped warhead. Without the Rosary and first Saturday devotion—without conversion, said the Virgin of Fatima—there would be the rise of Russia and the "annihilation" of nations—which may have meant the political absorption of surrounding countries like Ukraine but may also have meant atomic destruction. Fatima was largely a prophecy about the dangers of Communism, and the greatest temporal danger was confrontation between the superpowers. Such a confrontation would indeed have caused (and may still) flames to fall "as though they would set the world on fire."

But there's even more reason to believe that interpretation than the obvious ones I mention above, and some of the reasons are mysterious. Let's take a quick look at those now. According to Sister Lucia, the "great sign" prophesied at Fatima was an unusual display of the aurora borealis that occurred in 1938. This is fascinating because there are some who say the aurora caused atmospheric reflections identical to those caused by nuclear mushroom clouds. If that's true there is a direct connection between nuclear war and the Fatima warning.

Now let's get even more mysterious. In 1969, when a photographer took a picture of French nuclear testing on the Pacific island of Mururoa, images of Christ Crucified and the Blessed Virgin appeared in the stem and left of the rising cloud. Once more, the miraculous manifestation of Mary was connected with a nuclear warning.

Sister Lucia had said that it was up to the Pope as to when to publicly release the secret, but it was her opinion that it would be best to wait at least until after 1960. The reason, she said, was that the third secret would become *mas claro*—"clearer"—after that year.

And so it was. Looking back, the Sixties were a time of great evil and the decade in which the threat of nuclear annihilation was driven home by the Cuban missile crisis.

Now let's look at the 1970s. Four years after Mururoa, in 1973, were the revelations of Akita, Japan. There, a nun named Sister Sasagawa claimed she was told by the Virgin that if men did not repent—if we didn't get back to God and in a hurry—fire would "fall from the sky and wipe out a great part of humanity."

How does this relate to Fatima? The date of one of the Akita revelation was October 13—anniversary of the great miracle at Fatima—and occurred in the only nation ever to sustain the devastation of an atomic bomb!

Nor does it stop there. Seven years after *that*, on the very same day, October 13, in 1980, in Cuapa, Nicaragua, a seer named Bernardo Martinez saw the Blessed Mother. She appeared in a way that reminded him of a Fatima statue. And according to Martinez, who is now a priest, she told him that if mankind didn't change, it would *"hasten the arrival of a third world war."*

The next year, in 1981, as if to further stress the point, Mary began to appear as the Queen of Peace in Communist Yugoslavia at Medjugorje, saying that peace was in a state of *"crisis."* That same year, on May 13—anniversary of the first Fatima apparition—the Pope was shot in a way that brings to mind another part of the third secret that showed a "bishop in white" falling to gunfire (John Paul wore white the day he was shot and is technically "bishop of Rome"). What was the connection to Russia? Many believe the assassin, Mehmet Ali Agca, was part of a plot conducted by the Bulgarian KGB.

Now the plot thickens and the connections between Fatima, Communism, and nuclear war become even clearer. On March 25, 1984, Pope John Paul II consecrated the world and implicitly Russia to the Immaculate Heart of Mary, as requested in the first two secrets of Fatima. Less than two months after that consecration—on May 13, 1984, once more anniversary of the first Fatima apparition— one of the largest crowds in the history of Fatima gathered to celebrate and pray for Russia. That very day a massive explosion occurred in the Soviet Union—at Severomorsk—and *destroyed a third of the Northern Fleet's stock of surface-to-air missiles*—greatly lessening Russia's ability to strike and cause precisely what the secret warned about: falling fire!

If that isn't enough, years later, in 1993, Sister Lucia told a visiting Filipino cardinal, Ricardo Vidal, that the 1984 consecration by John Paul *"prevented an atomic war that would have occurred in 1985."* Prevented an atomic war! (This was the era when tensions were at a peak between the U.S. and Soviet hardliners such as Yuri Andropov and Konstantin Chernenko.)

The odds thus grow overwhelming that the third secret indeed had to do with Russia and nuclear warfare. As was shown in the vision, the flames of the sword were doused by the light of Mary, who was empowered by the 1984 consecration as well as prayers around the world, including at Fatima itself. Immediately after the consecration, there was the stunning, miraculous fall of Communism.

And so the bottom line is that the secret was a bit more dramatic—in fact much more dramatic—than what the secular media reported. What could be more dramatic than fire that sets the world aflame? What could be more serious? The third secret of Fatima predicted the shooting of the Pope and even more incredibly it showed an angel of chastisement hovering over our wayward planet.

Does this mean that the secret is totally fulfilled, that we're out of the woods? Hardly. Russia is showing signs of returning to its Cold War ways, and there is also China, the "red dragon." Communism is alive and all too well and so the image of Fatima—an image more than all else of heavenly fire, of purification, an image that pertains both to the past, present, and future—may well prove to be timeless.

Why are people waking up at 3 a.m.?

We just received e-mail concerning 3 a.m. Many Christians find themselves waking suddenly at this time (often right on the minute). I've been asking people about this for the past seven years. It often happens to Lisa and me. Recently, while giving a seminar in Connecticut to a group of about 40, nearly half (as I recall the count was 18) said that they often awoke at 3 a.m. and found themselves praying. They read the Bible or if they're Catholic say the chaplet of Divine Mercy or the Rosary or simply pray directly to Christ, which of course is the most powerful of all prayers.

Why three? Some speculate it's because spirits are "unleashed" at that time. Cultists reverse everything Christian and often witches and satanists do their rituals from midnight to 3 a.m. (a reversal of Christ's suffering from noon to 3 p.m. on Good Friday). In those rituals they're invoking demons who may be harassing us. Others believe that it's because 3 a.m. may have been when Christ rose from the dead. Send us your views. From time to time we have reports from e-mail correspondents (we can't vouch for authenticity, but will make clear it is from correspondents, not regular news sources). Maybe we'll get to the bottom of it!

More thoughts on the mystery of 3 a.m.

We received literally dozens of letters over the weekend on the mystery of 3 a.m.—whereby so many Christians seem to awake at the stroke of that hour. Just about everyone felt it was a call to prayer, often for God's mercy (see previous story and also a sample of the letters). Why is three a.m. significant? It has often been called the "witching" hour, and is the end of what I'm told are nightly witchcraft rituals. Many feel a dread or demonic presence and pray to chase it away. Perhaps the Holy Spirit is marshalling His forces. Others believe that in ancient times a day was 12 hours long and that Christ thus rose from the dead at 3 a.m. on Easter morning—an intriguing idea and if true one that would show His breaking the power of evil at that hour.

I can't remember all the times I've heard people say that such and such monumental event or vision or whatever happened at precisely 3 a.m. There are famous visions that occurred at that specific time, some that seemed good, some that did not seem holy. I remember seven years back when folks were passing around photos said to be Christ appearing at 3 a.m. to a seer in Africa. The problem was in the eyes, which looked neon red—catlike—and threatening. A clergyman tied into these events was recently removed from the Vatican.

I have seen other instances of dubious visions occurring at this time, although let me hasten to add that there have also been those that seemed authentic. As I mentioned, 12 a.m. to 3 a.m. is when satanists, reversing all that is good, declare a holy time (as we do between 12 and 3 *p.m.)*. We'll continue to try and get to the bottom of it.

’Tis the season to ask for blessings on *everything*

By Michael H. Brown

The first time I met the famous mystic, Maria Esperanza, I was astonished at her talents as a homemaker. Here was a woman who has the most gifts of any known mystic since Padre Pio—whose site of apparitions has official Church approval, who is sought after by crowds from around the world (tens of thousands have gathered at her events)—and yet at her house she is a gracious and humble mother who bakes and cooks exquisitely.

It is her spiritual touch. She prays, and it affects *everything*. It even makes the food taste better! We can do the same. It says in the Bible to pray without ceasing, and when we do (when we pray as we’re doing housework or dressing or driving, or for that matter buying gifts) everything goes better and there is a touch to what we do that’s hard to describe.

It’s the touch of our angels. They’re allowed to help in direct proportion to how much we pray, and Christmas is the time when we need to pray a whole lot. We need to pray for our families. We need to pray for deliverance. We need to pray for unity. We need to pray that every get-together is a joy and that old tensions disappear and that anything that haunts us is chased back into the darkness.

We should also pray about things we might not normally think to pray about. When it comes to gifts, the Spirit will lead us as to the best thing to buy or imbue what we have already purchased with a special grace. Pray that the gifts you bought will be touched in a special manner by the Holy Spirit—that an angel will accompany them—and that they’ll bring a special joy to those who receive them. The same is true of Christmas dinner: it’ll come out all the better if you pray before and during the preparation—not just repetitive prayers (though these are great), but also some real pleading to the Holy Spirit!

Pray about every single thing you have to do and every ingredient and every method and if the prayer is done with faith from the heart, it'll taste better than ever and bless those who eat it.

That's what Christmas is about: sharing His Spirit. And the best way to share it is by praying. You'll be amazed at how well things turn out, and how those little prayers may affect those around you in ways you didn't even expect.

"Towers" figure into many parts of Scripture

Anyone with remaining questions about whether the events of September 11 could be part of a chastisement need only search the Bible for the word "towers." There, the indications—the hints—come in a torrent. Throughout Scripture, towers figure prominently into God's judgments.

This is not "gloom and doom." This is Holy Scripture.

Take a look at *Judges* 9, where "all the men of the tower of Shechem also died, about a thousand men and women." In many instances the judgment comes from flames. "On every lofty mountain and on every high hill there will be streams running with water on the day of the great slaughter, when the towers fall," says *Isaiah* 30—mentioning two verses later "a consuming fire."

According to Scripture—indeed, according to the very passage above—such destruction is the lot of "rebellious children." It is the lot of those who add "sin upon sin." It's the lot of those who "weave webs that are not inspired" by God. It is for those who presume they can do anything and build high places for themselves instead of God.

"This guilt of yours shall be like a descending rift, bulging out in a high wall whose crash comes suddenly, in an instant," says *Isaiah* 30:13-14. "It crashes like a potter's jar, smashed beyond rescue."

"Therefore, her young men will fall in her streets, and all the men of war will be silenced in that day," declares the Lord of hosts in *Jeremiah* 49. "I will set fire to the wall of Damascus, and it will devour the fortified towers..."

Sin, says that same book, brings "a mound of ruins." It brings earthquakes [49:21]. It leads to—yes, terrorism.

"I am bringing terror upon you, from all round about you," says the Lord God of hosts in *Jeremiah* 49:5.

Edom would become an "object of horror," it warned; "every passer-by shall be appalled and catch his breath at all her wounds."

"He destroyed their fortified towers and laid waste their cities," adds *Ezekiel* 19—mentioning a "young lion" and the "sound of his roaring."

This is interesting because "Osama" (as in Bin Laden) means "roaring lion"!

"I will bring up many nations against you," says that same part of Scripture. "They will destroy the walls of Tyre and break down her towers."

It was the fate that in one case—*Ezekiel* 26—causes destruction to the richest metropolis. "The blow of his battering rams he will direct against your walls, and with his axes he will break down your towers," it says in a passage about the Lord sending Nebechadnezzar as a chastisement. "How have you perished, city most prized!"

On the day of wrath, the Bible makes clear, there is destruction; it is a day of "clouds and darkness, a day of trumpeter and battle cry against the fortified cities and the high corner towers." We remember too Babylon!

"I have cut off nations," says *Zephaniah* 3 for those who still don't believe that God chastises in this manner. "Their corner towers are in ruins. I have made their streets desolate."

Is there hope? Of course. There is always hope. The Old Testament makes clear the way for repentance—and avoiding just such chastisement. But pretending that God does not punish (calling such a notion "doom and gloom") is the devil's way of making us ignore it.

As for the New Testament: "Or take the eighteen who were killed by a falling tower in Siloam," says *Luke* 13:4-5. "Do you think they were more guilty than anyone else who lived in Jerusalem? Certainly not! But I tell you, you will come to the same end unless you reform."

Twin brothers and former marines reveal visions that changed their lives

Two burly former Marines, Joseph and Rocco Nasiatka of Pawcatuck, Connecticut—who are also twin brothers—have revealed to us what appear to be unique and credible apparitions of the Virgin Mary.

They're not seers; each saw her once. But it was something they could never forget. For Rocco, it happened in Viet Nam, about 18 miles from Da Nang. He was based with Delta Company, first battalion, Seventh Marines. One night at the end of June in 1968, Rocco, who operated an M-60 machine gun, was stationed on a ambush at what was called Hill 41. He was sitting there watching for the enemy as others slept when suddenly Mary was there with no forewarning, just hovering in front of his sights. "She was absolutely beautiful," he recounts. "I tell people flat out, I wasn't dwelling on the religious. I was dwelling on *survival*. And at that time we used to go out on night ambushes. What you do is basically look for the enemy and a lot of times you wouldn't see the enemy and it would be just mundane boredom. This one particular night I saw a vision of the Blessed Virgin Mary. She was elevated off the ground, she was in blue, and she said I was to be wounded, that my life was 'mitigated.' That was the word. I was to die in Viet Nam. I had felt that—I had felt before I left for Viet Nam that I had been marked for death, and others worried about this too—but I still did it because it was my duty, I was a Marine."

He had been marked to die but that fate was about to be lessened. It was going to be lessened because of prayers, says Rocco, now in his fifties.

Instead of death, the Lord was going to send him a physical suffering.

"She was barefoot and elevated off the ground," he continues about the apparition. "She said, 'How do you feel about a disability?' She said, 'It will be severe.' I said I could deal with it if my brain was intact."

The former Marine says he saw the Virgin with his eyes wide

open and in the pose of Our Lady of Grace, but all in blue, "more like an electric blue, vibrant, beautiful. She was all blue and she just appeared right in front of me."

The Virgin told Rocco his life was to be spared and when she foresaw that he would be wounded she pointed to her own left hand and said he would have a severe disability—specifically predicting what would occur a week later, something that, in retelling, still gives Rocco goose bumps. "Wow! You know? Then she came later and asked for like input, 'How do you feel about this,' and I said as long as my mind was intact, I can deal with a disability."

The prophecy was precisely fulfilled—in what is one of the most remarkable visitations we've heard about—a week later. While on night ambush on July 4, 1968, Rocco had rested his hand atop the machinegun's feed cover when his unit was fired upon. Four bullets ravaged his left hand while another hit between the fingers of his right hand. Meanwhile the left hand and its position atop the gun was just right to deflect the bullets from striking his head while the bullet in his *right* hand went through skin without touching bone! "When the Holy Mother talked to me, she'd said it would be my left index finger that would be amputated, and what they did was take a good portion of my hand because gangrene had set in," Rocco says. "They did take the finger off too. But the one on the right hand, if you could see it, you'd wonder how it could happen. It went through the skin only and didn't hit a bone, a pure miracle, plain and simple."

Born on Easter Sunday 1949 both Rocco and his brother Joseph had grown up in a very devout home, and in fact had begun making rosaries when they were 12. But they had lost their feel for religion in the Marines. Joseph was a sergeant who served in Guam while Rocco was in Viet Nam, and as Joseph says, the Marines "took the holiness out of us."

They do not look like standard seers. They look like they would be more at home working a dock than kneeling in a church. But as it happens, Joseph too has seen Mary. *His* apparition occurred 27 years after his brother's, while he was in his bedroom. She appeared out of the blue—once again was just *there*—and when she arrived, all else, everything in the room, disappeared.

"It was September 1995 that the Blessed Mother appeared to me," says Joseph. "When I saw her she was absolutely beautiful. I was a military policeman, and so [when the apparition later occurred] I took in a lot of details. She looked about 25 years of age, very beautiful, very small stature. She wasn't large. And she was barefoot.

"She had like a blue shawl and I asked her, point blank, why did you intervene for my brother, because I remembered that she had seen my brother in Viet Nam, and she said, *'It was your mother's tears and prayers that had gotten my attention.'* I asked her to explain to me why that would happen, and she made a gesture with her hands. And she said, 'In life there's a life stream,' and she said, *'Your brother was to die in Viet Nam.'* That's what she said. And she said, *'I asked the Father for mercy, and mercy was granted.'*

"I was very analytical," says Rocco. "I was questioning her. I told her I didn't understand that. When I said that, she spread her hands apart like Our Lady of Grace and said, *'I have great love for all of humanity'*—and when she said this there were waves of her love, her most beautiful love, her precious hands were apart, and there was like love coming from her hands into me like an *ocean.* It was rolling into me and it was beautiful. It was fantastic. When I saw her, everything else disappeared around me. She had roses strewn at her feet. She was about five-foot tall. The remarkable thing was the love coming out of her. I told my mother about it the next day. Somebody said it was because I was immersed in the faith, but that isn't so. I hadn't even been in a church. And then in October of that year, my mother suffered a series of heart attacks and what happened was that I actually came back to the faith at her deathbed. The Holy Spirit came into me."

Now, waiting to retire from jobs with the Groton Department of Utilities, the two brothers make rosaries that exude an indescribable grace. It's their mission. The Virgin had told them that they were to be holy and do many acts for her, and that's exactly what happened. She said we would be her servants and bring many people to Jesus. So now these two former Marines make rosaries! They have never charged money. They give them freely. They feel it must come from the "sweat of the brow." Tears come as they're doing them, and they wash some rosaries with those tears. They stopped counting at 1,000. The beads are not just among the most beautiful we've seen but imbued with a great spiritual feeling. Those to whom the rosaries are given have experienced beautiful things: healings, conversions, one woman who was saved from suicide. Occasionally they feel spoken to, and in 1996 Joseph was invited to consecrate to her due to the "dire times." He too still gets goose bumps. "I was told it would be like entering her ark of protection," says Joseph of his relation with the Virgin Mary, "and I knew this was what I was born for."

From the mailbag:

Once more, folks are waking at three a.m.

Once more, we're getting mail from people who say they're being awoken at 3 a.m., nearly as if a silent spiritual alarm goes off at precisely that hour. We've written about this before: how countless Christians of *all* denominations find themselves suddenly awake at that time and feel compelled to pray. "I am running into and hearing about a lot of people who had a sudden urge to pray either the night before or that morning, before the towers got hit," writes one viewer from Ohio. "Personally, I have been awakened a lot lately at 3 a.m. and the only way I can get back to sleep is to pray."

In the past we have wondered if it's an hour of mercy (the night-time version of the afternoon Divine Mercy chaplet hour), or whether it's connected to the fact that from midnight to three a.m. witches hold their rituals and unleash spirits that the Holy Spirit may be awakening us to pray away.

Who knows. Maybe the veil between worlds is thinnest at this hour. Many pray the Rosary or Divine Mercy chaplets, or read Scripture. These are all excellent. Prayer is so crucial right now. We need to pray more than to talk.

There are also viewers who have been hearing strange booming noises. This is interesting because the "1990 prophecy" we have been studying mentioned "strange loud rumblings" that would come at the time of regional chastisements. "Just wondering if more people have been reporting awakening around three a.m. to pray," writes another viewer from the West Coast. "This has happened a few times to me but none like 3:33 a.m. this morning (10/23). I had a dream of lying in bed and hearing and being shaken by what sounded like the biggest BOOM—like ten times louder than the loudest scariest thunder you've ever heard. Then, scared in the dream, I said four *Hail Marys* and the *Memorare*. I then awoke (tearful, perspiring) saying the Rosary (all fifteen decades) and the St. Michael prayer. This was a literal wake-up call to prayer. I had an inside feeling of hearing. 'I need you.' I think we all needed to pray, especially now."

Such noises have even made the newspapers in places like Lewiston, Maine. "More and more people were talking about bright lights, rumbling sounds, and rattling buildings," said the article. "The reports came from all over the area."

Others are seeing angels in the clouds or other heavenly formations. This we heard recently from Morrisville, Pennsylvania, where one viewer writes that he saw "two magnificent orange streaks about forty degrees above the horizon. I had never seen anything like it."

As it says in Scripture: there will be signs in the sky (*Luke* 21:25), and as we have pointed out, striking angelic images have been seen in the northern lights—as well as many demonic images in smoke from the World Trade Center.

It's as if the angels are touching down, and as they do—as they descend—the demons are dispersing and manifesting in all directions. They're being smoked out!

The angels are on the scene, and with them we are called at *all* hours to pray, pray, pray.

Marines who are twins and saw Virgin now are vehicles for Rosary miracles

Last month we brought word of two former Marines and twin brothers who separately had experienced apparitions of the Virgin Mary, one while he was stationed in Viet Nam, the other 27 years later. Their names are Joseph and Rocco Nasiatka of Pawcatuck, Connecticut, and they tell us that they saw the Virgin just as she appears above. "That image on the website was exactly what I saw, as close as you can get, but all in blue," notes Rocco, who experienced his sole apparition while manning an M-60 machine gun about 18 miles from Da Nang during his stint with the Delta Company, first battalion, Seventh Marines.

That was in June of 1968 and Mary had come to inform him that he would be severely wounded, which indeed occurred a week later. We have explained all that, but now want to look at what has happened since: what kinds of things have occurred recently, and what other experiences the two brothers, now in their fifties (and employed by the Groton Department of Utilities), have had. We do so because of the outpouring of response, and because there are indications that their ministry of making rosaries has been attached to miracles (indications that, of course, need to be documented). Indeed, those to whom they have given their hand-made beads have claimed everything from emotional healing and protection against car crashes to alleged remissions of cancer.

It is those "most in need" to whom the brothers minister, and they decline to take any money for the rosaries—which many find to glow beyond their remarkable, beautiful crystal and which are imbued with the result of their nearly palpable devotion. Both men formally consecrated themselves to the Virgin Mary after Joseph's apparition in 1995. They have made more than a thousand rosaries and the graces associated with them are reportedly numerous. Joseph says that in one case his wife had given a physical therapist at South County Hospital in Wakefield, Connecticut, a pair and the therapist had in turn given them to a daughter who later had an accident. The rosaries had been hung from the rearview mirror and the daughter got through a horrid crash with hardly a scratch. Recalls Joseph: "The car looked like it had been through a shredder, and there was only the rosary and the mirror, with streams of lights hitting the rosary when this woman went to see the daughter's wreck."

They know it is not them. They know they are "vessels." They have tried to remain "cloistered." They know those who really need them will find them—and it is to those they gladly minister. In one dream Joseph saw "seven flaming spiritual creatures" who were humanlike but both terrifying and majestic. He believes they represented the gifts of the Spirit. Often, the experiences come with little forewarning. Recounts Joseph: "We went to this restaurant and this woman who was a waitress heard that I was giving away rosaries, and she was wanting very much my rosary and it broke my heart that all my rosaries had been given away. But I had a Miraculous Medal that a priest had given me and I was thinking of giving her my Miraculous Medal instead of the rosary and the Blessed Mother in an inner allocution told me that she had written her name on my heart and for me to give this woman my Miraculous Medal. She knew it meant a lot to me because it was given to me by a priest. She had said, "I have not written my name among many hearts, but I have written my name upon yours,' and enough said." When the waitress came around Joseph gave her the medal and as he did the Holy Spirit entered the woman so strongly that some of those who worked with her were ready to call an ambulance. The woman was trembling and weeping but describing the experience as fantastic.

"Another time, I was given the image of a woman's face," says Joseph. "She worked in a post office in a town right near where my dad lived and I was told she was in much need of my rosary. I had seen her but didn't know her name, and I was told to go over to her and give her one of the healing rosaries. I immediately went over and gave her a rosary and I said, 'I don't know what your problems are, but I was told you are in much need.' Immediately, as if someone had turned on a spigot, the tears came flowing down from her eyes and she said, 'I'm speechless.' She put it around her neck and called me later on and said what happened was that she had severe back problems. She had some kind of an operation and it caused her to have severe problems and when she put the rosary on the rosary healed her."

There are other accounts of protection. In Ashaway, Rhode Island, was a woman who put a pair of the rosaries on her bedpost and a month later there was a freak accident. In this instance a car crashed through her home into her living room but stopped at the bedroom. In another case Joseph went to a Catholic gift shop to get a holy image for another person in need and just before he left felt "told" to take a healing rosary with him because he would be seeing a person in much need. It turned out to be a woman who owned the shop. "I went over in faith and again I presented my rosary to this woman and told her I didn't know what her circumstance was, but that I was told she was in much need of healing, and she was astonished. She said, 'Who told you?' I told the story and gave her a rosary I call the 'Sword of the Spirit,' and she started crying. What I found out was that she had just lost a 26-year-old daughter and she had donated one of her kidneys to try to save her daughter's life but it didn't happen and the mother was extremely heartbroken. The next time I came in, she said, 'I was heartbroken. I had lost all zest for life. But when I received that healing rosary I could feel God's love heal my heart.' Even though it was a terrible ordeal, she has moved on. She says she feels wonderful. That made me so happy. All these graces are to remind us to have oneness with Jesus through Mary."

The brothers, no-nonsense types, but totally open to God, believe the rosaries are the result of the Virgin's flow of God's power. "When the Blessed Mother was in front of me, I was absorbing those graces and that's why the rosaries are so powerful," says Joseph. "They're her graces. They are not of earth. When the Blessed Mother was standing in front of me, and she told me she had great love for all humanity, it was pretty much like Our Lady of Grace when the graces came out of her hands, and as I was standing there I actually was absorbing those graces, and as they were coming out of her they were coming out of me and that's why these rosaries are so powerful—because of her graces."

Often, the ministry of these two burly ex-Marines is to women and children. Joseph consecrated himself to the Immaculate Heart first, and then Rocco, who had not yet fully come to Mary despite his Viet Nam apparition, consecrated himself after a second experience.

This was in 1996, and unlike the apparition in Viet Nam, this time her voice came from an indistinct ball of blue light that appeared to him. "It was in my bedroom as I was praying," says Rocco, who like his brother has had only one full-scale apparition. "I wasn't forced to consecrate. I had to think about it and she said she wasn't forcing me. She doesn't say you must do that. She just said she would be pleased."

He consecrated himself and since that time the vocation of rosaries—something that they had been taught to do in childhood, but that they had lost touch with during their years as hardened Marines—has quietly exploded. They are constant witnesses to the Lord's goodness. They repeatedly see both small and great happenings. "God always gives help when you need it," says Joseph. "You just have to look for it."

Not everyone is healed. In fact, Joseph's own wife died of breast cancer. But so many have touched the goodness. At a spiritual level, the rosaries are nearly delectable. We have experienced them ourselves. They seem otherworldly. According to Rocco they were going to Adoration at St. Michael's Church one day when they encountered a relative with a friend who had cancer and while on Interstate 95 felt "told" to go immediately to this church. As it happens, the Nasiatka twins were in the parking lot and when the brothers prayed over her, she too trembled, broke into a sweat, and later claimed a remission had occurred at that point. "I saw her later and she was beaming," says the former Marine. "She said she was free of cancer. We tell people, don't look to us. We're just conduits."

The Lord heals those who are in His plan to be healed and does so in this case through faith—and the rosaries.

They are "shock waves" of goodness, says Joseph. The message is to think of one another. All they ask in return for a rosary is for people to do is something good for someone else. "It's God's way," Joseph says.

Lights in the sky: the devil's great modern deception

Since 1947, when a pilot named Kenneth Arnold spotted strange objects near Mount Rainier, Washington, mankind has been barraged by the reports: lights in the sky, "flying saucers," even alien abduction. It's no longer the stuff of the "lunatic fringe." It's out there on the radio, in the mainstream bookstores (where it now has its own section), and on network shows. In 1997 the nation was transfixed by reports on CNN and other news shows of inexplicable lights over Arizona.

In the coming days and weeks we'll be reporting aspects of this phenomenon because it has now reached a dangerous level. As we will show, there's a deeply spiritual aspect—an aspect that figures into the signs of our times—to unidentified flying objects, or UFOs. Some of them may be hallucination; some of the reports may be satellites; and for all we know, there may be life on other planets. We're not ruling out any of those possibilities—not even the chance that in cases like a strange crash at Roswell, New Mexico (which also occurred in 1947), reports of UFOs may be caused by the sighting of secret Air Force craft. Indeed, many of the reports come from the vicinity of military bases.

But there is a spiritual aspect here—a demonic deception—and it is as old as humanity.

You can go back to Cro-Magnon times and see caves painted with what look like otherworldly creatures and when you study them they begin to look like modern "ETs." In Sumerian, Babylonian, and Egyptian times was the belief in "gods" that were half human/half beast, bred with humans, and came from the stars. On the islands of Cyclades to the east of the Greek mainland is a statue of a goddess from 2500 B.C. that bears remarkable resemblance to wide-eyed "UFO" aliens. In 1500 B.C. Pharaoh Thutmose III saw silent, "foul-smelling" discs in the sky. The same was indicated in South America—where Indians likewise built pyramids thought to have occult powers. In Noah's time aliens were called Nephilim (*Genesis* 6:4) and immediately preceded the Flood.

They are as old as time itself and have the purpose of corrupting mankind. In our modern age, we are told that they are "legion" (*Mark* 5:9). In April of 1984 the National UFO Reporting Center in Seattle recorded four sightings for the month. By 1996 the same month of April had 83 sightings. And last month—March 2001—there were 238.

Although some of this is due to the internet and better reporting—and although we see just recently news that a UFO group disbanded in England for lack of sightings—from all indications the cases worldwide have continued to skyrocket. They are running parallel to societal evil as well as with signs in nature and they were foreseen at LaSalette, France, in 1846—where the Virgin Mary allegedly told two shepherd children that a time would come when *"the demons of the air together with the anti-Christ will perform great wonders on earth and in the atmosphere, and men will become more and more perverted."*

Whether or not we are in the final age of anti-Christ, we are in a very special time in which all manifestations of the supernatural are reaching a crescendo and we need to remember that as superintelligences demons are supremely deceptive. Just as they once masqueraded as gods or nature spirits and then as elves and fairies, so do they come in our own time as "spacemen" in accordance with current culture.

It is how they best deceive us. They are now loveable ETs acclimating us to their presence. And in olden times many of the people—adherents of the faith—were wise enough to see it. Charlemagne, who coalesced Christianity in Europe—and defeated the barbarians—was severely injured when a large sphere descended from the sky like lightning and caused his horse to rear up. During his reign there were so many "tyrants of the air, and their aerial ships," as he put it, that he declared them "evil." During the High Middle Ages, around the time of the bubonic plague, in the 1300s, there was an eruption similar to that of our own age. Eerie fireballs were seen above Paris, Florence, and Avignon, France—where the papal palace had moved. In some locales the plague was even said to descend like a ball of fire. "One such ball was fortunately spotted while hovering above Vienna and exorcised by a passing bishop," wrote an historian named Philip Ziegler. "It fell harmlessly to the ground and a stone effigy of the Madonna was raised to commemorate this unique victory."

It's no coincidence that art of this period shows the air full of devils pointing plague-tipped arrows nor is it a coincidence that during this time there had been eruption of materialism, sensuality, Church corruption, and witchcraft—which now also haunt our age.

In Kilkenny, Ireland, a friar named John Clyn sensed "the whole world, as it were, placed within the grasp of the Evil One."

Our mission—the mission of Christians everywhere—is to prevent this from happening again, and we must know the enemy to defeat him. We caution that no one should delve into UFO books, radio shows, or websites. Curiosity can kill the cat. Most such sites have an occult energy, and some are outright satanic. It's no happenstance that ufologists and New Agers go hand-in-hand. They come from the same source, and the fact that Satan is deceiving us with lights in the sky is obvious when we look at certain details. For example: UFO outbreaks and repeated sightings often occur over land where Indians performed rituals, or where modern witches have their woodland covens. This has been seen in places like Upstate New York (on a Tuscurora reservation near Niagara Falls, and near the Taconic Parkway north of New York City); at the Allagash watershed in northern Maine (where a so-called "abduction" occurred); Crestone, Colorado (where a New Age center now stands and where strange creatures have been reported since Indian times, including "ant" people); and Arizona—where, in areas like Phoenix, there is not only a history of ritual but massive burial mounds.

This is hardly to say that all the spirituality of Indians was evil. It's to say that the pagan aspect was in error. If you want to know what a demon looks like, recall the creatures in *Star Wars* (or the faces on some totem poles) and you'll get a fairly good idea.

Those who claim to have "close encounters" often find the experience terrifying. Afterward they report psychic phenomena—including ESP, precognition, and levitation, which indicate the preternatural nature of it—and also a sulfur smell, which since time immemorial has been associated with the demonic.

Aliens are often said to materialize and dematerialize, to even walk through walls, and so we have more evidence of their spiritual nature. If we believe such reports—if there is any credibility to such things—we must ask ourselves why a "spaceman" who can walk through walls and teleport would need a flying saucer.

As one expert, Guy Malone of Roswell, New Mexico (whose ministry is called "Alien Resistance") points out, aliens not only look demonic but in certain cases have fled when the name of Jesus is invoked.

Why would an extraterrestrial—if it was really an extraterrestrial—run from the name of God?

And why would an alien be created in such an ugly, frightening form?

Why do people wake up to find such creatures in a circle with their hands raised over the person?

Why do they cause nightmares?

And why do they return day after day and night after night for years—even haunting generations?

Why is it that we read reports of people who have had these experiences only after dabbling with the occult, and why do "abductees" need deliverance afterward?

Why are "crop circles," thought to come from UFOs (and most prevalent in England), often formed into what look like occult or ancient Egyptian or masonic symbols?

The descriptions of aliens connect to past artwork of demons (including old voodoo statues) and are anything but an image of God. This should be enough to raise our spiritual antennae. But as we will report in coming articles, there is more...much more... *stay tuned...*

Pope's historic visit to Ukraine accents mysterious nation

Pope John Paul II's historic visit to Ukraine—a nation that was once a republic of the Soviet Union—brought forth the drama of that country. It's a mysterious place. Situated right on the border between East and West, many believe it's a flashpoint for both political and mystical events—and many have long feared that it could be a major battleground if there is ever another world war.

It has certainly been a mystical battlefield. Few nations in the history of the world have suffered as Ukraine has, and few have had as many powerful apparitions. Throughout the nation are places of pilgrimage and magnificent icons showing the Mother of God holding her precious Son. Many of the icons have smiled, frowned, or shed actual tears. One such example is Zarvanystya—an incredibly powerful shrine that John Paul visited before he was Pope. (Indeed, some say he has Ukrainian blood; Poland borders the western part of the nation).

At any rate according to legend a monk found a radiant icon—a miraculous image of mother and Son—in a brook at Zarvanystya during the 13th century. In 1987—as Communism was beginning to loosen its grip, just before the collapse of the Iron Curtain—there was phenomena again.

"One day on my way to cut wheat, I stopped to see why there was a crowd around the well [at Zarvanystya]," said a saintly woman named Chornij Zenovia who had spent years in a Siberian concentration camp. "The people said they were seeing the Holy Mother. I knelt and started praying very hard and suddenly instead of the well I saw a big glow, like a mountain, and in it I saw a lady holding a baby in her arms. Personally I took it as a sign that Communism would soon disappear."

Although the KGB moved in (unleashing an attack with dogs and clubbing pilgrims), the apparitions continued through 1988.

Meanwhile the Virgin was appearing at many other places in this ancient, troubled territory.

At a monastery in Pochaiv, Ukraine, where Mary appeared

during the 12th century in a pillar of fire, she was spotted again, and near Ternopil she was seen above a steeple enshrouded in clouds. In Pidkamin I spoke to several people who witnessed a living picture or "tableaux" like the famous image at Knock.

For three days in July of 1987 hundreds came to catch sight of the Virgin on the exterior wall of a stone church called St. Parakovey's, her hand on an image of Jesus that looked about 8 or 9 years old.

Near Buchach, where manifestations of Mary had occurred at the end of both world wars, she was seen with the Infant in a light above Trinity Orthodox Church—reminding us that she is the mother of all.

In the basement of Pokrowa Catholic Church, where images of Mary had been seen in the 1950s, I saw human skulls unearthed by workmen renovating the church, men who told me that among the remains were the bones of small children and two decapitated priests.

Such is the mysterious Ukraine: few realize that its people suffered a holocaust in the 1930s, with somewhere between 4.6 million to ten million dying in a Soviet-induced famine—as many people, some scholars believe, as Jews who died in the Nazi Holocaust.

Few realize too that this mysterious land is where Chernobyl (which means "wormwood," see *Revelation*) exploded, and where (many believe) the Croatians and Serbians are from.

It is now the Croatians who are witness to Medjugorje...

Vicka reiterates comments on Virgin's "plan"

Medjugorje seer Vicka Ivankovic reiterated to *Spirit Daily* Wednesday that part of the Blessed Mother's plan is "about to unfold." She added, however, that "Our Blessed Mother did not tell me what part of the plan it was. I will tell you when I know."

There is no indication that the unfolding of a part of the Virgin's plan will involve the secrets of Medjugorje—prophecies that have been given to each of the six seers at this famous site in Bosnia-Hercegovina—and there is no tie-in whatsoever with the year 2000 nor with other more spectacular predictions.

The seers have always warned about overexpectation, exaggeration, and setting deadlines. They say only that events will occur within their lifetimes (they're now in their thirties). Although the word "soon" has been used, this has been said for years now and reminds us that in heaven's terminology, "soon" can even mean decades.

But speculation is intense that in some way, large or small, matters are beginning to shift at Medjugorje, where the Virgin has appeared since 1981, and this has come in part because of a recent message in which the Virgin mentioned a *"new time."*

"Dear children! Today I desire to open my motherly heart to you and to call you all to pray for my intentions," she had said. *"I desire to renew prayer with you and to call you to fast which I desire to offer to my Son Jesus for the coming of a new time—a time of spring. In this Jubilee year many hearts have opened to me and the Church is being renewed in the Spirit. I rejoice with you and I thank God for this gift; and you, little children, I call to pray, pray, pray—until prayer becomes a joy for you."*

Speculation has likewise been heightened because of the death last week of Father Slavko Barbaric, a long-time spiritual director of the apparitions. (See also story on Medjugorje and the bishop)

In the early days of the apparitions the Blessed Mother spoke about "plans" in terms of the local parish, the apparitions, the conflict against Satan, and "*God's design for the salvation of man-*

kind." She has often asked for prayers so that her plan can be fulfilled—without revealing, at least to the public at large, what the plan involves.

Muslims and Christians seek miracles at large "virgin's tree" near Cairo

An old gnarled sycamore in Egypt is attracting pilgrims—Christians and Muslims—from around the world. The tree is said to have miraculous effects such as healing and is at a spot where the Virgin Mary stopped and rested with Joseph and the Infant on their travels through this mysterious land two millennia ago.

Will it one day serve as the catalyst for true communion between religions? Will it bring Muslims—who acknowledge Mary as a very blessed historical figure—into understanding the power of Christianity while allowing Christians to find kinship with Muslims?

Many are those who rub the tree and massage it as if to absorb its essence. Actually, the original sycamore, known as the "Virgin's Tree," fell sometime in the 17th century and was replaced with a new sapling in 1672. In 1906 it fell again but was replaced with a shoot that was saved and nurtured to produce the large tree at which pilgrims now come to pray.

According to *The New York Times*, an early 19th-century traveler described the journey to the tree as a rugged trip along the Nile, through a strip of greenery that gave way to desert six miles from the walls of the inhabited city of Cairo.

"On approaching within a mile of the site of Heliopolis, the traveler passes by the village of El Matariya, where are pointed out an old sycamore, under the shade of which (according to tradition) the Holy Family reposed, and a well which afforded them drink," wrote Edward William Lane in his "Description of Egypt" in 1825.

Today the old village of Matariya is a densely populated, garbage-strewn neighborhood on the way to Cairo's airport, "a shabby maze of alleys and market streets near middle-class Heliopolis, where the prosperous and politically connected elite of the city make their home," notes *The Times*.

But there is mysticism in the air. A silence falls. There is the chirp of birds that seem in tune with the mood. Indeed, the tree isn't far from where the Virgin Mary appeared during the 1960s and 1970s over a Coptic church in Zeitun—apparitions approved by the Coptic hierarchy and witnessed by more than a million.

"I will ask Mary if she would ask Jesus to cure me from disease," said one recent visitor, George Sobhi, who had suffered a minor stroke. "I will pray for health."

According to the newspaper, last year the Egyptian government enclosed both the tree and the well that Mr. Lane mentioned inside a walled compound, set up a ticket booth and assigned police officers to guard it. However, the ticket has not deterred visitors. "For the love of Mary the virgin, nothing is too much," said a woman named Umm Badri, who came with her daughter-in-law today to embrace the tree. "She will cure us."

There must be a power here. There is excitement among those who visit—a sense of grace. Is it a sign of the times? Is it a missive from heaven to understand each other at this critical time?

The tie-ins keep coming on. It is noted that Fatima in Portugal—another famous spot—was named after royalty that took the name from the daughter of Mohammed. It is nearly as if the Virgin keeps beckoning those who follow Islam.

In addition to the apparitions at Zeitun, Mary has also appeared recently at Shentena El-Hagar, Assiut, and Edfu.

Mr. Sobhi and his cousin, meanwhile, had completed their slow walk around the compound, reported *The Times* last week. "They had stared in silence at the large modern painting of the Virgin Mary, seated by a spring against a charming background of orderly farms and forests, that the government installed in a tiny chapel near the tree."

"'Are you Muslim or Christian?' one pilgrim asked when she saw a foreigner. Then she displayed the small tattoo of a cross on her wrist, a typical decoration for Copts. 'It doesn't matter," she added quickly. 'We are all descended from Adam and we are all family. . .'"

Visions, dreams, and strange images tied to terrorist attack on U.S.

We hear from all over from those who had strange premonitions of the September 11 event. Here in Upstate New York we spoke to a friend who had a dream the night before the attack of an imposing man with a knife. It was striking enough to mention to his wife even before word came of the hijackings (which involved the use of sharp objects). "He looked very tall, like six and a half feet, and he did not look American," said this friend, a Eucharistic minister in a local chapel. "He looked Middle Eastern. And he was not alone. When I found out about the hijackings later that morning, I couldn't believe it." At a local restaurant, a waitress dedicated to the Rosary described a dream of two tall slabs exploding and crumbling. Another person we know expressed a distinct, uncanny feeling. "Something bad's going to happen," he warned his family—coming back a second time and saying, "Something *very* bad is going to happen." That was the evening of September 10. And the same is true around the world. In other parts we hear of folks awoken by unsettling dreams and in the months leading up to the attack we carried a number of articles about prophecies warning that foreign powers were conspiring to drag the U.S. into a war and that there was danger on our own soil. One prophecy, known now as the "1990 prophecy," said New York City would see its "pride broken" by 2002. There were also warnings last August that after the stem-cell decision America would quickly experience chastisement.

Clearly, there was agitation in the spirit world, and maybe you have other examples of omens leading up to the horrid event. We're told that on the evening of the attack the Virgin Mary appeared to Medjugorje seer Ivan Dragicevic crying and asking prayers for peace. While there is no indication that September 11 was part of any Medjugorje seers' secrets, there were clearly deep spiritual elements to the event. We have carried items on how demonic faces seemed to appear in the flames and smoke billowing from the World Trade Center. One came from a photographer named Mark Philips, whose photo appeared in the Associated Press. Some looking at it can see eyes, a nose, a mouth, and horns. We have seen other photos with a flurry of other such images. One reader and a neighbor saw swords in the sky above Long Island. These remind us of miraculous formations in clouds or photographs taken at sites of apparition. Somehow the camera occasionally catches glimpses of otherwise unseen presences. In the case of the Trade Center the question is whether such an image if valid is indicating that the devil was behind the attack (which in many ways, of course, he was) or whether it's heaven's way of showing the devil and his minions being purged—a symbol of the evil in our system.

We have also heard from folks who have had recent visions of a great battle being prepared, a battle between angels and devils. A seer had warned that a "great event" was coming, and Pat Hull, a Texas woman who allegedly saw this same seer in bilocation, had a similar admonition. "A great blackness of evil was being released," Pat had told us last August. "[The seer] said it that way. And God has held up His hand as long as He is going to, and He is going to take His hand down and there's nothing, nothing, that will stop this, this disaster, from happening. She didn't tell me what the disaster was. She didn't say any kind of a time. We got through with our visit and I wrote it all down. It was about 3:30 that afternoon. So our visit was between 3 and 3:30. I slowly sifted back. Even Friday [the next day] at noon, I still said to my daughter, I'm not all back yet, and I pointed up. I said, 'From here to over here I feel movement, I hear voices, there are angels, good spirits, they are getting ready for a mighty battle. I heard everything they were saying but I can't tell you what they said. They were rushing around going here and there like an army would getting ready to go in battle. That night, I didn't hear the voices anymore, but I sensed movement and feeling."

This is an important moment in both American and human history. If we take the event for what it was—a purging, a mercy, an evil that God allowed to set us right—we'll be okay. If we don't, there will be other visions, other dreams. . . and more such events.

If you want to lose weight try a diet designed by the Holy Spirit

By Michael H. Brown

Three years ago I decided to finally weigh myself. It had been years—maybe more than a decade. I had no idea what I weighed, and figured I was a bit overweight. My shirts and suits were getting pretty tight.

It was a scale my wife had bought after she was pregnant and when I got on it I was shocked. I weighed 201 pounds. I had no idea. The last time I could remember my weight I was something like 165. That was probably in the 1970s.

Put simply, I was getting obese. I wasn't alone. From what I read, the percentage of Americans now overweight is more than fifty percent. Too much sugar and salt and fat.

I was both surprised and distressed. Here I was, swimming every day and working vigorously in the yard, and I was nothing less than fat. How to lose it? I went right to our bedroom, sat down, and prayed from the heart (that's when prayers work!).

I prayed that I be given a way to lose weight, and immediately I felt an infusion of thought. I felt "told" to start drinking as much water as I could, to cut down on lunches, and to stop using the salt shaker.

That was about it. I never really thought much about salt, but what it does is cause inordinate water retention. When we eat too much it sends our bodies a signal to retain water because our systems need the water to dilute salt.

Think about how much salt we use these days! Even if we don't add it to our food, it's used in snacks, cheese, soup, ice cream, pizza, and even cereal in terrific quantities. Check for sodium content on the food labels. It's especially heavy in fast foods, instant dinners, and food served at just about any restaurant.

If you're overweight, there's a good chance that salt has a lot to do with it. In moderation it's a splendid treat, but overused it piles on the pounds and diminishes our overall health. There's probably no more hidden a source of obesity than salt content.

On the other hand, when we drink water, especially water with no chlorine (God's simplest and most powerful sustenance), the opposite happens. The more water we pump into our bodies, the more weight we lose. That sounds illogical but the reason is because water intake signals the body that it no longer has to retain so much water and water weighs a lot (about eight pounds a gallon).

I started drinking about eight glasses a day and couldn't believe how fast the pounds came off. In the first two weeks I lost a pound a day on "heaven's diet." For the next couple weeks it diminished to a loss of about half a pound a day. In all I've now lost about 30 pounds and am not really depriving myself. The lesson: pray. Ask for guidance about every physical need. The Holy Spirit even helps us with our weight. In fact, no one can help more. No matter how much they learn at medical school, they aren't able to fully master the intricacies of the human body but God can because He made it.

Give yourself the gift of being who you really are

Do you often feel funny around others? Do you get into funks about yourself? Do you let others influence your self-image? If that happens, it may be time to let *God* define who you are. It may be time to listen to what *He* thinks of you. It also may be time to shield yourself spiritually. For the simple fact of the matter is that others, in what they say or think, have a profound effect on our moods—and we often have to guard against this, especially on holidays.

You know the feeling: someone comes around and suddenly you begin to feel different—inferior, inadequate, uncomfortable. Suddenly, a change comes over you and a family or social occasion is less enjoyable than it should be. Sometimes, it affects us (as in the workplace, or with someone at home) on a constant basis.

Avoiding this means prayer. The more we pray, the more we are filled with the way God views us, and that's a very positive feeling because it's filled with love. The more we pray, the better grounded we are in social occasions—the more the views of others bounce off. The more we pray, the more we become humble, and a humble person has a strong self-definition that others can't jar.

When we know someone has a negative, antagonistic, or jealous view of us, we should forgive that person and pray for him or her *from our hearts.* We should take the time to really love that person as much as we can. We should return positive for negative.

As difficult as this may seem, once we make that breakthrough all the ill feelings which have come upon us from that person instantly vanish!

The best approach is prevention. Before a gathering, we should pray that any negative influence from others doesn't affect us in the least and we should pray for a shield against spiritual and especially jealous harassment. As it says in *Proverbs*, jealousy stings like hatred. It's the rage of man (6:34). It can seem overwhelming.

But with prayer it is not!

We don't have to let envy or simple dislike ruin an occasion. If we protect ourselves *before* social gatherings, make sure we ourselves have no envy, and then pray any time we begin to feel uneasy, the negativity will often disappear before it can take root.

At family gatherings, we should also avoid argumentation. Silence is often the safest way to navigate a discussion.

And we should say nothing negative. When we criticize others it brings a spirit that then opens us up to spiritual attack.

Before a gathering, ask God to guide you in everything you say and think and take the time to pray that your angel gets between you and any unpleasant influence. Ask Him to make you feel whole and comfortable—ask Him to give you great strength—and ask that the real *you* be recognized. If someone says something negative, don't respond in kind; turn the other cheek. But at the same time, don't let negativity burrow in. Don't let it *define* you. Ask God to dispel it. Ask God to remind you of who *you* are! Rebuke all the evil that may be hoisted upon you (do this in the silence of your heart, in the Name of Christ, since such an attack may be demonic), send love to the person affecting you, and pray for humility.

Humbleness is key. It is the ultimate defense. When we have humility our self-image is solid as a rock—and like a rock is impervious to the attacks of the enemy.

Worrying blocks God's faithful blessings

Hard as it might be to believe, we're not supposed to worry. Anxiety is against God's will. He doesn't want us to be anxious. He wants us at peace. He wants us suffused with a feeling of tranquility. And there's something else: anxiety binds up His blessings.

When we worry we prevent God from acting.

Now, of course, God can act if He chooses, and despite anxiety—despite our lack of faith—He often does. It's another example of His mercy. He puts up with a lot from us. But overall worrying inhibits Him from answering our prayers.

Why would that be? Why would anxiety interfere with our requests?

One of the tests of life is trust. God loves when through use of our free will we *trust* Him. He loves when we rely on Him totally. And as Jesus said (*Matthew* 6:25-32), "Look at the birds of the air, that they do not sow, nor reap nor gather into barns, and yet your heavenly Father feeds them. Are you not worth much more than they?"

Worry is the opposite of trust. In fact, it's *anti*-faith. "God commands you to pray, but He forbids you to worry," said St. John Vianney. As an American mystic, Sister Mildred Mary Ephrem Neuzil, said, "Worry is like a rocking chair: it doesn't get you anywhere."

Worrying is the opposite of faith and just as faith unlooses great blessings from heaven, worry *stymies* them. It says in *Proverbs* (28:20) that a faithful man will be richly blessed. "According to your faith will it be done to you," added Jesus (*Matthew* 9:29).

If we pray enough and have faith that our prayers will be answered, in God's time, they will, if they're good for us. On the contrary, when we pray and worry we're just treading water. We're on that rocking chair. In His mercy God may respond, but He may not bless as largely as He would otherwise. We may miss His largest blessings. Worry is belief that God will not protect us. It's different from caution. Naturally we have to be careful with what we do, *but not to the point of constant fretting.*

Jesus tells us that "the worry of the world" makes us "unfruitful." It chokes His words. For mysterious reasons we're supposed to exercise faith in our relationships, in our work, in our spiritual journey. In short: in everything. Have faith and you will have joy! "Which of you by worrying," asked Christ, "can add a single hour to his life's span?" (*Luke* 12:25).

A look back at prophecies – and nuggets of fascinating prescience

We have recently written about the accuracy of certain recent prophecies, especially those from Venezuelan mystic Maria Esperanza. We were reminded of more such instances by a call the other day from a priest in London. While we have explained how Esperanza correctly foresaw violent events, and foreign intrusion, as it turns out years ago she had specifically mentioned the World Trade Center. As the priest, Father Richard Foley, pointed out, on December 9, 1992, Maria told a group of visiting Americans that she saw "two huge towers with black smoke all around them." She had said they were in New York and asked pilgrims to pray about it. This was all recorded on page 181 of a book of ours, *The Day Will Come.* "Something was going to happen in America, she said, and indeed, a couple months later, on February 26, 1993, there was the first terrorist bombing at the World Trade Center," said the book.

While that pertained to the 1993 event, Esperanza has repeatedly returned to themes that we now see connected to the twin towers. It was Maria who last December and then again last March prophesied that something "big"—something which would shake the world—was about to happen involving foreign interests on American soil. In March she specified that a rumbling of some sort would occur in the area of New York-New Jersey and then on August 25 she said a "great event" would happen within "three weeks or three months."

As we all know now it ended up being three weeks—and as fate would have it, Esperanza was in the New York metropolitan area on the very day—beseeching prayers for New York and the United States and then, once events occurred, warning the U.S. not be be provoked into an endless war!

A look back at recent commentaries or prophecies from other sources yields similarly prophetic nuggets. For example, as we recently indicated, on page 184 of another of our books, *Prayer of the Warrior,* is the ironic warning that "Manhattan is at ground zero." That was published in 1993. The site of the Trade Center bombing is now famously known as "ground zero."

Then there is *The Final Hour.* On page 295 is quoted an alleged Irish seer named Beulah Lynch who saw rising seas and also "the destruction of tall, tall buildings that brought to mind New York."

Another alleged Irish seer, Christina Gallagher, warned on September 11, 1999, while speaking at the tip of Manhattan in the shadows of the World Trade Center, that "if Americans don't turn back to God, all of this will be destroyed."

As we recall an alleged seer from Boston warned long ago of a man with a turban who would afflict New York. . .

Meanwhile, just last winter, a seer from Ecuador named Pachi Borrero prophesied that as the Jubilee Year ended, after the first week of January, things would get rougher for the world, and just recently she has quoted an alleged locution telling her that "the angel is ready to sound the trumpet of water, blood, and fire."

As for Esperanza, she sees situations intensifying until the middle part of 2004 in this one wave of events. There may be other waves that follow, and these future ones may pertain to the secrets of Medjugorje—which prophesies major events that are expected to occur during the lifetimes of the seers (between now and around 2040, if there is normal longevity).

From what we can tell, none of the recent events are contained in the secrets of Medjugorje, at least not in those possessed by seers who have made extensive public comments about them. Thus, the events in the Medjugorje secrets may be a culmination of what is only beginning to build.

But last January the Medjugorje Madonna warned that Satan was "unchained," and we now see that very clearly—with terrorists in our very midst.

Trip to World Trade Center showed how Holy Spirit can give hints at subtle level

By Michael H. Brown

God speaks to all of us all of the time. It's just that too often, we don't take the time to listen. While there are times He grants us striking signs, for the most part He gives us hints. He is subtle. He deals at the level of the subconscious. He hints to us about our health, what we should eat, who we should associate with, where we should go and what we should do. He "speaks" to us about our jobs, our spirituality, our children.

Often this is done through "intuition" and "coincidences." And sometimes, there are prophetic elements. This may have occurred on October 22, 1999, when we took a trip to Manhattan for research about potential coming disasters. We thought there might be a disaster in store for New York—an earthquake or hurricane—and to get an idea of what kind of damage it might cause, we spent most of our time at the South Tower of the World Trade Center. We went to the observation level at the 110th floor, where we took notes on what kind of destruction might be ready to occur to the surrounding area during a future event—not realizing we were standing on it!

Our next stop was across the way, at the city's Emergency Management Office, which was also part of the Trade Center complex.

There we spoke to the director, Jerry Hauer. One of the topics: anthrax.

The emergency center itself was a new one in a structure that they believed was impervious to a future event—fortified against potential 200-mile-an-hour winds and with an entrance on the third floor (in case of flood). This building too, housing the very emergency management office, would later vanish in the disaster of September 11!

If that's not coincidental enough, the previous August, on another trip to New York, for the same purpose, we had focused on the Rockaways, where Flight 587 would later crash.

Coincidence? Or signals from God? Often, it's hard to tell. Often, we forget to pray about such episodes. When the book we were working on, *Sent To Earth,* came out in November of 2000, there was another "coincidence": the title of chapter 40 was "Ground Zero." There was also the sad coincidence of one of my best friends, who, the last time I saw him, told me he was going to take a new job at the World Trade Center. Though not because I sensed danger, but for other reasons, I urged him twice to stay out on Long Island. He died in the South Tower on September 11. And then there was a book a long while ago, *Prayer of the Warrior*, which came out in 1993. Without even knowing what I was doing, I had written (on page 184), in discussing current evil, "it is a spiritual war, and Manhattan is at ground zero."

Does this mean that there are no natural disasters in sight for New York, and that the regional event, the "ground zero," it would experience is now through? We would urge folks to continue to pray, and we note that one man we have written about foresaw both terrorism in New York *and* natural events. It's time to pray, and in the clarity of prayer, to discern hints, signs, and coincidence—to discern danger.

God speaks to all of us all the time but sometimes we're too hard-headed to listen.

Prayer from Our Lady of America

Prayer to the Immaculate Conception as written by Sister Mildred Mary Neuzil of Ohio at the behest of Our Lady on October 5, 1956:

"O Immaculate Mother, Queen of our country, open our hearts, our homes, and our Land to the coming of Jesus, your Divine Son. With Him, reign over us, O heavenly Lady, so pure and so bright with the radiance of God's light shining in and about you. Be our Leader against the powers of evil set upon wresting the world of souls, redeemed at such a great cost by the sufferings of your Son and of yourself, in union with Him, from that same Savior, Who loves us with infinite charity.

"We gather about you, O chaste and holy Mother, Virgin Immaculate, Patroness of our beloved Land, determined to fight under your banner of holy purity against the wickedness that would make all the world an abyss of evil, without God and without your loving maternal care.

"We consecrate our hearts, our homes, our Land to your Most pure Heart, O great Queen, that the kingdom of your Son, our Redeemer and our God, may be firmly established in us.

"We ask no special sign of you, sweet Mother, for we believe in your great love for us, and we place in you our entire confidence. We promise to honor you by faith, love, and the purity of our lives according to your desire.

"Reign over us, then, O Virgin Immaculate, with your Son Jesus Christ. May His Divine Heart and your most chaste Heart be ever enthroned and glorified among us. Use us, your children of America, as your instruments in bringing peace among men and nations. Work your miracles of grace in us, so that we may be a glory to the Blessed Trinity, Who created, redeemed, and sanctifies us.

"May your valiant Spouse, St. Joseph, with the holy Angels and Saints, assist you and us in 'renewing the face